Beginning Database Design

From Novice to Professional

Clare Churcher

Apress

Beginning Database Design: From Novice to Professional

ISBN-13 (pbk): 978-1-4302-4209-3

ISBN-13 (electronic): 978-1-4302-4210-9

President and Publisher: Paul Manning
Lead Editor: Jonathan Gennick
Technical Reviewer: Stéphane Faroult
Editorial Board: Steve Anglin, Ewan Buckingham, Gary Cornell, Louise Corrigan, Morgan Ertel, Jonathan Gennick, Jonathan Hassell, Robert Hutchinson, Michelle Lowman, James Markham, Matthew Moodie, Jeff Olson, Jeffrey Pepper, Douglas Pundick, Ben Renow-Clarke, Dominic Shakeshaft, Gwenan Spearing, Matt Wade, Tom Welsh
Coordinating Editor: Anita Castro
Copy Editor: Chandra Clarke
Compositor: SPi Global
Indexer: SPi Global
Artist: SPi Global
Cover Designer: Anna Ishchenko

Distributed to the book trade worldwide by Springer Science+Business Media New York, 233 Spring Street, 6th Floor, New York, NY 10013. Phone 1-800-SPRINGER, fax (201) 348-4505, e-mail orders-ny@springer-sbm.com, or visit www.springeronline.com.

For information on translations, please e-mail rights@apress.com, or visit www.apress.com.

Apress and friends of ED books may be purchased in bulk for academic, corporate, or promotional use. eBook versions and licenses are also available for most titles. For more information, reference our Special Bulk Sales–eBook Licensing web page at www.apress.com/bulk-sales.

Any source code or other supplementary materials referenced by the author in this text are available to readers at www.apress.com. For detailed information about how to locate your book's source code, go to www.apress.com/source-code.

To Neville

Contents at a Glance

Contents

viii

Foreword

When I wrote the foreword to the first edition of *Beginning Database Design*, I expressed my hopes to see this book become a popular classic. I felt that it deserved to be so. As the technical reviewer, I had thoroughly enjoyed Clare's skill in turning a subject that is often presented dryly into a vivid and interesting book, and her skill in dissecting the thought process that lets you go from functional requirements to the design of a database that will be able to keep data consistent, grow, and bear the load. *Beginning Database Design* doesn't enunciate, like so many books, quasi-divine rules with pretentious jargon. It explains the goals, the common mistakes, why they are mistakes, and what you should do instead. It brings to light the logic behind the rules, all in a short and very readable book.

There is much satisfaction in seeing five years later that my hopes have been fulfilled, and that *Beginning Database Design* has become one of the leading titles on this important topic—databases are everywhere and database design belongs to the core body of knowledge of any serious software developer. This edition has retained all the qualities that made the first one successful, including Clare's lucid writing and humor, and if the page count has increased it has mostly been to include exercises allowing readers to test their understanding and compare their solutions to the answers that are provided. As the technical reviewer once again, I was in a privileged position to witness the small improvements—there wasn't that much to improve—that Clare has brought to her book, clarifying a sentence here, improving an example there. There is a great quote by Saint-Exupéry, the author of *The Litte Prince*, that says that perfection is achieved not when there is nothing left to add, but when there is nothing left to remove. I am sure that Clare will agree with me that this remark, written with aircraft engineering in mind, applies to database design as well. I also feel that there is nothing to remove from this book.

Stéphane Faroult
Database, SQL, and Performance Consultant
RoughSea Limited

About the Author

Clare Churcher (B.Sc. [Honors], Ph.D.) has designed and implemented databases for a variety of clients and research projects. She is currently the Head of the Applied Computing Department at Lincoln University in Lincoln, Canterbury, New Zealand. Clare has designed and delivered a range of courses including analysis and design of information systems, databases, and programming. She has received a university teaching award in recognition of her expertise in communicating her knowledge. Clare has road-tested her design principles by supervising over 70 undergraduate group database design projects. Examples from these real-life situations are used to illustrate the ideas in this book.

About the Technical Reviewer

Stéphane Faroult first discovered relational databases and the SQL language back in 1983. He joined Oracle France in its early days (after a brief spell with IBM and a bout of teaching at the University of Ottawa) and soon developed an interest in performance and tuning topics. After leaving Oracle in 1988, he briefly tried to reform and did a bit of operational research; but after one year, he succumbed again to relational databases. He has been continuously performing database consultancy since then, and founded RoughSea Limited in 1998. He is the author of *The Art of SQL* (O'Reilly, 2006) and of *Refactoring SQL Applications* (O'Reilly, 2008).

Acknowledgments

Thanks to my family, friends, and colleagues who helped with the two editions of this book. First of all, I want to say thanks very much to my husband, Neville, for introducing me to this subject a long time ago and for always being prepared to offer advice and support. Thanks also to all my friends and colleagues at Lincoln University for their interest and input. Most of the examples in these books are based on scenarios that have cropped up during my teaching at Lincoln. So, a big thank you to my students for all the quirky insights, understandings, and misunderstandings they have introduced me to over the last 19 years.

Thanks again to my editor Jonathan Gennick for suggesting I write a second edition and providing helpful suggestions, and also to Stéphane Faroult for his good-humored expertise as technical reviewer.

Introduction

Everyone keeps data. Big organizations spend millions to look after their payroll, customer, and transaction data. The penalties for getting it wrong are severe: businesses may collapse, shareholders and customers lose money, and for many organizations (airlines, health boards, energy companies), it is not exaggerating to say that even personal safety may be put at risk. And then there are the lawsuits. The problems in successfully designing, installing, and maintaining such large databases are the subject of numerous books on data management and software engineering. However, many small databases are used within large organizations and also for small businesses, clubs, and private concerns. When these go wrong, it doesn't make the front page of the papers; but the costs, often hidden, can be just as serious.

Where do we find these smaller electronic databases? Sports clubs will have membership information and match results; small businesses might maintain their own customer data. Within large organizations, there will also be a number of small projects to maintain data information that isn't easily or conveniently managed by the large system–wide databases. Researchers may keep their own experiment and survey results; groups will want to manage their own rosters or keep track of equipment; departments may keep their own detailed accounts and submit just a summary to the organization's financial software.

Most of these small databases are set up by end users. These are people whose main job is something other than that of a computer professional. They will typically be scientists, administrators, technicians, accountants, or teachers, and many will have only modest skills when it comes to spreadsheet or database software.

The resulting databases often do not live up to expectations. Time and energy is expended to set up a few tables in a database product such as Microsoft Access, or in setting up a spreadsheet in a product such as Excel. Even more time is spent collecting and keying in data. But invariably (often within a short time frame) there is a problem producing what seems to be a quite simple report or query. Often this is because the way the tables have been set up makes the required result very awkward, if not impossible, to achieve.

Getting It Wrong

A database that does not fulfill expectations becomes a costly exercise in more ways than one. We clearly have the cost of the time and effort expended on setting up an unsatisfactory application. However, a much more serious problem is the inability to make the best use of valuable data. This is especially so for research data. Scientific and social researchers may spend considerable money and many years designing experiments, hiring assistants, and collecting and analyzing data, but often very little thought goes into storing it in an appropriately designed database. Unfortunately, some quite simple mistakes in design can mean that much of the potential information is lost. The immediate objective may be satisfied, but unforeseen uses of the data may be seriously compromised. Next year's grant opportunities are lost.

Another hidden cost comes from inaccuracies in the data. Poor database design allows what should be avoidable inconsistencies to be present in the data. Poor handling of categories can cause summaries and reports to be misleading or, to be blunt, wrong. In large organizations, the accumulated effects of each department's inaccurate summary information may go unnoticed.

Problems with a database are not necessarily caused by a lack of knowledge about the database product itself (though this will eventually become a constraint) but are often the result of having chosen the wrong attributes to group together in a particular table. This comes about for two main reasons:

The creator does not have a clear idea of what information the database is meant to be delivering in the short and medium term

The creator does not have a clear model of the different classes of data and their relationships to each other

This book describes techniques for gaining a precise understanding of what a problem is about, how to develop a conceptual model of the data involved, and how to translate that model into a database design. You'll learn to design better databases. You'll avoid the cost of "getting it wrong."

Create a Data Model

The chasm between having a basic idea of what your database needs to be able to do and designing the appropriate tables is bridged by having a clear data model. Data modeling involves thinking very carefully about the different sets or classes of data needed for a particular problem.

Here is a very simple textbook example: a small business might have customers, products, and orders. We need to record a customer's name. That clearly belongs with our set of customer data. What about address? Now, does that mean the customer's contact address (in which case it belongs to the customer data) or where we are shipping the order (in which case it belongs with information about the order)? What about discount rate? Does that belong with the customer (some are gold card customers), or the product (dinner sets are on special at the moment), or the order (20% off orders over $400.00), or none of the above, or all of the above, or does it depend on the boss's mood?

Getting the correct answers to these questions is obviously vital if you are going to provide a useful database for yourself or your client. It is no good heading up a column in your spreadsheet "Discount" before you have a very precise understanding of exactly what a discount means in the context of the current problem. Data modeling- diagrams provide very precise and easy-to-interpret documentation for answers to questions such as those just posed. Even more importantly, the process of constructing a data model leads you to ask the questions in the first place. It is this, more than anything else, that makes data modeling such a useful tool.

The data models we will be looking at in this book are small. They may represent small problems in their entirety, but more likely they will be small parts of larger problems. The emphasis will be on looking very carefully at the relationships between a few classes of data and getting the detail right. This means using the first attempts at the model to form questions for the user, to find the exceptions (before they find you), and then to make some pragmatic decisions about how much of the detail is necessary to make a useful database. Without a good data model, any database is pretty much doomed before it is started.

Data models are often represented visually using some sort of diagram. Diagrams allow you to take in a large amount of information at a glance, giving you the ability to quickly get the gist of a database design without having to read a lot of text. We will be using the class diagram notation from UML to represent our data models, but many other notations are equally useful.

Database Implementation

Once you have a data model that supports your use cases (and all the other details that you have discovered along the way), you know how big your problem is and the type of detail it will involve. You now have a good foundation for designing a suitable application and undertaking the implementation.

Conceptually, the translation from data model to designing a database or spreadsheet is simple. In Chapters 7 through 9, we will look at how to design tables and relationships in a relational database (such as Microsoft Access), which represent the information in the data model. In Chapter 12, we also look at how this might be done in an object-oriented database or language (e.g., JADE, Visual Basic), and for problems with not too many classes of data, how you might capture some of the information in a spreadsheet product such as Microsoft Excel.

The translation from data model to database design is fairly straightforward; however, the actual implementation is not quite so simple. A great deal of work is necessary to ensure that the database is convenient for the eventual user. This will mean designing a user interface with a clear logic, good input facilities, the ability to quickly find data for editing or deleting, adaptable and accurate querying and reporting features, the ability to import and export data, and good maintenance facilities such as backup and archiving. Do not underestimate the time and expertise necessary to complete a useful application even for the smallest database! Considerations such as user interface, maintenance, archiving, and such are outside the scope of this work but are well covered in numerous books on specific database products and texts on interface design.

Objective of This Book

Setting up a database even for a small problem can be a big job (if you do it properly). This book is primarily for beginners or those people who want to set up a small, single-user database. The ideas are applicable to larger, multiuser projects, but there are considerable additional problems that you will encounter there. We do not look at problems to do with concurrency (many users acting together), nor efficiencies, nor how you manage a large project. There are many excellent books on software engineering and database management that deal with these issues.

The main objective of this book is to ensure that the people starting out on setting up a database have a sufficient understanding of the underlying data so that any effort expended on actual implementation will yield satisfying results. Even small problems are more complicated than they appear at first sight. A data model will help you understand the intricacies of the problem so that some pragmatic decisions can be made about what should be attempted. Once you have a data model that you are happy with, you can be confident that the resulting database design (if implemented faithfully) will not disappoint. It may be that after doing the modeling you decide a database is not the appropriate solution. Better to decide this early than after hours of effort have gone into a doomed implementation.

CHAPTER 1

■ ■ ■

What Can Go Wrong

The problem with a number of small databases (and quite probably with many large ones) is that the initial idea of how to record and store the data is not necessarily the most useful one. Often a table or spreadsheet is designed to mimic a possible data entry screen or a hoped-for report. This practice may be adequate for solving the immediate problem (e.g., storing the data somewhere); however, mimicking a data entry screen or report in your design inevitably leads to problems as the requirements evolve. It can make it difficult, if not impossible, to get information for different reports or summaries that were not originally envisaged but nevertheless should be available given the data collected.

This chapter gives examples drawn from real life to illustrate some very basic types of problems encountered when data is stored in poorly designed spreadsheets or tables. These are real examples that I have encountered in my own design work. They do not come from a textbook or out of an exam paper. Some of the data has been removed or altered to protect the identities of the guilty.

Mishandling Keywords and Categories

A common problem in database design is the failure to properly deal with keywords and categories. Many database applications involve data that is categorized in some way; products or events may be of interest to certain categories of people, and customers may be categorized by age, interest, or income (or all three). When entering data, you usually think of an item with its particular list of categories or keywords. However, when you come to preparing reports or doing some analyses, you may need to look at things the other way around. You often want to see a category with a list of all its items or a count of the number of items. For example, you might ask, "What percentage of our customers is in the high-income bracket?" If keywords and categories are not stored correctly initially, these reports can become very difficult to produce.

Example 1-1 describes a case in which information about how plants are used was recorded in a way that seems reasonable at first glance, but that ultimately works against certain types of searches that you would realistically expect to be able to perform.

1

EXAMPLE 1-1. THE PLANT DATABASE

Figure 1-1 shows a small portion of a database table recording information about plants. Along with the botanical and common names of each plant, the developer decides it would be convenient to keep information on the uses for each plant. This is to help prospective buyers decide whether a plant is appropriate for their requirements.

plantID	genus	species	common_name	use1	use2	use3
1	Dodonaea	viscosa	Akeake	shelter	hedging	soil stability
2	Cedrus	atlantica	Atlas cedar	shelter		
3	Alnus	glutinosa	Black alder	soil stability	shelter	firewood
4	Eucalyptus	nichollii	Black peppermint gum	shelter	coppicing	bird food
5	Juglans	nigra	Black walnut	timber		
6	Acacia	mearnsii	Black wattle	firewood	shelter	soil stability

Figure 1-1. *The plant database*

If we look up a plant, we can immediately see what its uses are. However, if we want to find all the plants suitable for hedging, for example, we have a problem. We need to search through each of the use columns individually. Producing a report of all hedging plants would require some logic along the lines of: "IF use1 = 'hedging' OR use2 = 'hedging' OR use3='hedging'." Also, the database table as it stands restricts a plant to having three uses. That may be adequate for now, but if that three–use limit changes, the table would have to be redesigned to include a new column(s). Any logic will need to be altered to include "OR use4='hedging'," and at the back of our minds we just know that whatever number of uses we choose, eventually we will come across a plant that needs one more. The carefully collected data has unfortunately been saved in a manner that is difficult to use and maintain.

In Example 1-1, the real shame is that all the data has been carefully collected and entered, but the design of the table makes it extremely difficult to answer a question such as, "What plants are good for shelter?" The developer has done better than many in separating the uses into individual columns. Often data like this can be found stored in a single column separated by commas or other punctuation. (E.g., an entry in a single column for uses might read: "shelter, hedging, soil stability.") This is even more difficult to manage than the design in Figure 1-1.

The problem is that the database was designed principally to satisfy the user's immediate problem, which is: "I need to store all the info I have about each plant." The developer thought of the data in terms of a single type or class, Plant, and he saw each use as an attribute of a plant in much the same way as its genus or common name. This is fine if all you want to know are answers to questions like, "What uses does this plant have?" The approach is not so useful when going in the other direction, searching for plants having a given use.

In Example 1-1, we really have two sets or classes of data, Plants and Uses, and we are interested in the connections between them. The data modeling techniques described in the rest of the book are a practical way of clarifying exactly what it is you expect from your data and helping you decide on the best database design to support that.

Jumping ahead a bit to see a solution for the plant database problem, you can quite quickly set up a useful relational database by creating the two tables shown in Figure 1-2. (Some extra tables would be even better, but more about that in Chapter 2.)

plantID ▾	genus ▾	species ▾	common_name ▾
1	Dodonaea	viscosa	Akeake
2	Cedrus	atlantica	Atlas cedar
3	Alnus	glutinosa	Black alder
4	Eucalyptus	nichollii	Black peppermint gum
5	Juglans	nigra	Black walnut
6	Acacia	mearnsii	Black wattle

Table Plants

plant ▾	use ▾
1	soil stability
1	hedging
1	shelter
2	shelter
3	firewood
3	soil stability
3	shelter

Table Uses

Figure 1-2. *An improved database design to represent Plants and Uses*

An end user with modest database skills would be able to set up the appropriate keys, relationships, and joins and produce some useful reports. A simple query on (or even a filtering or sorting of) the Uses table will enable the user to find, for example, all shelter plants. There is no restriction now on how many uses a plant can have. The initial setup is slightly more costly, in time and expertise, than for the single table described in Example 1-1, but these separate tables will be able to provide a great deal of additional information.

Example 1-1 shows us one way we can satisfactorily deal with categories. Unfortunately, there are other problems in store. In Example 1-1, the categories were quite clear cut, but this is not always the case. Example 1-2 shows the problems that occur when categories and keywords are not so easily determined.

EXAMPLE 1-2. RESEARCH INTERESTS

An employee of a university's liaison team often receives calls asking to speak to a specialist in a particular topic. The liaison team decides to set up a small spreadsheet to maintain data about each staff member's main research interests. Originally, the intention is to record just one main area for each staff member, but academics, being what they are, cannot be so constrained. The problem of an indeterminate number of interests is solved by adding a few extra columns in order to accommodate all the interests each staff member supplies. Part of the spreadsheet is shown in Figure 1-3.

personID	...	...	...	interest 1	interest 2
152				Computing education	
275				Computer visualisation	Simulation
282				Scientific visualization	Statistics
292				Visualisation of data	Computing education
890				Databases	Scientific visualisation

Figure 1-3. *Research interests in a spreadsheet*

We are able to see at a glance the research interests of a particular person, but as was the case in Example 1-1, it is awkward to do the reverse and find who is interested in a particular topic. However, we have an additional problem here. Many of the research interests look similar but they are described differently. How easy will it be to find a researcher who is able to "visualize data"?

3

As in Example 1-1, the table has been designed taking just one class of data into consideration: in this case, People. Really, though, we have two classes, People and Interests, and we are concerned with the connections or relationships between them. A solution analogous to that in Example 1-1 would be much more useful in this case, too.

Creating a table of people is reasonably straightforward, but the table of interests poses some problems. In Example 1-1, the different possible uses were fairly clear (hedging, shelter, etc.). What are the different possible research interests in Example 1-2? The answer is not so obvious. A quick glance at the data displayed shows eight interests, but it is reasonable to assume that "visualisation" and "visualization" are merely different spellings of the same topic. But what about "scientific visualisation" and "visualization of data"—are these the same in the context of the problem? What about "computer visualisation"? Any staff member with one of these interests would probably be useful for an outside inquiry about how to visualize some data.

Having decided on two classes of data, People and Interests, we now need to clearly define what we mean by them. People isn't too difficult—you might have to think about which staff members are to be involved and whether postgraduate students should also be included. However, Interests is more difficult. In the current example, an interest is anything that a staff member might think of. Such a fuzzy definition is going to cause us a number of problems, especially when it comes to doing any reporting or analysis about specific interests. One solution is to predetermine a set of broad topics and ask people to nominate those applicable to them. But that task is far from simple. People will be aggrieved that their pet topic is not included verbatim and hours (probably months) could be wasted attempting to find agreement on a complete list. And this list may well comprise a whole hierarchy of categories and subcategories. Libraries and journals expend considerable energy and expertise devising and maintaining such lists. Maybe such a list will be useful for the problem in Example 1-2, but then again maybe not.

Having foreseen the difficulties, you may decide that the effort is still worthwhile, or you may reconsider and choose a different solution. In the latter case, it may well be easier for the liaison team to make a stab at the most likely individual and let a real human being sort out what is required. In just the three-month period prior to drafting this chapter, I have seen three different attempts at setting up spreadsheets or databases to record research interests. Each time, a number of hours were spent collecting and storing data before the perpetrator started to run into the problems I've just described. None of the databases is being maintained or used as envisioned.

Repeated Information

Another common problem is unnecessarily storing the same piece of information several times. Such redundancy is often a result of the database design reflecting some sort of input form. For example, in a small business, each order form may record the associated information of a customer's name, address, and phone number. If we design a table that reflects such a form, the customer's name, address, and phone number are recorded every time an order is placed. This inevitably leads to inconsistencies and problems, especially when the customer moves from one address to another. We might want to send out an advertising catalog, and there will be uncertainty as to which address should be used. Sometimes the repeated information is not quite so obvious. Example 1-3 illustrates one such case.

EXAMPLE 1-3. INSECT DATA[1]

Team members of a long-term environmental project regularly visit farms and take samples to determine the numbers of particular insect species present. Each field on a farm has been given a unique code, and on each visit to a field a number of representative samples are taken. The counts of each species present in each sample are recorded.

---

[1] Clare Churcher and Peter McNaughton, "There are bugs in our spreadsheet: Designing a database for scientific data" (research report, Centre for Computing and Biometrics: Lincoln University, February 1998).

Figure 1-4 shows a portion of the data as it was recorded in a spreadsheet.

	A	B	C	D	E	F
1	farm	field	date	sample	springtail	fungus_beetle
268	1	ADhc	Aug-11	1	2	0
269	2	ADhc	Aug-11	2	2	0
270	1	ADhc	Aug-11	3	7	0
271	1	ADhc	Aug-11	4	3	2
272	1	ADhc	Aug-11	5	3	0
273	1	ADhc	Aug-11	6	3	9
274	1	ADhc	Aug-11	7	2	1
275	1	ADhc	Aug-11	8	6	1
276	1	ADhc	Aug-11	9	2	1
277	1	ADhc	Aug-11	10	5	3
278	1	ADhc	Aug-11	11	0	0
279	1	ADhe	Aug-11	1	0	6
280	1	ADhe	Aug-11	2	1	1
281	1	ADhe	Aug-11	3	5	2

Figure 1-4. Insect data in a spreadsheet

The information about each farm was recorded (quite correctly) elsewhere, thus avoiding that data being repeated. However, there are still problems. The fact that field ADhc is on farm 1 is recorded every visit, and it does not take long to find the first data entry error in row 269. (The coding used for the fields raises other issues that we will not address just now.)

On the face of it, the error of listing field ADhc under farm 2 instead of farm 1 in Figure 1-4 doesn't seem like such a big deal—but it is avoidable. The fact that the farm was recorded in this spreadsheet means that the data is probably likely to be analyzed by farm, and now any results for farms 1 and 2 are potentially inaccurate. And how many other data entry errors will there be over the lifetime of the project? Given that the results in Example 1-3 came from a carefully designed, long–term experiment and were to be statistically analyzed, it seems a shame that such errors are able to slip in when they can be easily prevented.

It is important to distinguish the difference between data input errors (anyone can make typos now and then) and design errors. The problem in Example 1-3 is not that field ADhc was wrongly associated with farm 2 (a simple error that could be easily fixed), but that the association between farm and field was recorded so many times that an eventual error became almost certain. And errors such as these can be very difficult to detect.

Another piece of information is also repeated in the spreadsheet in Example 1-3: the date of a visit. The information that field ADhc was visited on Aug-11 is repeated in rows 268 to 278, creating another source of avoidable errors (e.g., we could accidentally put Aug-10 in row 273). Such an error would affect any analyses based on date.

The repeated visit date information in Example 1-3 also gives rise to an additional and more serious problem: what do you do with miscellaneous information about a particular visit (e.g., it was raining at the time—quite important if you are counting insects)? Is it just included on one row (making it difficult to find all the affected samples), or does it go on every row for that visit (awkward and compounding the repeated information problem)? In fact, the weather information in this case was recorded quite separately in a text document, thereby making it impossible to use the power of the software to help in any analyses of weather.

Techniques described more fully in later chapters would have prevented the problems encountered in Example 1-3. Rather than thinking of the data in terms of *the counts in each sample*, the designer would have thought about Farms, Fields, Visits, and Insects as separate classes of data in which researchers are interested both individually and together. For example, the researchers may want to find information about fields with particular soil types or visits undertaken in fine weather conditions. Figure 1-5 shows how separating information

5

about fields and visits into separate tables not only reduces problems with repeated information, but allows more data (soil types for fields, weather conditions for visits) to be easily added. The Counts table still suffers the same problems as the tables in Examples 1-1 and 1-2, but that can be addressed. We will return to this example in Chapter 4.

field ▾	farm ▾	soil ▾
Adhc	1	
Adhe	1	
Mvhe	2	
MVhc	2	

Table Fields

visitID ▾	field ▾	date ▾	conditions ▾
113	Adhc	Aug-06	Fine
114	Adhe	Aug-06	Fine
115	Adhc	Sep-06	Rain
116	Adhe	Sep-06	Overcast

Table Visits

visitID ▾	sample ▾	springtail ▾	fungus_beetle ▾
113	1	2	0
113	2	2	0
113	3	7	0
113	4	3	0
113	5	0	2
113	6	3	1

Table Counts

Figure 1-5. *An improved database design for the insect problem*

Designing for a Single Report

Another cause of a problematic database is to design a table to match the requirements of a particular report. A small business might have in mind a format that is required for an invoice. A school secretary may want to see the whereabouts of teachers during the week. Thinking backward from one specific report can lead to a database with many flaws. Example 1-4 is a particular favorite of mine, because the first time I was ever paid real money to fix up a database was because of this problem (clearly student record software has moved on a great deal since then!).

EXAMPLE 1-4. ACADEMIC RESULTS

A university department needs to have its final–year results in a format appropriate for taking along to the examiners' meeting. The course was very rigidly prescribed with all students completing the same subjects, and a report similar to the one in Figure 1-6 was generated by hand prior to the system being computerized. This format allowed each student's performance to be easily compared across subjects, helping to determine honors' boundaries.

ID	Name	S001	S002	S103	S104	S202	S310	S331	GPA
982208	Jo Brown	A+	A	A	A+	A	B+	B+	8.6
986667	Helen Green	A	A	A+	A	A	B+	B+	8.5
987645	Peter Smith	A	B+	A-	A-	B+	A-	B	7.5

Figure 1-6. Report required for students' results

A database table was designed to exactly match the report in Figure 1-6, with a field for each column. The first year the database worked a treat. The next year the problems started. Can you anticipate them?

Some students were permitted to replace one of the papers with one of their own choosing. The table was amended to include columns for option name and option mark. Then some subjects were replaced, but the old ones had to be retained for those students who had taken them in the past. The table became messier, but it could still cope with the data.

What the design couldn't handle was students who failed and then reenrolled in a subject. The complete academic record for a student needed to be recorded, and the design of the table made it impossible to record more than one mark if a student completed a subject several times. That problem wasn't noticed until the second year in operation (when the first students started failing). By then, a fair amount of effort had gone into development and data entry. The somewhat curious solution was to create a new table for each year, and then to apply some tortuous logic to extract a student's marks from the appropriate tables. When the original developer left for a new job, several years' worth of data were left in a state that no one else could comprehend. And that's how I got my first database job (and the database coped with changing requirements over several years).

Example 1-4 is particularly good for showing how much trouble you can get into with a poor design. The developer could see the problem from the point of view of the required report. He thought in terms of one class: Student. In reality, at the very minimum, we have two classes, Student and Subject, and we are interested in the relationship between them. In particular, we would like to know what mark a particular student earned in a particular subject. Chapter 4 will show how an investigation of a Many–Many relationship such as the one between Subject and Student would have led to the introduction of another class, Enrollment. This allows different marks to be recorded for different attempts at a subject. Taking this approach the oversight concerning how to deal with a student's failure would have been discovered, and this whole sorry mess would have been avoided.

Summary

The first thoughts about how to design a database may be influenced by a particular report or by a particular method of input. Sometimes the driver for a database is simply that some valuable information has come to hand and needs to be "put somewhere." The hurried creation of a database or spreadsheet can lead to a design that cannot cope with even simple changes to the information you would like to retrieve. It is important to think carefully about the underlying data, and design the database to reflect the information being stored rather than what you might want to do with the data in the short term.

TESTING YOUR UNDERSTANDING

Exercise 1-1

A school is planning some outdoor activities for its students. The staff wants to create a database of how parents can help. The secretary sets up the database table in Figure 1-7 to keep the information.

last_name ▾	first_name ▾	phone ▾	contribution ▾	contribution2 ▾
Smith	Jane	4623598	Food preparation	Driving
Green	Rob	8965431	Transport	
Henry	James	9576342	Camping Gear	Cooking
Wang	Li	9612345	Cooking	

Figure 1-7. Initial database table for recording parent contributions

What problems can you foresee in making good use of this information?

Suggest some better ways that this information could be stored.

Exercise 1-2

A small library keeps a roster of who will be at the desk each day. They have a database table as shown in Figure 1-8.

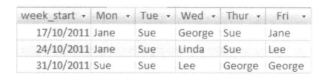

week_start ▾	Mon ▾	Tue ▾	Wed ▾	Thur ▾	Fri ▾
17/10/2011	Jane	Sue	George	Sue	Jane
24/10/2011	Jane	Sue	Linda	Sue	Lee
31/10/2011	Sue	Sue	Lee	George	George

Figure 1-8. An initial database table to record roster duties

What problems can you foresee in making good use of this information?

Suggest some better ways that this information could be stored.

8

CHAPTER 2

■ ■ ■

Guided Tour of the Development Process

The decision to set up a small database usually arises because there is some specific task in mind: a scientist may have some experimental results that need safekeeping; a small business may wish to produce invoices and monthly statements for its customers; a sports club may want to keep track of teams and subscriptions.

The important thing is not to focus solely on the immediate task at hand but to try to understand the data that are going to support that task *and other likely tasks*. This is sometimes referred to as *data independence*. In general, the fundamental data items (names, amounts, dates) that you keep for a problem will change very little over a long time. The values will of course be constantly changing, but not the fact that we are keeping values for names, amounts, and dates. What you do with these pieces of data is likely to change quite often. Designing a database to reflect the type of data involved, rather than what you currently think is the main use for the data, will be more advantageous in the long term.

For example, a small business may want to send invoices and statements to its customers. Rather than thinking in terms of a statement and what goes on it, it is important to think about the underlying data items. In this case, these items are customers and their transactions. A statement is simply a report of a particular customer's transactions over some period of time. In the long term, the format of the statement may change, for example, to include aging or interest charges. However, the underlying transaction data will be the same. If the database is designed to reflect the fundamental data (customers and transactions), it will be able to evolve as the requirements change. The type of data will stay the same, but the reports can change. We might also change the way data is entered (transactions might be entered through a web page or via e-mail), and we might find additional uses for the data (customer data might be used for mail–outs as well as invoicing).

Arriving at a good solution for a database project requires some abstraction of the problem so that the possibilities become clear. In this chapter, we take a quick tour of how we will approach the process from initial problem statement, through an abstract model, to the final implementation of a (hopefully) useful application. The diagram in Figure 2-1 is a useful way of considering the process.

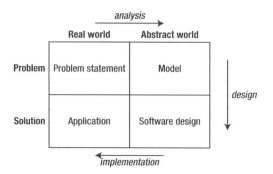

Figure 2-1. The software process (based on Zelkowitz et al., 1979[1])

Using Figure 2-1 as a way of thinking about software processes, we will now look at how the various steps relate to setting up a database project by applying those steps to Example 1-1, "The Plant Database."

Initial Problem Statement

We start with some initial description of the problem. One way to represent a description is with *use cases*, which are part of the *Unified Modeling Language* (UML),[2] a set of diagramming techniques used to depict various aspects of the software process. Use cases are descriptions of how different types of users (more formally known as *actors*) might interact with the system. Most texts on systems analysis include discussions about use cases. (Alistair Cockburn's book *Writing Effective Use Cases*[3] is a particularly readable and pragmatic account.) Use cases can be at many different levels, from high-level corporate goals down to descriptions of small program modules. We will concentrate on the tasks someone sitting in front of a desktop computer would be trying to carry out. For a database project, these tasks are most likely to be entering or updating data, and extracting information based on that data.

The UML notation for use cases involves stick figures representing, in our case, types of users, and ovals representing each of the tasks that the user needs to be able to carry out. For example, Figure 2-2 illustrates a use case in which a user performs three as yet unknown tasks. However, those stick figures and ovals aren't really enough to describe a given interaction with a system. When writing a use case, along with a diagram you should create a text document describing in more detail what the use case entails.

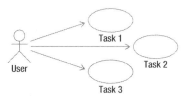

Figure 2-2. UML notation for use cases[4]

---

[1] Marvin V. Zelkowitz, Alan C. Shaw, and John D. Gannon, *Principles of Software Engineering and Design* (Englewood Cliffs, NJ: Prentice-Hall, 1979), p. 5.

[2] Grady Booch, James Rumbaugh, and Ivar Jacobsen, *The Unified Modeling Language User Guide* (Boston, MA: Addison Wesley, 1999).

[3] Alistair Cockburn, *Writing Effective Use Cases* (Boston, MA: Addison Wesley, 2001).

[4] The diagrams in this book were prepared using Rational Rose (http://www.rational.com/). The software was made available under Rational's Software Engineering for Educational Development (SEED) Program.

Let's see how use cases can be applied to the problem from Example 1-1 in the last chapter. Figure 2-3 recaps where we started with an initial database table recording plants and their uses.

plantID ▾	genus ▾	species ▾	common_name ▾	use1 ▾	use2 ▾	use3 ▾
1	Dodonaea	viscosa	Akeake	shelter	hedging	soil stability
2	Cedrus	atlantica	Atlas cedar	shelter		
3	Alnus	glutinosa	Black alder	soil stability	shelter	firewood
4	Eucalyptus	nichollii	Black peppermint gum	shelter	coppicing	bird food
5	Juglans	nigra	Black walnut	timber		
6	Acacia	mearnsii	Black wattle	firewood	shelter	soil stability

Figure 2-3. Original data of plants and uses

If we consider what typical people might want to do with the data shown in Figure 2-3, the use cases suggested in Example 2-1 would be a start.

EXAMPLE 2-1. INITIAL USE CASES FOR THE PLANT DATABASE

Figure 2-4 shows some initial use cases for the plant database. The text following the figure describes each use case.

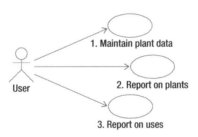

Figure 2-4. First attempt at use cases for the plant database

Use case 1: Enter (or edit) all the data we have about each plant; that is, plant ID, genus, species, common name, and uses.

Use case 2: Find or report information about a plant (or every plant) and see what it is useful for.

Use case 3: Specify a use and find the appropriate plants (or report for all uses).

As explained in the previous chapter, if the data is stored as in Figure 2-3, we cannot conveniently satisfy the requirements of all the use cases in Example 2-1. It is easy to get information about each plant (use case 2) by looking at each row in the table. However, finding all the plants that satisfy a particular use is extremely awkward. Have a go at finding all the plants suitable for firewood. You have to look in each of the use columns for every row.

Analysis and Simple Data Model

Now that we have an initial idea of where we are heading, we need to become a little abstract and form a model of what the problem is really about. In terms of Figure 2-1, we are moving across the top of the diagram.

A practical way to start to get a feel for what the data involves is to sketch an initial data model that is a representation of how the different types of data interact. UML provides class diagrams that are a useful way of representing this information. There are many products that will maintain class diagrams, but a sketch with pencil and paper is quite sufficient for early and small models. A large portion of this book is about the intricacies of data modeling, and the following sections provide a quick overview of the definitions and notation.

Classes and Objects

Each *class* can be considered a template for storing data about a set of similar things (places, events, or people). Let's consider Example 2-1 about plants and their uses. An obvious candidate for our first class is the idea of a `Plant`. Each plant can be described in a similar way in that each has a *genus*, a *species*, a *common_name*, and perhaps a *plantID* number. These pieces of information, that we will keep about each plant, are referred to as the *attributes* (or *properties*) of the class. Figure 2-5 shows the UML notation for a class and its attributes. The name of the class appears in the top panel, and the middle panel contains the attributes. For some types of software systems, there may be processes that a class would be responsible for carrying out. For example, an `Order` class related to an online shopping cart might have a process for calculating a price including tax. These are known as *methods* and appear in the bottom panel. For predominantly information–based problems, methods are not usually a major consideration in the early stages of the design, and we will ignore them for now.

Figure 2-5. *UML notation for a class*

Each plant about which we want to keep data will conform to the template in Figure 2-5; that is, each will have (or could have) its own value for the attributes *plantID*, *genus*, *species*, and *common_name*. Each individual plant is referred to as an *object* of the `Plant` class. The `Plant` class and some objects are depicted in Figure 2-6.

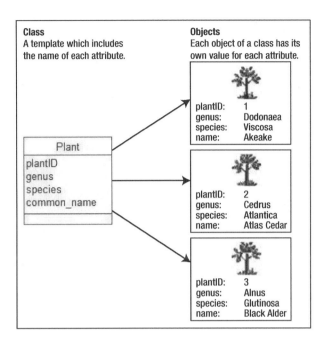

Figure 2-6. A class and some of its objects

The *Plant* class could include other attributes, such as typical height, lifespan, and so on. What about the uses to which a plant can be put? In the database table in Figure 2-3, these uses were included as several attributes (*use1, use2*, and so on) of a plant. In Example 1-1, we saw how having uses stored as several attributes caused a number of problems. What we have here is another candidate for a class: *Use*. In Chapter 5, we will discuss in more detail how we can figure out whether we need classes or attributes to hold information. Our new class, *Use*, will not have many attributes, possibly just *name*. Each object of the *Use* class will have a value for *name* such as "hedging," "shelter," or "bird food." What is particularly interesting for our example is the *relationship* between the *Use* and *Plant* classes.

Relationships

One particular plant object can have many uses. As an example, we can see from Figure 2-3 that Akeake can be used for soil stability, hedging, and shelter. We can think of this as a relationship (or association) between particular objects of the *Plant* class and objects of the *Use* class. Some specific instances of this relationship are shown in Figure 2-7.

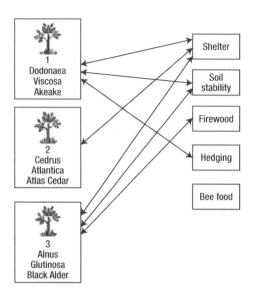

Figure 2-7. Some instances of the relationship between Plant and Use

In a database, we would usually create a table for each class, and the information about each object would be recorded as a row in that table as shown in Figure 2-8. The information about the specific relationship instances would also be recorded in a table. For a relational database, you would expect to find tables such as those in Figure 2-8 to represent the plants and relationship instances shown in Figure 2-7. We will look further at how and why we design tables like these in Chapter 7. For now, just convince yourself that it contains the appropriate information.

plantID	genus	species	common_name
1	Dodonaea	viscosa	Akeake
2	Cedrus	atlantica	Atlas cedar
3	Alnus	glutinosa	Black alder
4	Eucalyptus	nichollii	Black peppermint gum
5	Juglans	nigra	Black walnut
6	Acacia	mearnsii	Black wattle

Table Plant

Plant	Use
1	soil stability
1	hedging
1	shelter
2	shelter
3	firewood
3	soil stability
3	shelter

Table Plant Uses

Figure 2-8. Plant objects and instances of the relationship between Plants and Uses expressed in database tables

In UML, a relationship is represented by a line between two class rectangles, as shown in Figure 2-9. The line can be named to make it clear what the relationship is (e.g., "can be used for"), but it doesn't need to have a name if the context is obvious. The pair of numbers at each end of the line indicates how many objects of one class can be associated with a particular object of the other class. The first number is the minimum number. This is usually 0 or 1 and is therefore sometimes known as the *optionality* (i.e., it indicates whether there must be a related object). The second number is the greatest number of related objects. It is usually 1 or many (denoted n), although other numbers are possible. Collectively, these numbers can be referred to as the *cardinality* or the *multiplicity* of the relationship.

14

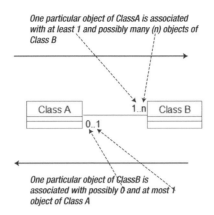

Figure 2-9. *A data model expressed as a UML class diagram*

Relationships are read in both directions. Figure 2-9 shows how many objects of the right–hand class can be associated with one particular object of the left–hand class and vice versa. When we want to know how many objects of *ClassB* are associated with *ClassA*, we look at the numbers nearest *ClassB*.

A great deal can be learned about data by investigating the cardinality of relationships, and we will look at the issue of cardinality further in Chapter 4. The current chapter concentrates on the notation for class diagrams and what the diagrams can tell you about the relationships between different classes. Figure 2-10 shows some relationships that could be associated with small parts of some of the examples you saw in the Chapter 1.

	Left to Right	Right to Left
Plant 0..n — 0..n Use	One particular plant may have no uses or it could have any number	One particular use may have no plants associated with it, or it may have many plants
Person 1..n — 0..n Interest	One person may have lots of interests or may have none	Each interest has at least one person associated with it and maybe several
Customer 1..1 — 0..n Transaction	One customer may have several transactions but might not have any	Each transaction is associated with exactly one customer
Visit 1..1 — 1..n Sample	A visit has at least one sample associated with it and maybe many	Each sample comes from a single visit

Figure 2-10. *Examples of relationships with different cardinalities*

15

Figure 2-10 is consistent in that the phrases in the right-hand columns accurately describe the diagrams. Whether each diagram is appropriate for a particular problem is quite a different question. For example, in the first row in Figure 2-10, why would we want a use that has no plants associated with it? It is questions like this that help us to understand the intricacies of a problem, and we will discuss these in Chapter 4. At the moment, none of the problems have been sufficiently defined to know if the diagrams in Figure 2-10 are accurate, but they are reasonable first attempts.

Further Analysis: Revisiting the Use Cases

Using the notation for class diagrams, we can make a first attempt at a data model diagram to represent our plants example. We have a class for both plants and uses, and the relationship between them looks like Figure 2-11.

Figure 2-11. First attempt at a data model for plants example

We now need to check whether this model is able to satisfy the requirements of the three use cases in Figure 2-4:

Use case 1: Maintain plant information. We can create objects for each plant and record the attributes we might require now or in the future. We can create use objects, and we can specify relationship instances between particular plant and use objects.

Use case 2: Report on plants. We can take a particular plant object (or each one in turn) and find the values of its attributes. We can then find all the use objects related to that plant object.

Use case 3: Report on uses. We can take a particular use object and find all the plant objects that are related to it.

So far not too bad. But let's look a bit more carefully. Use case 1 is really two or maybe three separate tasks. If we consider how the database will actually work in practice, it seems likely that the different uses (hedging, shelter, etc.) would be entered right at the start of the project and be updated from time to time. Entering information about uses is a task that a user might want to perform independently of any specific plant information. At some later time, the same user, or someone else, may want to enter details of a plant and relate it to the uses that are already recorded.

These are important questions to consider about any use cases related to input. How will it be done in practice? Will different people be involved? Will bits of the data be entered at different times? Answering these questions is the first part of the analysis, where we have to get inside the users' heads to find out what they really do. (Don't ever rely on them telling you.)

■ **Tip**   For data entry or editing, separate the tasks done by different people or at different times into their own use cases.

Now let's look at use case 2 where we want to report about plants. We can find out more about the problem by probing a bit more deeply into how the user envisages the reporting of information about plants. Think about the following dialog:

> *You*: Would you like to be able to print out a list of all your plants to put in a folder or send to people?
>
> *User*: That would be good.
>
> *You*: What order would you like the plants to be listed in?
>
> *User*: By their genus, I guess. Alphabetical?
>
> *You*: Genus? So you'd like, for example, all the Eucalyptus plants together.
>
> *User*: Yep, that would be good.

At this point in the conversation, we see another level of the problem. (Give yourself bonus points if you've already thought of the issue I'm about to describe.) If we look carefully at the data in the original table, we can see that it appears that each genus includes a number of species, and each of these species can have many uses. Another question can confirm whether we understand the relationship between genus and species correctly.

> *You*: So each species belongs to just one genus? Is that right?
>
> *User*: That's right.

We can see that asking questions about the reporting use cases in the initial problem statement is another excellent way to find out more about the problem.

■ **Tip** For data retrieval or reporting tasks, ask questions about which attributes might be used for sorting, grouping, or selecting data. These attributes may be candidates for additional classes.

We now realize that we have a new class, *Genus*, to add to our data model. Why is it important to include this new class? Well, if genus remains as simply an attribute of our original `Plant` class, we can enter pretty much any value for each object. Two objects with genus *Eucalyptus* might end up with different spellings (almost certainly if I were doing the data entry). This would cause problems every time we wanted to find or count or report on all *Eucalyptus* plants. The fact that our user has mentioned that grouping by genus would be useful means that it is important to get the genus data stored appropriately. Our revised data model in Figure 2-12 shows how genus can be represented so that the data is kept accurately.

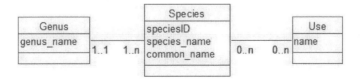

Figure 2-12. *Revised data model for our plant problem*

17

We now have a set of genus objects, and each plant must be associated with exactly one of them. You will see in Figure 2-12 that we have also renamed the *Plant* class to *Species*, as it is the species, or type of plant, about which we are keeping information, not actual physical plants. This opens the way for future extension of the model to keep information about actual plants if we so wish (e.g., when each was planted, when it was pruned, and so on).

Entering the values of each genus will likely be a separate job from entering data for each species, so it should have its own use case. We don't want or need to enter a new object for the *Eucalyptus* genus every time we enter a new species.

Example 2-2 shows the amended use cases. See how the reporting use cases can now be much more precisely defined in terms of the data model.

EXAMPLE 2-2. REVISED USE CASES FOR THE PLANT DATABASE

Figure 2-13 shows the revised use cases for the plant problem. Text following the figure describes each use case.

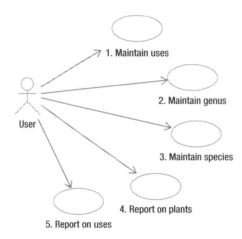

Figure 2-13. *Revised use cases for the plant problem*

Use case 1: Maintain uses. Create or update a use object. Enter (or update) the name.

Use case 2: Maintain genus. Create or update a genus object. Enter the name.

Use case 3: Maintain species. Create a species object. Generate a unique ID, and enter the species and common name. Associate the new species object with one of the existing genus objects and optionally associate it with any number of the existing uses.

Use case 4: Report plant information. For each genus object, write out the name and find all the associated species objects. For each species object, write out the species and common name. Find all the associated uses and write out their names.

Use case 5: Report use information. For each use object, write out the name. Find all the associated species objects, and write out for each the associated genus name and the species and common names.

What we have done here is taken some initial use cases and explored the details (e.g., how would you like the plants ordered in the report?). This led us to update the class diagram. We then looked at how the new class diagram copes with the tasks we need to carry out. This is an iterative process and forms the main part of the analysis of the problem. After a few iterations, we will have a much clearer idea of what the users want and what they mean by many of the terms they use.

Design

After a few iterations of evaluating the use cases and class diagrams, we should have an initial data model and a set of use cases that show in some detail how we intend to satisfy the requirements of the users. The next stage is to consider what type of software would be suitable for implementing the project. For a database project, we could choose to use a relational database product (such as MySQL or Microsoft Access), a programming language (for example, Visual Basic or Java), or for small problems maybe a spreadsheet (such as Microsoft Excel) will be sufficient.

Here is a brief overview of how the design might be done in a relational database. We consider the details more thoroughly in Chapters 7 to 9, so if you don't follow all the reasoning here, don't panic. For those readers who already know something about database design, please excuse the simplifications.

In very broad terms, each class will be represented by a database table. Because each species can have many uses and vice versa, we need an additional table for that relationship. This is generally the case for relationships having a cardinality greater than 1 at both ends (known as Many–Many relationships). (There will be more about these additional tables in Chapter 7.) The tables are shown in Figure 2-14 as they would look in Microsoft Access. Three tables correspond to the classes in Figure 2-12 and the extra table, *PlantUse*, gives us somewhere to keep the relationships between plant species and uses (Figures 2-7 and 2-8). The other relationships between the classes can be represented within the database by setting referential integrity between the four tables (more about this in Chapter 7).

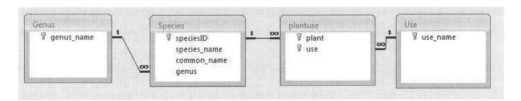

Figure 2-14. *Representing classes and relationships in Microsoft Access*

For those readers who know a bit about database design we have included an attribute *speciesID* in the *Species* table, which is a number unique to each species. This notion of having one attribute (or possibly a combination of attributes) that uniquely identifies each object is important, and we will look at it more in Chapter 8. In a relational database, these unique identifiers are known as *key fields* and they are shown with a small key in Figure 2-14. (We could also have added an extra ID field in the *Use* and *Genus* tables, but as the names are unique we have chosen not to do so.) We have also introduced some additional attributes to help create the relationships between the tables. For the *Species* table we have included an attribute, *genus*, and have insisted that its value must come from an entry in our table *Genus*. (This new attribute is referred to in technical jargon as a *foreign key*, and the insistence that it match an existing value in the Genus table is known as *referential integrity*—more about this in Chapter 7.) The line between the *Genus* and *Species* tables says that the *genus* field in the *Species* table is a foreign key and so must have a value that exists in the *Genus* table. This design means we won't ever have to worry about different spellings of *Eucalyptus*. Similarly, we have included foreign key attributes, *use* and *plant*, in the *PlantUse* table.

19

We have now done some analysis to understand the details of the problem and represented those details with use cases and a class diagram. We have also started a design for a relational product such as Access, SQL Server, or MySQL that represents our class diagram as tables. We can now think about implementing the database.

Implementation

We will not be going into the intricacies of how to implement a database in any particular program, but it is useful to see where the analysis is leading us in general terms. The data model in Figure 2-12 can be represented very accurately in a relational database product such as MySQL or Microsoft Access as shown in Figure 2-14. The first stage in the implementation is to set up these tables and the foreign keys that represent the relationships, and then input some data. Figure 2-15 shows some of the data that would be in relational database tables set up according to the design in Figure 2-14.

Table Genus

Table Species

(The value of genus must be one of the values in the Genus table)

Table Use

Table PlantUse

(The value of plant must be one of the values in the Species table.
The value of use must be one of the values in the Use table)

Figure 2-15. Example data in tables for the plant database

We have now implemented our design, but we still need to provide convenient ways to maintain and retrieve the data. This means we have to provide forms and reports that will efficiently satisfy the requirements in our revised set of use cases.

Interfaces for Input Use Cases

We need to provide the users of our plant system with a nice way to input their data. The use cases for maintaining genus and use data are easily taken care of. We can enter the data directly into the appropriate table usually via an interface such as a form or a web page. The use case for maintaining species information is a little trickier. We need to update two tables: $Species$ (for the data about each species) and $PlantUse$ (because we need to specify which uses each species is associated with). Some database products have utilities to facilitate the entry of data into two tables simultaneously, usually via a form. Alternatively, we might have a web page with a script to insert the data into the appropriate tables.

Figure 2-16 shows a very basic form for entering data about a particular species, It was created using the Form Wizard in Microsoft Access. This form allows us to enter data that will end up as one row in the $Species$ table and several rows in the $PlantUse$ table (one for each use for this particular species). The form also provides convenient ways to establish the relationships between a species and its genus and uses by providing drop-down lists that will contain each of the possible genus or use objects. This is one possible solution to satisfy the requirements of use case 3 (maintaining species data) in an accurate and convenient way.

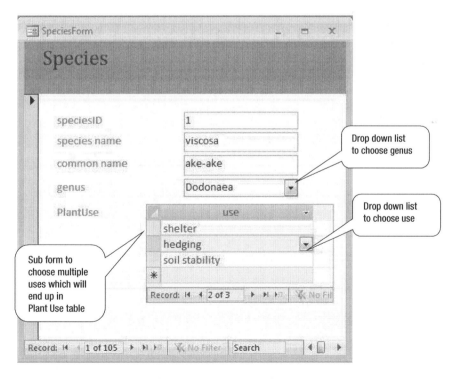

Figure 2-16. A form to satisfy the use case for maintaining species data

21

Reports for Output Use Cases

With the data stored in separate tables, the reporting and querying facilities in database products make extracting (simple) information reasonably straightforward. We will not go into the detail of how to set up queries and reports now, but we will look at two possible reports that would satisfy our reporting use cases. Most good report generators allow the data to be selected, ordered, and grouped in various ways. By grouping on either genus or use, we can quite simply provide the information to satisfy the two reporting use cases from Figure 2-13. Figure 2-17 shows a report grouped by uses and shows the plants that are appropriate for each use. The report was created very simply using default options in the Access Report Wizard.

PlantUse

Use	ID	Genus	Species Name	Common Name
bird food				
	4	Acacia	melanoxylon	Tasmanian blackwood
	7	Alnus	incana	grey alder
	28	Eucalyptus	nichollii	Black peppermint gum
coppicing				
	30	Eucalyptus	gunnii	cider gum
	4	Acacia	melanoxylon	Tasmanian blackwood
	28	Eucalyptus	nichollii	Black peppermint gum
firewood				
	6	Alnus	glutinosa	Black alder
	3	Juglans	nigra	black walnut
hedging				
	1	Dodonaea	viscosa	ake-ake

Figure 2-17. *A simple report satisfying the use case for providing information on plants suitable for a specific use*

We could create a similar report to Figure 2-17, by grouping our data by genus instead of use. However, there are many different ways to access information from the database. Figure 2-18 shows a very simple web page view of our Access database. It allows users to select a genus and to see the associated species and uses (the web page was developed with Microsoft Expression Web).

genus name	speciesID	species name	common name	use
Dodonaea	1	viscosa	ake-ake	shelter
Dodonaea	1	viscosa	ake-ake	hedging
Dodonaea	1	viscosa	ake-ake	soil stability

Dodonaea ▼

Figure 2-18. *A simple web page front end satisfying the use case for returning plant information grouped by genus*

Summary

We have now taken the complete trip from original imprecise problem statement to a possible final solution for our very simple plants and uses example. The steps are summarized here and illustrated in Figure 2-19.

1. Express the problem in terms of what a user might want to achieve. For a database problem, this will typically be in terms of the data to be stored and the information that needs to be retrieved. Sketch some initial use cases and a data model.

2. Think about other possible uses of the information and how the data might be usefully ordered or grouped. Undertake an iterative analysis process of reconsidering the data model and the use cases, until you are satisfied that you have a complete and precise understanding of the problem. For larger problems, this stage may include making some simplifying or other pragmatic choices. The bulk of this book will concentrate on this phase of the process.

3. Choose the type of product to manage the data and create an appropriate design. For a relational database, this will involve designing tables, keys, and foreign keys. Different structures will be required if the project is to be implemented in some other type of product such as a programming language or a spreadsheet. The design phase is discussed more fully in Chapters 7 to Chapter 9.

4. Build the application. For a relational database, this will include setting up the tables and developing forms and reports to satisfy the use cases. The mechanics of how to do this in any particular product is outside the scope of this book, but there are numerous how-to books available that will help you.

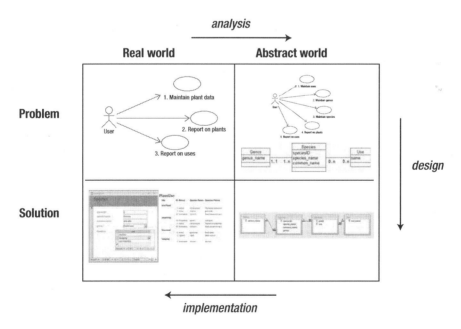

Figure 2-19. *The development process for our simple database example*

23

TESTING YOUR UNDERSTANDING

Exercise 2-1

A small sports club keeps information about its members and the fees they pay. The secretary wants to be able to record when members pay and print a report similar to that in Figure 2-20.

last_name	first_name	phone	type	gender	fee	date_paid
Smith	Jane	563201	Full	F	220	21/09/2011
Wilson	Harry	375967	Full	M	220	19/09/2011
Green	Bert	439871	MidWeek	M	150	
Jones	Bert	295784	Social	F	80	
Smith	Sharon	387648	MidWeek	F	150	16/08/2011

Figure 2-20. Membership data for a small club

a) Think about when the different pieces of data might be entered. Sketch an initial use case diagram for data entry.

b) Consider what different things you are keeping information about and sketch a simple class diagram.

c) What options could you suggest to the club for different ways a report could be presented? Does your class diagram have the information readily available?

CHAPTER 3

■ ■ ■

Initial Requirements and Use Cases

In this chapter, we consider part of the first step from real-world problem to eventual real–world solution as described in Chapter 2. First we need to make sure we really understand the problem. This may sound obvious, but it is surprising how often people set about implementing a database before they understand the problem completely. There are two things we need to do: understand what tasks need to be carried out by all the people who will use the system, and then figure out what data needs to be stored to support them. Use cases and class diagrams as shown in Figure 3-1 are a great way to start to consolidate our understanding of a problem.

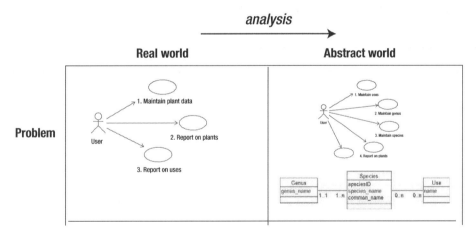

Figure 3-1. *The first step: developing an abstract model of the real-world problem*

First, we have to *fully* understand the real problem. It is not enough to have a rough idea of what a business or club or scientist does. One of my favorite quotations comes from Peter Coad and Ed Yourdon's book *Object Oriented Analysis*,[1] in which they have this to say about analyzing an air traffic control system:

> *The analyst needs to immerse himself in the problem domain so deeply that he begins to discover nuances that even those who live with air traffic control every day have not fully considered.*

While the people involved are the experts in their particular real-world problem, they seldom need to think in an abstract way about the details. Exceptions and irregularities can just be "dealt with" as they arise. In a manual system, someone can scribble a note, post an additional invoice, or adjust some totals. However, an automated system cannot be so forgiving, and possible irregularities need to be considered right from the start.

People will not usually volunteer information about the little oddities of their problem, and even when questioned will often not recognize that they might be important. Answers such as "No, not really," or "Hardly ever," or "Umm, no, I don't think so, umm, well maybe," are a sign that a complication exists that needs to be understood before any design of a database should proceed further.

As you have seen in the previous chapters, databases are often set up to solve one immediate problem with little regard for what may come next or how sometimes the situation may vary from the norm. In Example 1-4, "Academic Results," tables were set up to record students' marks without considering the (sadly not altogether uncommon) case of a student having to repeat a subject.

In this chapter, we look at ways to get an initial, accurate overview of the problem and express this with use cases. Then, having understood all the definitions, details, exceptions, irregularities, reasonable extensions, and uses of the system (gasp), we have to ensure that our abstract model captures the most important features accurately. It is, after all, the abstract model that will eventually be implemented.

You may be designing your own database, or perhaps you are designing one for someone else. In either case, there are two views of the problem. One is the concrete, real-world view from the person who will be the eventual user (I will call this person the client), and the other view is the more abstract model from the person who is designing and possibly developing the system (I'll call this person the analyst). If you are designing your own database, then wear two hats and swap them as necessary.

As a good understanding of a real–world problem depends so critically on the client and analyst being able to understand each other, we will take a moment to look at the two different views of a problem.

Real and Abstract Views of a Problem

The analyst sees the problem in a mostly abstract way. For the type of database problems we are considering, the processing can mostly be separated into:

- Entering, editing, or otherwise maintaining data.

- Extracting information from the database based on some criteria. This view of the problem is shown in Figure 3-2.

---

[1] Peter Coad and Ed Yourdon, *Object Oriented Analysis* (Upper Saddle River, NJ: Yourdon Press, 1991).

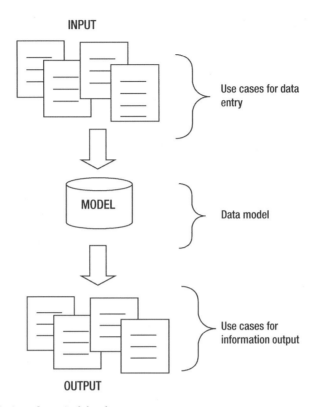

Figure 3-2. *An analyst's view of a typical database system*

The first thing an analyst must do is understand the client's problem in sufficient detail to help determine the input and output requirements (both immediate and potential). These can be expressed in use cases. The analyst then needs to develop a data model that will support those requirements. As you shall see in later chapters, the data model provides considerable insight into the details of a system, so the use cases and data model are often developed in tandem.

Establishing the use cases is not a simple problem. Users or clients seldom have a clear idea of the whole process. Many database projects fall into one of the two categories described in the next sections, and it is useful to look at these from the client's perspective.

Data Minding

A data–minding project involves a client who has data that needs to be looked after. This is often the case for research results. A scientist may devise an experiment to collect data that will allow a specialist statistical analysis to be undertaken. The analyst's responsibility here is to think ahead and ask questions about how else the data might be used, and store it in such a way as to allow for the immediate and possible future requirements. This process is depicted in Figure 3-3.

27

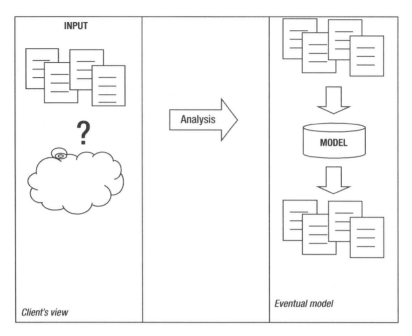

Figure 3-3. The analysis of a data-minding problem

A careful analysis at this stage helps prevent the very common and infuriating situation of knowing the data is "in there" but not being able to "get it out" conveniently. Predicting the potential output requirements, given the type of data that is being collected, is one of the most difficult aspects of storing data.

Task Automation

Many projects involve a client with a job that needs to be automated. This could be a small business, club, or school that has been keeping records by hand or with software that needs to be updated. Maybe they are looking to transfer their data to a database with a web interface. These clients usually have a clear idea of what they do. The analyst's job here is to separate what the client *does* from what needs to be *recorded* and *reported*, and recast the problem as shown in Figure 3-4.

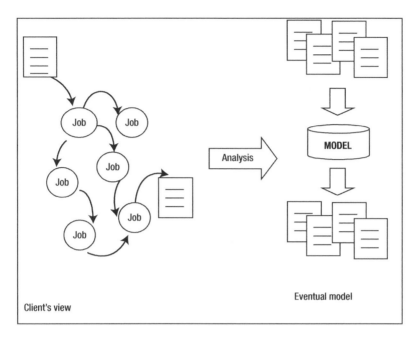

Figure 3-4. *The analysis of a task automation problem*

A typical description for a task automation problem at a local school might go like this:

When parents call up to say that children are sick, we have to let their classroom teachers know, and if it's sports day and the child is on a school team, the sports teacher might have to sort out substitutes. Then we need to count up all the days missed to put on the child's report. The Department of Education needs the totals each term, too.

Recording the absence and being able to report it in several ways are clearly prime requirements. However, what about the sports teams? Does the system need to differentiate those children on teams (and if so does it need to know which teams)? Does the system need to know on which dates there are interschool matches? Probably not. Differentiating what the client *does* (if it's sports day, tell the sports teacher) from what needs to be *recorded* is part of the scoping process. The eventual solution for the sports part of the problem may be as complicated as recording all the details about teams, substitutes, and match dates, or may be as simple as handing the sports teacher a list of everyone who is absent each day and letting her sort it out.

Every problem is different, so we need a general framework for discovering and representing the intricacies of a database problem. A good start is to determine answers to the following questions:

- What does the user do?

- What data are involved?

- What is the main objective of the system?

- What data are needed to satisfy this objective?

29

- What are the input use cases?

- What is the first data model?

- What are the output use cases?

The preceding steps are iterative. As we learn more about the problem, we will probably have to return to the early steps and adjust them. We will work through these steps in the context of Example 3-1.

EXAMPLE 3-1. MEAL DELIVERIES

Visitors to the city staying in local motel or hotel rooms are offered a service that will deliver to them a variety of fast food or takeaway meals (pizzas, burgers, Indian takeout, and so on). A visitor phones the company and places an order for some meals. A driver is selected and dispatched to pick up the meals from the appropriate fast-food outlets. The driver delivers the meals to the customer, receives the payment, and informs the depot. He also fills in a time sheet, which he returns to the depot later.

One of the reasons given for wanting to automate this currently manual process is to be able to produce statistics about the numbers of orders taken and about the time taken to complete orders.

What Does the User Do?

"What does the user do?" is a question particularly relevant to task automation problems. As a start, it is useful to list the jobs that the user regularly undertakes. Here is a starting list of tasks undertaken in the current manual meal deliveries example:

- Receptionist records details of order (address, phone number, meals, total price).

- Receptionist selects a driver and gives him the information about the order.

- Driver picks up meal(s) from fast food outlet(s).

- Driver delivers meal(s) and informs the depot.

- Driver hands in time sheet at the end of his shift.

- Receptionist or manager produces weekly and monthly statistics.

The first five of the preceding tasks may involve entering data into the system, while the last task involves reporting on information already in the system.

What Data Are Involved?

The tasks described in the previous section are very much stated from the users' point of view and are what physically take place. We need to step back a bit, put on our analysts' hats, and think about what data, if any, need to be recorded or retrieved at each step.

It is useful to start by thinking about what a typical order might involve. Let's say a family is in a motel for the night and rings up for curries for mum and dad and pizzas for the kids. Brainstorm about what data could be recorded at each step of the job. Some possibilities are shown in Table 3-1.

Table 3-1. *Physical User Tasks and Related Data*

Task	Physical Jobs	Data That Could Be Recorded
1	Take order.	Order number, address, phone, name, meals, price, time.
2	Dispatch driver.	Driver's name (or ID?), order number, time, outlets to visit.
3	Pick up meals.	Order number, time of picking up each meal.
4	Deliver meals.	Order number, time of delivery.
5	Enter time sheet.	Anything other than what we already have for each order? Sign-in time, sign-out time?

Let's look at some of the questions each of these jobs might raise:

Take order: Recording the information about an order seems fairly straightforward. We need to be able to identify an order easily. We could refer to the customer and the time of placing the order, but generally assigning an order number will make it easier to track the order through its various stages. The information about the customer is fairly obvious. We need to at least record where the meals are to be delivered and how to get in touch with the customer. What about the meals that have been requested? How do we record this information? Presumably the customer is choosing from some list of available meals. Should the system be able to somehow provide that list of meals to the receptionist so that a selection can be made? What about price? If we have data about the meals, we will know the price. Is there some other cost that needs to be entered? Is there a mileage charge perhaps?

Dispatch driver: First up, we need to think about how we know which driver is going to deliver the order. Does the system need to keep track of the whereabouts of drivers and determine which driver is the most appropriate? Does the receptionist choose from a list of drivers on duty? Does the system need to keep track of which drivers are available or which are currently on a delivery? If all the drivers are busy, what happens?

Having decided on a driver, we then need to tell him about the order (two curries, two pizzas). Do we also tell him where to go to get them (e.g., are there several pizza outlets from which to choose)? Does the system need to record which outlets provided the meal for this order? If the outlets for pizzas and curries are far apart, might two drivers be involved?

Pick up meals: What do we want to record about a driver picking up a meal? Do we want the system to be able to tell us the current stage of an order (e.g., "Curries were picked up at 8:40, pizzas have not been collected yet")? Do the eventual statistics need to be separated into times that meals were picked up and times that meals were delivered, or will overall times do?

Deliver meals: If statistics on time are important, recording the time the meals were delivered will be essential.

Enter time sheets: Assuming that time sheets are currently managed manually, looking at an existing time sheet will be very helpful. It is possible that the manual time sheet will contain some of the information we have already discussed. Is there any data that we have not recorded yet? Does the system need to record information about pay rates and payments made to the drivers? We discuss looking at existing manual forms again in the section "Finding Out More About the Problem."

What Is the Objective of the System?

Clearly, a system to record meal deliveries could be quite small or very large depending on how much of the information in the previous section we decide to record. With our analysts' hats on, we need to sort out the main objectives and provide pragmatic solutions (as opposed to all-encompassing ones).

One common problem if you are working with other people is that when you ask questions similar to the ones described in the previous section, your clients may become quite enthusiastic about broadening the scope of the system to include more and more. They will soon settle down, though, when they realize that extras come at a cost.

It is important not to see everything that *could* be automated as something that *should* be automated. Many jobs are much more conveniently done manually and often a task or a decision is better for having some human involvement. A good example is assigning demonstrators to laboratory classes. While the database may have all the information about requirements and availability, the actual matching up may be better done by a real person who has additional information (e.g., who has a tendency to sleep in, who is likely to fall out with whom, who is likely to be most patient at 5:30 on a Friday afternoon).

It is best to keep the scope of the problem as small and tightly defined as possible in the early stages of the analysis. Satisfy the most pressing requirements first. A properly designed database should not be too difficult to expand later as necessity dictates or as time and funds allow. Let's think about the meal delivery example. The initial incentive for developing the database was to provide summary information about the orders and the times involved. Information about orders in a summary might include the total number of orders and/or their combined value, probably within some timeframe (weekly or monthly). This information might allow the company to identify some trends and adapt its business accordingly.

Let's think about the time statistics. How detailed should they be? Here is where you need to be imaginative. A question such as "What statistics do you want about time?" may not elicit adequate detail from a client. If it doesn't, you might try to think of what could be achieved and try some more specific questions. Here are a few suggestions:

- Do you need to have statistics to back up statements such as "Our meals are delivered within 40 minutes" or "Our average delivery time is 15 minutes"?

- Do you need to be able to break down the delivery time to see where the delays are? For example: How long does an order typically have to wait before a driver becomes available? What proportion of the time is spent waiting for the meals to be prepared? What is the average time taken to deliver a meal from outlet to customer?

- Do you need to be able to break these statistics down by driver? For example, to find out if any drivers are regularly slower than others?

- Do you need to be able to break these statistics down by outlet? For example, do you need to see the average waiting times for each outlet to determine whether any are significantly slower?

The purpose of these questions is to determine the most pressing requirements. Let's assume that for this small business the main objective is just to get some idea of the overall times from phone call to delivery. Asking the other questions may (or may not) lead the client to become too ambitious: "I never thought of that. What a good idea. Throw that in as well."

Before everyone gets carried away, it is essential to consider how realistic it is to obtain data sufficiently reliable to fulfill these extra ideas. The main objective of overall delivery times isn't too difficult. It requires the time of the call to be logged, as well as the time of final delivery. Any more detail than that comes at significant cost. Drivers will have to be constantly recording times or informing the depot at each stage of the process. Will an extra receptionist be required to cope with maintaining all this extra data? If these extras are not essential to the client, the scope should exclude them. If, however, the extra information is one of the main purposes of acquiring the system, there are still issues to consider. How accurate will the data be? If drivers suspect that times are being recorded next to their names, might they feel pressured into being less than accurate sometimes? Setting up a complicated system to analyze inaccurate numbers is a waste of everybody's time and money.

Let's assume that after some careful thought it is agreed that only the total delivery time is required. We can now restate the main objectives of the project:

To record orders for meals so that summaries of the number, value, and overall time taken to process orders can be retrieved for different time periods.

What Data are Required to Satisfy the Objective?

We can now revisit each of the tasks in Table 3-1 with the more clearly stated objective in mind. After further consultation with the client, we can produce some more precise descriptions of the tasks, such as the ones below.

Take order: If we are to provide statistics by month or week, we will need to record a date. The client has confirmed that there is a price list of different meals, and it would be useful for the receptionist to be able to make selections from this list. We will therefore need an additional task: to enter and maintain information about meals and their prices. The client confirms that the cost of the order is just the total cost of all the meals.

Dispatch driver: We need to know how a driver is chosen and determine what we need to record. Let's assume we discover that the drivers are assigned to be on duty for various time units. Obviously, being able to maintain and print out duty rosters would be useful. However, automating rosters doesn't directly contribute to our main objective. It is agreed to leave the rosters outside the scope of the system for now. The receptionist will use information available independently of the database (probably a list of names pinned to a notice board) to determine who should be assigned to deliver an order.

Even though the receptionist will assign the driver manually, we still need to consider what the system will need to record. How important is the accuracy of the driver information? If we want to keep data about what particular drivers do (for example to calculate pay or analyze performance) then keeping accurate information is important. If, for this system, it is only necessary to be able to contact the driver to place the order and check its progress, then a contact phone number on the order will be sufficient. This needs to be clarified with the client with a question such as, "Is it important for you to know how many orders were delivered by different drivers?" Let's say for now that this is not required in the initial stages.

Where does the driver go to pick up the pizzas? Is it part of the system to suggest or record the outlet? Once again, if the purpose of the statistics is to streamline the business, knowing where each driver traveled and how long they had to wait at various outlets would be essential. Given that we have determined that this is not the main objective, we decide not to maintain information about outlets for now.

Pick up meals: We agreed with the client that only the overall time from initial contact to final delivery of an order is required. This means we do not need to record the times at every stage of the process. Even if we don't record the pickup times, might it still be useful to know that a meal has been picked up and is on its way to the customer? Certainly this will be useful information when there is a delay or a problem. However, to satisfy our main objective, it is not necessary for the system to record information about the status of a delivery. If there is a problem, the receptionist has a contact number for the driver and can call him and find out the stage of the order. So in the first instance, we need to record nothing about picking up meals.

Deliver meals: If we want to have statistics on overall delivery times, we clearly need to record the time that each meal is delivered. We don't need to be concerned at this stage how that information gets into the database. The driver may call the depot or write the time on a time sheet for entering later. At this stage, we are only concerned that the system is capable of storing the delivery time for each order. When the order is delivered, the receptionist also needs to know that the driver is free to take another order. We decided in the section about dispatching drivers that for now these decisions would be independent of the database. The receptionist would probably just make a manual note that the driver was able to take a new order.

Enter time sheets: We already have the driver's name, information about the order, and delivery times recorded. Is there anything else we need to record at this step? Let's say that a look at the current manual time sheets confirms that we already have all the information we need.

We have gone to a lot of trouble to ask questions to clarify the scope of the problem and the data necessary to support that. The decisions to which we have come are hypothetical. They are not right or wrong. Even for a real problem there will not be right or wrong answers; we can only ever hope for a good pragmatic solution. If the database is designed sensibly, being able to add additional information or increase the scope should be reasonably straightforward at a later stage. It may take considerable time to come to some decision about the size and scope of the system, so having arrived at some agreement, it is important to clearly express what the new scope is. Example 3-2 restates the problem in light of our rethink.

EXAMPLE 3-2. RESTATEMENT OF MEAL DELIVERY PROBLEM

The system will record and provide information about meals and their current prices. It will maintain data about orders including the date, the meals requested, and contact information for the customer and the driver assigned to the delivery. It will also maintain the time the order was placed and the time it was finally delivered. Given this, the system will be able to provide summary information about the number and value of orders within particular time periods and also summaries of the time taken for total processing of orders. The system will not maintain any additional information about drivers nor about which drivers were associated with a particular order. The system will not maintain any information about outlets nor which were used for any particular order.

What are the Input Use Cases?

Recall that use cases are simply textual descriptions of the ways users interact with the system. There are many different levels of use case from very high-level descriptions of objectives to very low–level tasks. The most useful level for our purposes of trying to understand and describe a database system is the user task level. In his book *Writing Effective Use Cases*,[2] Alistair Cockburn describes this as something small enough "that a user could do in less than about twenty minutes and then go off and have a coffee." He also says it should be a job "significant enough so that if a user did several of the tasks in a day he could use it as evidence for a raise." So something like "manage the orders for the business" would be too broad for a task and "look up driver's phone number" would probably be too insignificant.

---

[2] Alistair Cockburn, *Writing Effective Use Cases* (Boston, MA: Addison Wesley, 2001).

Now that we have a clearer idea of the objectives and the scope of the system, we can return to our list of jobs that involve data entry (which appears earlier in Table 3-1) and decide what interaction with the system needs to take place at each point. The interactions are shown in Table 3-2.

Table 3-2. *Physical User Tasks for Data Entry and Interaction with the Proposed System*

Task	Physical Job	Interaction with System
0	Record available meals.	Enter and maintain data about each item that can be ordered (ID, description, current price).
1	Take order.	Enter order data (order number, time, address, phone) and the ID of each meal required (assume for now that prices don't change).
2	Dispatch driver.	Record driver's contact number with appropriate order.
3	Pick up meals.	Nothing.
4	Deliver meals.	Record delivery time for the appropriate order (here or possibly at the next step).
5	Enter time sheet.	Nothing.

The interactions in Table 3-2 form the basis for our first attempt at writing down some data entry use cases. How big should each use case be? Should we combine some tasks or split others into more than one use case? The overriding consideration is readability and communication. At the first pass, about five to ten use cases is enough (and not too many) to give a clear view of the components of a small problem.

We could consider combining all the tasks that involve data about an order into one use case (i.e., entering the original order, adding the driver contact, and updating the delivery time). However, for this problem these tasks are all quite separate, performed at different times, and possibly by different people. It may not be possible to assign a driver to an order immediately (during busy times we may have to wait to see which driver becomes available first), so entering the driver contact data should be a separate task from entering the order. Similarly, recording the delivery time is a separate task performed at a different time. Each of these tasks to do with updating an order are central to the whole business and will be repeated several times a day, so it is reasonable to consider providing each with its own use case. However, the mechanics of adding the driver contact and adding the delivery time are almost identical in that information about a particular order has to be found and then updated. We can (if we feel like it) combine these into one use case called, for example, "Update Order Status."

Thinking about updating the status of an existing order leads us to ponder how the user will be able to locate a particular order. It might be useful to provide lists of orders yet to be assigned a driver or yet to be delivered. We will not look at specific user interface design at this stage (i.e., how such a list would be presented or how a user might select the appropriate one); however, making such information available will be important. We have enough data stored to be able to find orders with no driver contact number or no delivery time. Given that this information will be almost essential to the receptionist and it is readily available in the system, we will add reporting on uncompleted orders as a use case also. Example 3-3 shows the use cases so far.

EXAMPLE 3-3. INITIAL USE CASES FOR MEAL DELIVERIES

Figure 3-5 shows the initial use cases for the meal delivery problem, and the text for each use case is given after the figure.

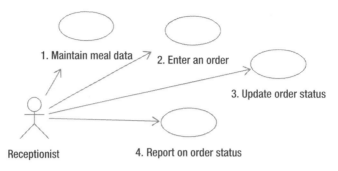

Figure 3-5. Use cases for meal deliveries

- **Use case 1**: Maintain meal data. Enter and update data on meals (ID, description, current price).

- **Use case 2**: Enter an order. Enter initial order information (order number, date, address, phone) and for each meal record the ID. (This assumes prices do not change. We will consider price changes later in the chapter in the section "Changing Prices.") Each meal must be one that is already in the system.

- **Use case 3**: Update order status. For a particular order already in the system, add driver contact number or delivery time.

- **Use case 4**: Report on order status. Retrieve all orders satisfying required status (e.g., no driver contact number or no delivery time).

What Is the First Data Model?

Now that we have some idea of the data we need to maintain, we can sketch a first data model for the problem. We clearly have data about at least two separate things, orders and the types of meals that can be supplied, and so have two classes as shown in Figure 3-6. The objects of the Meal class will be each of the meal types that appear on the menus in a client's motel or hotel room.

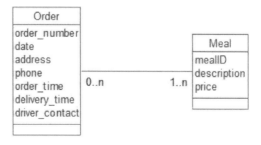

Figure 3-6. First attempt at a data model for meal delivery database

In Figure 3-6, we have separated each of the pieces of data we are recording and put them as attributes in the most likely class. Let's recap from Chapter 2 what a model like Figure 3-6 means. Reading from left to right, we have that a particular order (e.g., "to Colombo Street at 8:30 on April 1st") can involve one or more meal types. From right to left, we have that each type of meal (e.g., chicken vindaloo) could appear on many orders but may not appear on any (e.g., no one may ever want to order spinach and anchovy pizza). Just in case there is any confusion, when we talk about a meal, we mean a type of meal as it appears on the menu. We don't mean that a particular portion of curry may end up on more than one order!

Note that this model is only a first attempt and overlooks some important details that we will consider later in the chapter.

What Are the Output Use Cases?

We now need to reconsider the required reporting and summarizing tasks in terms of the data we are keeping, as in the data model in Figure 3-6. We have already determined that it would be useful to report on orders awaiting the assignment of a driver or orders yet to be delivered, and have included that in use case 4 in Example 3-3.

Let's think about the statistics on orders and delivery times that are part of our main objective. The statistics on orders can be found by considering the Order objects. We can find the value of each order by summing the prices of each meal associated with that order, given (for now) that prices remain constant. We can also determine the time taken for each order by subtracting the order_time from the delivery_time. By selecting those order objects that are in the date period of interest, we can determine different statistics about the times (e.g., averages or totals) during a particular week or month or whatever is required. We have enough information stored in our data model to satisfy the requirements of our main objective.

It is useful at this point to look at the data we are storing and see what other information can be deduced. Given the data we have, what other statistics could we supply? How about grouping all the orders for a particular type of meal? It might be useful to ask the client whether, given that much of the information is already stored, they like to know how much gross income came from pizzas, or how many people ordered curries, or if orders containing particular types of meals took longer to deliver. Do we have the information in a form that would make this type of report readily available?

We have information about particular meals (e.g., a chicken vindaloo or a lamb korma) but it is not easy to find out about different categories of meals (pizzas versus curries). Maybe it would be useful to introduce a new attribute or class, Category. Each meal could then be assigned a particular category. We will look more closely at whether something like a category should be an attribute or a class in Chapter 5, but for now take my word for it that a Category class would be a good idea. This is only a small extension to the problem and may provide considerable additional information for little extra effort or cost. With our analysts' hats on, we should at least discuss this addition with the client.

Even if we don't include an additional Category class, we still need at least one further use case to deal with the statistical output. Because all the reports are broadly similar, we can describe them quite clearly in one use case as shown in Example 3-4.

EXAMPLE 3-4. STATISTICAL REPORTING USE CASE FOR MEAL DELIVERIES

Figure 3-7 shows the use case for reporting statistics.

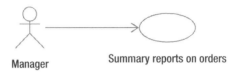

Manager   Summary reports on orders

Figure 3-7. Use case for reporting statistics

Use case: Summary reports on orders. (This assumes constant prices.)

For each completed order with a `date` *in the required time period:*

- Find all the associated meals and retrieve their `prices,`

- If required calculate the time of the order by subtracting `order_time` from `delivery_time.`

- If required, group orders by smaller time periods (day, week, etc.).

- Average and/or total prices/times.

More About Use Cases

We have been using very simple descriptions in our use cases. However, they can contain much more information, good examples of which can be found in Alistair Cockburn's book *Writing Effective Use Cases*. This book goes into more detail than I do here as it includes the analysis of larger projects where the specification of requirements for contractual purposes is more critical. In this book, we are using use cases not so much as a contractual specification document but as a way to clarify and learn more about the proposed project, its scope, and its complexities.

There are no hard-and-fast rules about what use cases should include or how they should be presented. The overriding consideration is that they should be readable and provide a clear and complete description of what each task involves.

Let's take a closer look at some further aspects of use cases.

Actors

We use an *actor* as a representation of a user of our database. In order to take into account all the different ways our users might interact with the database, it is useful to consider all the different *types* of people our users may encompass.

In our example of the meal delivery service, you will see that in Figures 3-5 and 3-7 we distinguish two actors: receptionist and manager. It is not necessary to become too concerned about which people are associated with particular use cases. What is important is to consider the different *roles* of people likely to interact with the system and see the problem from the perspective of each. For a small business, these roles might be carried out by one or two people in total. For larger organizations, a single role might have many people associated with it (many data entry operators, for example). It becomes a case of putting on different hats and looking at the problem from different points of view.

Here are some broad categories of roles people might have, with examples from our meal delivery service.

Clerical/data entry operators: Users in this role deal with entering or updating raw data (e.g., entering order details or finding an order to enter a delivery time).

Supervisors: Users in this role deal with day-to-day details. They may require lists of transactions, rosters, and so on. For our meal delivery database, these users would probably deal with things such as a list of which orders have not yet been delivered or details of specific orders to follow up on problems.

Managers: Managers are more likely to be interested in summaries rather than day-to-day details (e.g., the total number of orders for each day during the last week or the average time of delivery for today's orders). They may also require very general summaries that show trends and which can be used for forecasting and strategic management decisions (e.g., value of orders per month over the last two years).

Thinking from the point of view of these different roles (or actors) can give a great deal of information about what the system will need to provide to be most useful.

Exceptions and Extensions

The textual description of each use case is the place to include any exceptions or problems that might occur. For our simple example, there are not too many. We might include what to do about orders that run past midnight so as to get the elapsed time correct (I hate dealing with times!). We might also include what happens if an order is not completed for some reason. This is quite tricky. We need to differentiate orders that have been cancelled from those that have not yet been delivered so our report on the status of current orders is correct. Every time we ask for those orders not yet delivered, we don't want to include all the discontinued orders from the beginning of time. Here are two possibilities: cancelled or terminated orders could be deleted from the system, or we could add a new attribute, status, to the Order class that could have values such as ordered, delivered, cancelled, and so on. The second option is more advisable in that it seems wasteful to delete information that is already in the system, and it is quite probable that a manager would be very interested to know what percentage of orders were cancelled (and very possibly why-but that introduces yet another level of complexity). Any additions such as keeping track of cancelled orders would have to be reflected in the use cases and data model.

As you can see, thinking about the things that can go wrong at each step helps our understanding of the problem.

Use Cases for Maintaining Data

Maintaining data includes three activities: storing new values, altering existing values, and deleting data. The three updating tasks can be combined into one use case (e.g., maintain meal data). While they are all separate jobs and are likely to be done at different times, they don't really individually satisfy the criteria for a user task given previously. A user could not really use the fact that she had corrected many misspellings of a meal description as evidence for a raise. Database software provides facilities to carry out data maintenance activities. If we create a table for meal data, the software will almost certainly provide utilities to allow us to add new meals, find particular ones (based on the value of one or more attributes), update the values for a particular meal, or delete a meal entirely. So for many classes, it is quite reasonable to include these maintenance activities in one use case and leave the particulars for when we design a user interface at some later point.

For some tasks, it may be sensible to separate out different aspects of maintaining a particular class of data. In our meal delivery example, we have separated entering orders from updating orders (e.g., adding the driver contact and delivery time) because these are quite significant and separate parts of the receptionist's job and they will certainly happen at different times. Considering the entering and updating tasks separately encouraged us to think about how a receptionist might conveniently find the appropriate order to update its status, and so led us to provide reports on the status of current orders.

Whether these aspects of maintaining the order data should be in separate use cases is a matter of opinion, and the deciding factor should be what is most readable and provides the best communication. As we only have a few use cases, leaving these separate seems reasonable; but if the scope, and therefore the number, of use cases grew, then clarity might be better served by combining them.

Use Cases for Reporting Information

For many clients, reporting tasks are probably the most significant part of the database system. We need to be able to extract objects that meet some criteria and then do something with them: display them on a screen or web page, write them out in a report, group them together, count them, or average or total some attribute value(s).

As we have seen, it is very useful to consider how we might want to select or group the objects when producing a report. In the meal delivery example we considered grouping orders by the type of meal and quickly realized that a broader definition of *meal category* might prove useful. Asking detailed questions about reports early on is a good investment because it will have an impact on the classes that will be required.

How many use cases do you need for reports? Once again be guided by readability. The use case in Figure 3-7 includes quite a few similar but different possibilities and is fairly easy to read. If we were to include other quite different reports (rosters, invoices, and so on) then each should have its own use case.

The mechanism for choosing which report to print or which orders to include (this week's or this month's) is not a matter for this part of the analysis. We defer these decisions until the user interface is designed. All that matters at this stage is that the data are stored in such a way as to make the reports possible.

Finding Out More About the Problem

We have considered a number of questions that need to be answered to understand and scope a project, and we have presented the questions as a dialog between client and analyst. A great deal of information is also available from other sources. The existing forms and reports that the client (business, researcher, club, etc.) is using are an excellent way to get an overview of a project. These documents can provide a wealth of detail and can be the source of a number of interesting questions. Having a close look at input forms and reports right at the start can improve the understanding of the problem and form a great basis for a line of detailed questioning.

It is important to realize that you are looking at the forms and reports to find out about the problem (not to find out about the forms and reports). Empty forms give an indication of the data the client expects to be recorded. However, much more information will come from filled-in forms. Here you are likely to find many of the irregularities and exceptions. Look for fields that are not filled in or are marked "not applicable." Look for options that are crossed out and another written in by hand. Look for fields that have two values in them or for explanatory notes written by hand on the bottom or back of the form. It is these details that will really give you some insight into the complexities of the problem.

Existing reports also give you a guide as to what information is currently accessible to the client. But bear in mind that this project has possibly been commissioned because the existing reports are unsatisfactory in some respects. Inspecting the existing reports can give rise to interesting questions. Look for gaps in the rows or columns. Look for blanks as opposed to zeros. Question any negative numbers. Ask for definitions of amounts.

What Have We Postponed?

Our analysis of the meal delivery example is nowhere near complete because we need a bit more expertise with data modeling to represent some of the complexities. For those concerned about the oversights, here are some of the things that we still have to consider. We will look at these issues again in more depth in later chapters.

Changing Prices

The `Meal` class has an attribute that we have called `price`. This is the current price of a meal, and clearly it will change over time. When a new order is placed, we need to know the current price that is recorded with the meal information. If the prices change and we run a report about old orders, as described in the use case in Figure 3-7, we will have a problem. The only prices we are storing are the current prices, so we will not necessarily find the total cost of particular orders when they were placed, but instead will find how much those same orders would cost at today's current prices. There are a number of ways to remedy this. The simplest in this case would be to include another attribute in the `Order` class to contain the total value of the order *at the time of ordering*. This will then be unchanged at a later date when the meal prices change.

Meals That Are Discontinued

Another thing that is certain to change over time are the meals being offered. Adding new meals doesn't raise any problems; however, removing a meal is trickier. If we remove a meal, we have to consider what happens to old orders in the system that are associated with that meal. We probably want to retain this historical data, so we may choose never to remove any meals that are associated with orders.

We then have the problem that our set of meals includes some that should not be associated with new orders. One way to deal with this is to add an attribute, `available`, to the `Meal` class that indicates whether the meal can be ordered at the present time. We would need to alter our use case for entering an order to say that only meals that are *available* can be included. Our reporting use cases, however, would probably include all meals that were ordered during the reporting period.

Quantities of Particular Meals

What if our customer orders two chicken vindaloos? We can associate the `Order` object with the `Meal` object, but where do we keep the information about how many of this particular meal is to be delivered for this order? This is a very serious oversight, and to fix it requires a new class between the `Order` and `Meal` classes. This often happens when we have Many–Many relationships. We will discuss this further in Chapter 4.

Summary

The first part of the analysis process is to understand the main objectives and the scope of the project. The analyst's job is to get inside the heads of all the different types of people who will use the system to understand what they require now and what they are likely to need in the future. The process is iterative but is likely to include the following steps:

- Determine the main objective of the system.
- Determine the jobs different users do in an average day.

- Brainstorm the data that could be associated with each job.

- Agree on the scope of the project and decide on the relevant data.

- Sketch data input use cases, consider exceptions, and check existing forms.

- Sketch a first data model.

- Brainstorm the possible outputs given the data being collected.

- Sketch information output use cases.

- Check that the data model can readily provide the output information

TESTING YOUR UNDERSTANDING

Exercise 3-1.

Consider the scenario described at the beginning of this chapter:

When parents call to say that children are sick, we have to let their classroom teachers know, and if it's sports day and the child is on a school team, the sports teacher might have to sort out substitutes. Then we need to count up all the days missed to put on the child's report. The Department of Education needs the totals each term, too.

Run through the steps in the summary section and sketch some use cases and an initial data model. Assume that the main objectives are to record the absences for the classroom teacher, for school reports, and for statistics given to the Department of Education.

CHAPTER 4

■ ■ ■

Learning from the Data Model

In the previous chapter, we attempted to extract the essential tasks involved in a real-world problem and express them with use cases. We also made a first attempt at determining the data that are necessary to support those tasks and formed an initial data model, which we depicted with a class diagram. In this chapter, we look more closely at the data model to see how it can further our understanding of a database system.

A data model is a precise description of the data stored for a real-world problem, in much the same way that a mathematical equation describes a real-world physical event, or an architectural drawing describes the plan of a building. However, like a mathematical equation or an architectural plan, the data model is neither a complete nor an exact description of a real situation. It will always be based on definitions and assumptions, and it has a finite scope. For example, a high school student's simple mathematical equation to describe the path of a ball tossed into the air will probably make assumptions about the constancy of the gravitational force and the absence of air resistance, and will likely assume low speeds where relativistic effects can be ignored. The equation is precise and correct for the assumptions that have been made, but it does not reflect the real problem exactly. It is, however, a good, pragmatic, and extremely useful description that captures the essentials of the real physical event.

A data model has similar benefits and limitations to a mathematical equation. It is a model of the relationships among the *data items* that are being *stored* about a problem, but it is not a complete model of the real problem itself. Constraints on money, time, and expertise will always mean that problems will need to be scoped and assumptions made in order to extract the essential elements. It is crucial that the definitions and assumptions are clearly expressed so that the client and the analyst are not talking at cross-purposes.

In the early stages of the analysis, as client and developer are trying to understand the problem (and each other), the details will necessarily be vague. In this chapter, we look at how the initial data model can be used to discover where definitions and scope may need to be more rigorously expressed.

Review of Data Models

The essential aspects of a data model were defined in Chapter 2. We will revisit these by way of an example that will highlight some additional features. Think about a small hostel that provides a number of single rooms for school groups visiting a national park. The hostel has a small database to keep track of its rooms and the people currently in residence. Because the hostel primarily deals with groups of students with a single point of contact, the idea of a group is central to their business model. It is still important to know which rooms particular students or teachers have been allotted. An initial data model to capture this information is shown in Figure 4-1.

You can see that there is a 1–Many relationship between the Group and Guest classes. Reading from left to right in Figure 4-1, we have that a particular group is related to one or more guests, and from right to left that a particular guest is associated with exactly one group. Figure 4-1 also depicts a 1–1 relationship between Guest and Room. Reading left to right, we have that each guest must be associated with one room and in the other

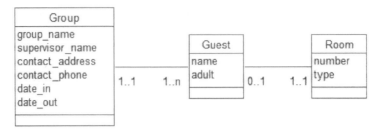

Figure 4-1. *Initial data model for the current occupancy of a small hostel*

direction that a room can be associated with at most one guest but maybe none. In normal speak, we have that groups consist of a number of guests, and each guest has a room. Rooms are for one guest only, and they may not all be full. Some possible instances of these objects and relationships are shown in Figure 4-2. We have

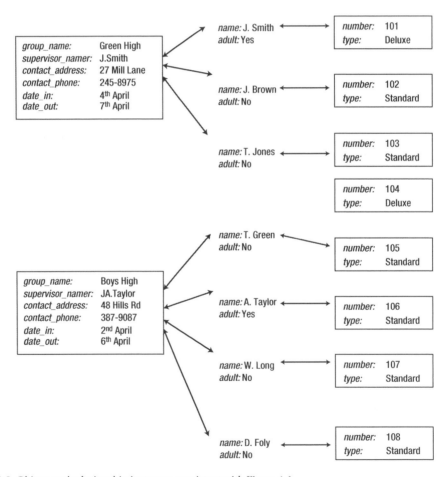

Figure 4-2. *Objects and relationship instances consistent with Figure 4-1*

two groups: Green High with three associated guests, and Boys High with four. Each of the guests is associated with one room (and some rooms are empty). Take a little time to convince yourself of how the class diagram in Figure 4-1 represents the situation.

Notice that room 104 is empty as is allowed by the data model (a room does not have to be associated with a guest). Now that we have read what the data model tells us in a mechanical way, let's think a little bit more deeply about what the model is telling us about the real problem and how it is being handled.

What is the definition of a *group* for this hostel? We see that in the example data in Figure 4-2 the Boys High group consists of four people. There is only one arrival date and departure date for the entire group and just the one set of contact information that applies to all the group members. In this respect, our definition of *group* is a little different from what we might expect in normal conversation. It is not a set of people who all know each other and feel as though they belong together, but a set of people with the same arrival and departure dates and common contact information. For the most part this model will work well for the hostel, but there will be the odd exceptional case. What would we do if A. Taylor and W. Long need to leave the Boys High group a day early? How could we record this information? There is no place to store dates with Taylor's or Long's Guest object, and there is only room for one departure date to be stored with the Boys High Group object. Within this model, we could capture this information by creating another Group object for Taylor and Long (Boys High Early Leavers, say) with a different set of dates. That would cope with knowing who is coming and going when. If it is essential, however, that the system needs to record that these two groups of Boys High people are somehow "together," the data would need to be modeled differently.

The data model also tells us that a guest *must* belong to a group. What else does this tell us about the definition of a group? What about a lone traveler wishing to stay at the hostel? Given that the hostel is primarily set up for groups of people this is unlikely, but it can be accommodated within the model. We can have a group with just one guest. In this respect, the definition of *group* for this database problem is once again different from the way the word is used in normal conversation. We would not generally refer to a *group of one person*; however, for this data model that is a possibility that might eventuate.

So our original data model, which at first glance looked quite simple, has told us quite a bit about how the problem is being dealt with. It has led us to a precise definition for a *group*:

A group is a set of guests with common contact information and with identical arrival and departure dates. A separate group will need to be formed for each different set of arrival and departure dates. A group can have one or more guests associated with it.

By being careful with the definition of the Group class, we have avoided needing special cases for groups with more than one set of dates or for guests traveling alone. This keeps the problem and its solution simple. Of course, if the majority of guests were lone travelers, we would rethink the problem and model it in an entirely different way.

In the rest of this chapter, we will look at questions we can ask about small pieces of a data model in order to learn more about the problem at hand. The questions we will look at only apply to relationships between two classes, but they can open up a great deal of discussion about the problem. As more is understood about a problem, what we learn from the data model can be reflected in the use cases. The questions we will consider are as follows:

- **Optionality:** Should it be 0 or 1?

- **Cardinality of 1:** Might it occasionally be 2?

- **Cardinality of 1:** What about historical data?

- **Many–Many:** Are we missing anything?

Optionality: Should It Be 0 or 1?

As described in Chapter 2, the optionality of one end of a relationship is the smallest number of objects that can be associated with an object at the other end. This is usually 0 or 1. For example, in Figure 4-1, reading the relationship between guest and room from left to right, we have that a particular guest *must* be associated with a room (optionality 1), whereas reading the relationship from right to left, we see that a particular room may have no related guest (optionality 0).

Optionalities can provide a great deal of information about the definitions of classes and the scope of the problem. We will look at a few small examples, each of which illustrates some aspect of deciding on the appropriate optionality.

Student Course Example

Consider the data model in Figure 4-3, which shows a relationship between students and courses in which they enroll.

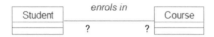

Figure 4-3. *Data model for students enrolling in courses*

On first sight this is quite trivial: a student can enroll in many courses, and a course can have many students enrolled in it. What about the optionalities? Can a student be enrolled in no courses? Our normal conversational definition of a student is someone who is studying or, more accurately, is formally enrolled in a course (which is quite different really!). What is our definition of student for this database? It has been a long time since I've been able to be described as a student in normal conversation, but I am quite sure I still feature in the student database at my former university. For the purpose of this example then, we might define a student as someone who is, or has been, enrolled in a course.

Does it make any sense to have a "student" in our database that is not and has never been enrolled in any courses? What about a person who has been accepted into a university but has not yet made final decisions about any specific courses? Is this person a student? The university would certainly want to keep information about such a person (her ID, name, address, and so on). We can accommodate this situation by expanding our definition of a student to include people accepted by and/or registered with the university.

What about a person who has contacted the university and asked to be sent information about enrollment? Any typically cash-strapped institution will want to keep information about such a person. Asking this question starts to involve issues about the scope of the problem as well as the definition of a student. It is important that questions such as "Exactly who are these people you call students?" are considered right at the start of the analysis process. Is the system to include contact details for everyone who has ever expressed an interest in attending the university, or is the scope to be restricted (at least for the time being) to records of current and former students?

Clearly, only the client can answer these questions. It is useful to see how careful consideration of the details of even the most simple data model can lead to important questions about much wider aspects of the problem. Asking whether a student must be enrolled in a course may seem pedantic at first, but until we can answer that question clearly, we have not even begun to understand the problem we are trying to solve.

Reading the relationship from right to left and questioning whether a course must have a student enrolled in it leads to a similar debate about how we define a course. What data might we want to keep about a course? Think about all the different situations we might need to deal with. We might need to consider former, current, or proposed courses; popular courses offered more than once concurrently (two streams); and unpopular courses that are on the books but lack students. You cannot come up with absolute answers without being able to discuss the situation with a client, but you can come up with some possible definitions for consideration.

Customer Order Example

Here is an easier example. (Or is it?) We keep information on customers and the orders they place. Our first instinct is to say that customers can place many orders and each order is placed by one customer. This can be represented as in Figure 4-4.

Figure 4-4. *Data model for customers placing orders*

What about the optionalities? Consider the relationship from left to right. Can a customer be associated with no orders? This depends on the definition of a customer. For the purposes of many businesses, it might be *anyone I am hopeful of selling something to.* A working definition such as *anyone who has ever placed an order and other people who are to be sent catalogs* seems reasonable and suggests an optionality of 0 (i.e., customers in our database have not necessarily placed an order). However, this definition should probably spark a few questions such as, "Do you want to be able to identify people who have previously placed orders but who are now fed up with being sent catalogs?"

Reading the relationship from right to left, we want to know whether each order *must* have an associated customer. This seems trivial. What is the point of an order if we don't know who it is for? If an order arrives in the mail with no name or address, it would be reasonable to say that it should not be entered in the database, and so from this perspective we can insist that every order must have a customer (optionality 1).

However, there is a subtle difference between knowing for whom an order has been placed and relating it to a customer object in the database. A written order may come in the mail from Mrs. Smith of Riccarton Road. While we know who placed the order, that is different from associating it with a customer. We may have to create a new object if Mrs. Smith is a new customer, or we may be faced with deciding which of the existing three Mrs. Smiths this order is from. The problem of distinguishing customers with similar details or deciding whether two or more entries in the customer database actually refer to the same real person can be difficult. Once again, we are not trying to solve any of these issues just now. We are simply using the data model to make us think clearly about some of the issues we will have to confront.

Insect Example

Here is another example of how investigating the optionalities of a relationship can lead to questions about the scope of the problem. Figure 4-5 shows part of a possible data model from Example 1-3 in which farms were visited and several samples of insects were collected. A `Visit` object would contain information about the date and conditions of a particular visit and would be associated with several `Sample` objects. Each sample object would contain information about the number of insects collected.

Visit			Sample
	?..1	?..n	

Figure 4-5. *Data model for collecting samples*

47

Asking whether a sample *must* be associated with a visit is like the question in the previous section about whether an order *must* have a customer. If for this research project our samples only come from farms, it is reasonable that we had to visit a farm to collect them, and so each sample should always be associated with a visit. However, if the scope of the database is broader, with records of samples that have been stored for years and whose origin is uncertain, we may have to reconsider. If we insist that a sample is associated with a visit then we will not easily be able to record information about these historical samples.

Asking whether each visit must have an associated sample (should the optionality at the sample end be 0 or 1?) leads to an interesting question. Is it possible that at some time we may want to record visits to farms for reasons other than collecting samples? These questions may seem trivial, but the broad understanding of the larger problem can only be improved.

A Cardinality of 1: Might It Occasionally Be Two?

Every part of a problem is susceptible to exceptional occurrences. During the analysis of a situation, it is important to think carefully about different scenarios to ensure that the database will be able to cope adequately with all the data that may eventuate. Some "exceptions" are really complications that have been overlooked. Real life and real problems are always complicated. Even something as simple as *write down your usual address* can have hidden difficulties, as many children in shared custody discover when they have to fill out an address on a school form. It might seem picky to insist on asking "Might a person have more than one usual address?" but thousands of modern-day families cannot be shrugged off as exceptional.

In this section, we will look at how to deal with "exceptions" that do not warrant a complete overhaul of the problem but nevertheless are likely to turn up during the lifetime of the database. We have already seen an example of a likely exception earlier in this chapter in the hostel data model. There we considered the case in which some members of a group might want to leave before the others. In the hostel data model, rather than complicating the problem by allowing each group to have several dates, we redefined what we meant by *group* for the purposes of storing the data (i.e., a set of people arriving and leaving on the same dates).

The following sections provide some other examples where a different definition can help cope with some foreseeable, but unusual, events.

Insect Example

In the previous section we looked at the example of a scientist visiting a farm to collect insect samples. Some insects might behave differently if it is fine or raining so it may be important to record information about the weather when the sample was collected. To record the weather conditions consistently, the scientist may decide to choose from one of a number of categories. Introducing a Weather class with objects for the different conditions (e.g. fine, overcast, raining) can ensure that this information is recorded consistently. Part of a possible class diagram to represent the data is shown in Figure 4-6.

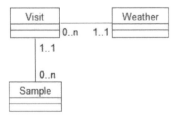

Figure 4-6. *Associating a weather category with a visit*

48

Reading the relationship between weather category and visit from left to right, it is reasonable that a visit will have one weather type that describes it, but there might also be occasions when a thunderstorm arrives while the last few samples are being collected. If so, do we care? The answer will, of course, depend on the client, but it is up to the analyst to ask the question and propose some possibilities.

At one extreme, the conditions under which each individual sample is collected may be vital. In this case, it might be more sensible to associate each sample with its own weather condition, as shown in Figure 4-7.

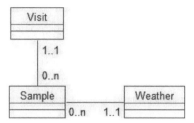

Figure 4-7. Associating each sample with a weather category

This latter solution may be overkill when the majority of visits have stable weather conditions. It seems pointless to record the same weather condition for each of 50 samples. A compromise solution may be to say that, if the weather changes markedly, we will create another visit. This way all visits have a single associated weather type, and we can cope with the "exceptional" case by redefining what we mean by a visit. For example:

A visit is a time spent on a farm during constant weather conditions on a single day. It is possible to have more than one visit to a farm per day.

This compromised solution is similar to our redefinition of a group for people with different departure and arrival dates in the hostel example. The data model remains unchanged, but our revised definition of a visit is in place for the inevitable day when lightning strikes, so to speak.

Sports Club Example

Here is another little snippet of a database problem. A local sports club may want to keep a list of its membership and the team for which each member currently plays (SeniorB, JuniorA, Veteran, etc.). One way to model this data is shown in Figure 4-8.

Figure 4-8. Members and their current teams

The data model as it stands does not require all members to be associated with a team (optionality 0 at the team end). This means members may be purely social or may miss out on being selected for a team. However, we should still ask questions about the maximum number of teams with which a member might be associated. For example, "Can a member play for more than one team and, if so, do we care?" The data model clearly does not allow for historical records to be kept. If a player is promoted from one team to another, he will simply be

49

associated with the new team, and we will lose information about his association with his previous team. If the scope of the database is simply to record current affiliations of members with teams, then that is OK. (If not, just wait a few moments until the next section.)

Even if we are only keeping information on current team membership, we are always going to come across the situation where injury or sickness necessitates a member of one team filling in for another team for a particular match. How will this affect the data model? This is a question of scope. Why are we keeping this data and what information do we want to be able to extract from the database? If we want to keep track of which players played in particular matches, our data model is woefully inadequate. We will need to introduce a `Match` class and consider other complications (see Chapter 5).

However, the scope of the problem may simply be to record a person's *main* team. This may be to enable team members to be on a list to be phoned if a match is canceled or if there is to be a rescheduled practice or a social outing. If this is the case, the cardinality of 1 in the data model in Figure 4-8 is fine, so long as it is understood that the relationship *plays for* means a player's *main* team rather than just any team they may play for.

A Cardinality of 1: What About Historical Data?

We have had a number of examples of relationships with a cardinality of 1 at one end. A room has one guest; a club member plays for one team. In both these cases, we have been careful to add the word *currently* because over time a room will have many guests and a player many teams. An important question is, "Do we want our system to keep track of previous guests or previous team affiliations?" This is often overlooked during the analysis, and sometimes the oversight does not become evident for some time. A sports club will find its system just fine for the first season but may get a surprise when the next year's teams replace the previous ones, which are then lost forever. In this section, we will look at a few different examples to illustrate how we can manage historical data.

Sports Club Example

To illustrate how the sports club might lose its historical data, let's look at some simple data as it might be kept in a database table. If each member is associated with just one team, that team becomes a characteristic of the member, and the relationship can be represented as an attribute in the `Member` class as in Figure 4-9.

member_no	last_name	first_name	team
152	Abell	Walt	SeniorB
103	Anderson	James	JuniorA
276	Avery	Graeme	JuniorA
287	Brown	Bill	JuniorA
298	Burns	Lance	Veteran

Figure 4-9. Members and their current teams

The following season when Bill Brown graduates to the SeniorB team, his previous association with the JuniorA team will be lost. If the historical data are important, the problem must be remodeled to reflect the fact that members will be associated with many teams over time. A revised model is shown in Figure 4-10.

50

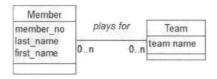

Figure 4-10. Members and the teams for which they play

Departments Example

Figure 4-11 is an example that often appears in textbooks. Reading from left to right, we have that each department has one employee as its manager. But clearly this means one at a time. Over time, the department will have several different managers.

Figure 4-11. Each department has a manager.

The important question for this situation is, "Do we want to keep track of former managers?" Why are we keeping information about managers at all? If it is just to have someone to call when something goes wrong, probably the current manager is all that is required. However, if we want to know who was in charge when something went wrong last year, we will need to keep a history. The data model will need to change so that a department can be associated with several managers as in Figure 4-12.

Figure 4-12. A department has several managers over time.

We will see in the next section how the introduction of an intermediate class will allow us to keep the dates for each manager.

Insect Example

Here is a real example of a problem arising in our scientific database of insect samples. To put the data in perspective, we need to know that the main objective of this long-term project was to see how the numbers of insects change as farming methods evolve over the years. The farms selected represented different farming types (organic, cropping, etc.). Throughout the duration of the project, each farm was visited several times to collect samples. Figure 4-13 shows part of an early attempt at a data model.

Figure 4-13. Visits to farms of different types

51

At first the data model in Figure 4-13 seemed to be serving its purpose adequately, but this was only because the farming types had not changed during the time the project had been running. However, real trouble was in store. A farm can only be associated with one farm type in this model. When a farm did eventually change, say from a conventional cropping farm to an organic farm, the previous farming type would be lost if the database was set up this way.

A farm can only be associated with one farming type *at a time*. The important question to ask is, "Might the type change over time, and is it important for the system to record that historical data?" In this case, it was critical to the whole experiment to keep information about the history of the farm types, but no one had noticed the problem because the time frames for change were very long.

A Many–Many: Are We Missing Anything?

We have come across quite a few Many–Many relationships in our examples so far. For example, a student can enroll in many courses, and a course can have many students enrolled in it. If we widen the scope of some of the examples to include historical data, as in the previous section, a number of 1–Many relationships will become Many–Many relationships (i.e., departments may have many managers, members many teams, and farms many types over a length of time).

Often we find that we need to keep some additional information about a Many–Many relationship. In the sports team example, we altered the model of members and teams to allow a member to be associated with more than one team. However, if we look at the model in Figure 4-10, we have no idea *when* those associations occurred. The historical data will not be of much use without a date attached somewhere. But where will the date go? In Figure 4-10, we have two classes: Member and Team. The date does not belong as an attribute of Member because it will be dependent on which team we are interested in. Similarly, the date cannot be an attribute of the Team class because there will be different dates for each of the players. This problem occurs often and is usually remedied by the introduction of a new class.

We need to ask the question:

Is there any data that we need to record that depend on particular instances of each of the classes in our Many–Many relationship?

In this example, the question would be:

Is there any data that depend on a particular player and a particular team?

And the answer is:

Yes—the dates that player played for that team.

Figure 4-14 shows how an intermediate class can be incorporated into the Many–Many relationship so that data that depend on a particular pairing of objects from each class can be included.

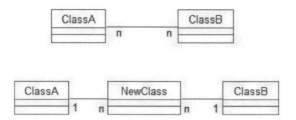

Figure 4-14. *Introducing a new class in a Many–Many relationship*

In situations where we have data that depend on instances of both classes in a Many–Many relationship, the Many–Many relationship is replaced by a new class and two 1–Many relationships. The many ends of the new relationships are always attached to the new intermediate class. We will see what this means for some of the examples we have already examined.

Sports Club Example

Let's reconsider the member and team problem. We'll put some attributes in the classes to make it clearer what information each is maintaining. The model is shown in Figure 4-15.

Figure 4-15. *Many–Many relationship between members and teams*

As we have already mentioned, the date that a particular member plays for a particular team cannot live in the Member class (because a member will play for many different teams over time) nor can it live in the Team class. Figure 4-16 introduces a new intermediate class, Contract, in the same way as was done in Figure 4-14.

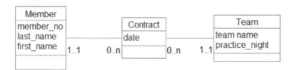

Figure 4-16. *Intermediate class, Contract, to accommodate the date a member played for a team*

Reading from the middle class outward, the model tells us that each contract is for exactly one team and exactly one member. Reading from the outside inward, we see that each member can have many contracts as can each team. Figure 4-17 shows some objects that might occur in such a data model.

53

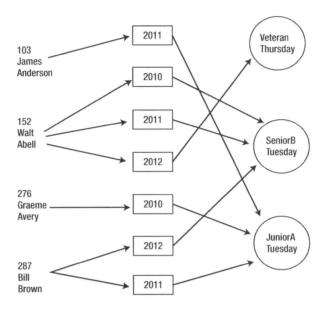

Figure 4-17. Some possible objects of the Member, Contract, and Team classes

We can now see what years members played for particular teams. We can see that Bill Brown (287) played for the JuniorA team in 2004 and for the SeniorB team in 2005. These data would be stored in database tables as shown in Figure 4-18.

member_no ▾	last_name ▾	first_name ▾
152	Abell	Walt
103	Anderson	James
276	Avery	Graeme
287	Brown	Bill
298	Burns	Lance

Member

team_name ▾	practice_night ▾
JuniorA	Tuesday
SeniorB	Tuesday
Veteran	Thursday
Under 18	Monday

Team

member ▾	team ▾	year ▾
103	JuniorA	2011
276	JuniorA	2010
287	JuniorA	2011
287	SeniorB	2012
152	SeniorB	2010
152	Veteran	2012
152	SeniorB	2011

Contract

Figure 4-18. Data for players, contracts, and teams

54

Student Course Example

Let's now return to the Many–Many relationship of students enrolling in courses (Figure 4-3). This isn't just a historical problem, although we clearly will want to know when the student completed the course. But even if we were only keeping student enrollments for a single year or semester, we should still look to see whether there is missing information that might require an extra class. The question that needs to be asked is:

Are there any data that I want to keep that are specific to a particular student and his or her enrollment in a particular course?

One obvious piece of data that fits the preceding criteria is the result or grade. Once again, we cannot keep the grade with the Student class (because it requires knowledge of which course) nor with Course class (because the grade depends on which student). In the same way as we dealt with this situation in Figure 4-14, we can introduce a new class, Enrollment, between the Student and Course classes as shown in Figure 4-19.

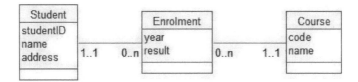

Figure 4-19. *Intermediate class to accommodate the result (and the year)*

A student and a course can each have many enrollments, and a particular enrollment is for exactly one student and one course. If we were to draw some objects, we would get a picture very like that in Figure 4-17 with students, enrollments, and courses replacing players, contracts, and teams.

Meal Delivery Example

As a final example of when we might need an additional class to keep information about a Many–Many relationship, let's look again at the meal delivery problem (Example 3-1) from the previous chapter. The initial data model had a Many–Many relationship between types of meal and orders. A particular type of meal (a chicken vindaloo, say) might appear on many orders, and a particular order may include many different meal types, as shown in Figure 4-20.

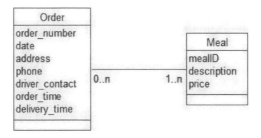

Figure 4-20. *Orders for different meal types*

What happens if a family orders three chicken vindaloos, one hamburger, and one pork fried rice? Where do we put these quantities? The quantity cannot be an attribute in the Order class (for this order there are three quantities and they each depend on the particular meal) nor in the Meal class (for there will potentially be hundreds of orders involving a particular type of meal, each with different quantities).

Once again, our problem of where to put the additional data is solved by including a new class as shown in Figure 4-21.

Figure 4-21. *Orders for different types of meal–with additional class to store quantities*

For some problems, it can be difficult to come up with a meaningful name for the intermediate class. In such a case, it is always possible to use a concatenation of the two original class names as we have done here with Order/Meal. We could maybe have called the class Orderline, in this example, as it represents each line in the order (i.e., a meal and the quantity). You might find it helpful to sketch some objects of the three classes in Figure 4-21 to clarify what is happening.

We can also use this new intermediate class to solve one of the other problems we deferred in Chapter 3. This was the problem of coping with the price of a meal changing over time. In the Meal class in Figure 4-21, we can define the price attribute as being the current price for that type of meal. An order placed for that meal today will be at that price. How do we know what was charged for this type of meal on an order several months ago? To deal with the problem of changing prices, we can include an attribute, price, in the intermediate class Order/Meal. This will be the price charged for a particular meal on a particular order and will not change when the current price changes in the Meal class. This way we have a complete history of the prices for each meal on each order. A price attribute in this intermediate class can allow us to keep historical data and also to deal with "unusual" situations such as specials or discounts. We are always keeping the price that was actually charged for that type of meal on that particular order.

The question that needed to be asked about the original Many–Many relationship in Figure 4-20 was:

Are there any data we need to store about a particular meal type on a particular order?

And the answer is:

Yes, the quantity of that meal type ordered and the price being charged for that meal type on the order.

When a Many–Many Doesn't Need an Intermediate Class

A few Many–Many relationships contain complete information for a problem without the need for an intermediate class in the data model. Problems that involve categories as part of the data often do not require an additional class. Example 1-1, "The Plant Database," involved plants and uses to which they could be put. The original data model is repeated in Figure 4-22.

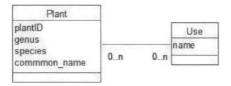

Figure 4-22. *Plants and their uses*

We can ask the question, "Is there any information we want to keep about a particular species and a particular use?"

In this case, the answer is probably, "No." A Many–Many relationship that doesn't require any additional information often occurs when we have something that belongs to a number of different categories; for example, a plant has many different uses and all we want to know is what they are.

It is possible, however, that in a different situation we might want to record whether a particular plant is excellent or just reasonable at hedging. Or we may want to note how many of a particular species are needed to be sufficient for attracting bees. In both these cases, we might need an intermediate class. Try sketching a new model for these situations.

Summary

Even at the very early stages of analysis, a simple data model can provide us with a number of questions. The answers to these questions will help us to understand a problem better. The resulting clarifications to the problem should eventually be reflected in the use cases and may affect the final model and the eventual implementation.

In this chapter, we have suggested some questions about a single relationship between two classes. Some of the questions we have discussed are reviewed here.

> **Optionality:** Should it be 0 or 1? Considering whether an optionality should be 0 or 1 might affect definitions of our classes; for example, "Would a student who was not enrolled in any courses still be considered a student for the purposes of our database?"

> **A cardinality of 1**: Might it occasionally be 2? We need to consider whether there might be exceptional cases in which we might want to squeeze two numbers or categories into a box designed for one; for example, "What happens if the weather changes during a visit?" Redefining a class might help out for the exceptional cases, as in, "If the weather changes, we will call it two visits."

> **A cardinality of 1:** What about historical data? Always consider whether the 1 in a relationship really means "just one at a time." For example, "A department has one manager. Do we want to know who the previous managers of the department were?" If so, the relationship should be Many–Many.

> **Many–Many:** Are we missing anything? Consider whether there is information we need to record about a particular pairing of objects from each class; for example, "What might we want to know about a particular student and a particular course?" If there is such information (e.g., the grade), introduce a new intermediate class.

57

TESTING YOUR UNDERSTANDING

Exercise 4-1.

Figure 4-23 shows a first draft of modeling the situation where a publishing company wants to keep information about authors and books. Consider the possible optionalities at each end of the relationship `writes` and so determine some possible definitions for a book and an author.

Figure 4-23. *Consider possible optionalities for authors writing books.*

Exercise 4-2.

Figure 4-24 shows a possible data model for cocktail recipes. The Many–Many relationship `uses` can be navigated in either direction. To find out the ingredients in a Manhattan or to discover the possible uses for that bottle of Vermouth. What is missing?

Figure 4-24. *Cocktails and their ingredients. What is missing?*

Exercise 4-3.

Part of the data model about guests at a hostel is shown in Figure 4-25. How could the model be amended to keep historical information about room occupancy?

Figure 4-25. *How could this be amended to keep historical information about room occupancy?*

CHAPTER 5

■ ■ ■

Developing a Data Model

In the previous chapters, you've seen how to determine the requirements of a database problem by considering the tasks users of the system need to carry out. Tasks were represented with use cases, and a simple data model was developed to represent the required data. In Chapter 4, you saw that a great deal can be learned about a problem by questioning some of the details of simple relationships, particularly the number of objects involved at each end of a relationship. In this chapter, you'll be introduced to a few problems that frequently occur in order to enlarge your armory for attacking tricky situations.

Attribute, Class, or Relationship?

It is never possible to say that a given data model is *the* correct one. We can only say that it meets the requirements of a problem within a given scope, and subject to certain assumptions or approximations. If we have a piece of data describing some person or thing or event, it is possible that there may be different ways of representing that information. In this section, we look at a simple problem, described in Example 5-1, for which various pieces of data may be represented as an attribute, class, or relationship depending on the overall requirements of the problem.

EXAMPLE 5-1: SPORTS CLUB

Let's say we are keeping information about current teams for a sports club. The club wishes to keep very simple records of the team name, its grade, and the captain. As a start we could have a class to contain this information as shown in Figure 5-1.

Figure 5-1. Simple class for Team

59

In Figure 5-1, each of the pieces of information we are capturing about a team, the name, grade, and the name of the captain is represented by an attribute. With this model, we can find the values of the attributes for any given team, but that is about all we can do. Of course, that may be all we want to do!

In previous chapters, we saw that it is important to consider how the data being stored might be used in the future. With the data in Figure 5-1, it is quite likely we may want to find all the teams in a given grade. Will the simple data model allow this? It is certainly possible to find all the **Team** objects with a given value for the **grade** attribute; however, to obtain reliable data, we would require the data entry to be exact. We would not get an accurate list of all teams in senior grade if the value of the **grade** attribute for different objects was variously recorded as "Senior," "snr," "Sen Grade," "Senior Grd," and so on. We saw a similar problem in Example 2-1 where we wanted to ensure plant genus information (like *Eucalyptus*) was always spelled correctly. If reliable recording and extracting of data about grades is important for our sports club, we need a data model that will ensure grades are recorded consistently. This can be done by representing the grade of a team as a class as in Figure 5-2. Each possible grade becomes an object of the **Grade** class, and each team is related to the appropriate **Grade** object.

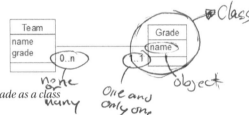

Figure 5-2. Representing a team's grade as a class

Therefore, depending on the requirements of the project, we might choose to represent the grade as an attribute of **Team** (if the consistency of the spelling is not important) or as a class of its own (if we think we may want to find all the teams belonging to the same grade, for example).

Now consider the **captain** attribute in Figure 5-1. It's unlikely that a person will captain more than one team at a time, so a query analogous to the one in the previous section (find all the teams Jenny currently captains) is unlikely to be a high priority. However, there may be some additional data about a captain that we might like to keep: perhaps her phone number and address. In the context of a sports club, it is highly likely that this information already exists in some membership list. We very possibly have another class, **Member**, that keeps contact information about all the members of the sports club. If so, we can represent a team's captain as a relationship between the **Team** and **Member** classes as shown in Figure 5-3. A particular object of the **Member** class is the captain of an object of the **Team** class.

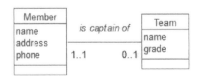

Figure 5-3. Representing captain as a relationship

Once again, depending on the problem, we have different ways to represent a team's captain. We might choose to represent the captain as an attribute of **Team** or as a relationship between **Member** and **Team**. The determining factor here will be whether the problem requires information about members in general.

60

Some useful questions to ask when considering whether to represent information as an attribute, class, or relationship are summarized here:

- "Am I likely to want to summarize, group, or select using a given piece of information?" For example, might you want to select teams based on grade? If so, consider making the piece of information into a class.

- "Am I likely now or in the future to store other data about this piece of information?" For example, might you want to keep information such as phone and address about a captain? Does (or should) this information already exist in another class? If so, consider representing the piece of information as a relationship between the classes.

Two or More Relationships Between Classes

How would the model in Figure 5-3 change if we also wanted to keep information about the people playing for a team? We may need to know their names and phone numbers. Keeping all this information as attributes of the **Team** class will rapidly become unwieldy. We would need attributes such as **player1Name**, **player1Phone**, and so on. Once again, we probably have the information we require about players already in a **Member** class. The fact that particular members play for a particular team can therefore be represented as a relationship between the classes. This is very similar to the situation in Example 2-1 where plant objects were related to particular use objects. Figure 5-4 shows the addition of this relationship between **Member** and **Team** in our data model.

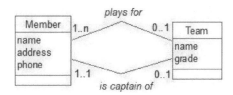

Figure 5-4. *Different relationships between Member and Team*

We now have two relationships between our **Member** and **Team** classes. One is about which members play for the team (could be many). The other is about which member is the captain of the team (just one). The model in Figure 5-4 also allows for members who do not play for or captain any teams (they may be social members of the club). Such members would simply not be linked to a team.

You may be wondering whether a captain of the team should always be one of the players in that team. The model as drawn in Figure 5-4 does not have anything to tell us about such a constraint. There are a number of ways to represent constraints such as this. It is possible to make the constraints part of the relevant use case. For the use case describing entering information about a team, we would say that the captain has to be one of the players. The *Object Constraint Language (OCL)*, developed by the Object Management Group,[1] to supplement the Unified Modeling Language, UML, provides a formal specification for constraints. I will not delve into formal methods in this book, preferring to draw attention to these additional constraints in the use case text.

Another situation in which it is possible to consider two relationships between classes is when we have historical data. Example 5-2 revisits the **Rooms**, **Groups**, and **Guests** example that we first examined in Chapter 4.

---

[1] http://www.omg.org/

61

EXAMPLE 5-2: SMALL HOSTEL

A small hostel consists of single-occupancy rooms. Typically, groups of people (e.g. school classes) stay at the hostel. We will expand the problem from Chapter 4 by keeping information about previous guests as well as current guests. A room will have many guests over time.(For simplification, we will assume that a guest only stays once and in one room.) The revised model is shown in Figure 5-5.

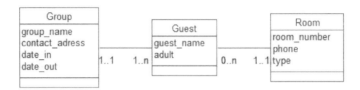

Figure 5-5. Model for a single occupancy room having many guests over time

The hostel primarily caters to groups of visitors and so the check–in and check–out dates belong with the group rather than each individual guest.

What can we find out from the model in Figure 5-5? If we have some query about a guest, we can easily find his room number, and we can also find the length of the stay by checking the dates of the related group object. Things become a little more complicated if we want to find the name of the guest currently occupying a room (say there has been a complaint about noise). There are an increasing number of guests associated with each room over time, so how do we go about finding the current one? One way would be to search through all the guests associated with the room and check their associated group information to find one with a **date_out** value in the future. Another likely task is to retrieve a list of empty rooms. To do this, we would have to find those rooms without a guest belonging to a group with a **date_out** in the future.

These solutions are quite feasible, but for tasks that are likely to be required regularly, they are complicated and tedious. A different option is to consider having a second relationship between **Room** and **Guest** for the *current* guest. All guests will be associated with a room as in Figure 5-5, but we add an additional relationship between the current guest and the room. This is shown in Figure 5-6.

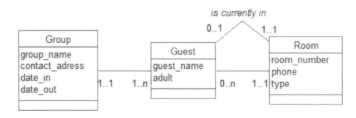

Figure 5-6. Alternative model for a room having many guests over time

With the data model in Figure 5-6, we can find the current guest with reference to objects of only two classes (**Room** and **Guest**). With the model in Figure 5-5 we needed to inspect date attribute values of the **Group** object as well. To find empty rooms, we can now simply look for all rooms that have no current guest.

There are a few problems with modeling the data in this way as some extra updating is required to keep the data consistent. For example, when a group checks out, we will have to update the **date_out** in **Group**, and we will also have to remove each *is currently in* relationship instance to reflect that the room is now empty. This extra maintenance step is caused because we are in effect storing the same piece of information in more than one way. While the *retrieval* of information about empty rooms and current guests is simpler for the model in Figure 5-6, the *updating* of data is more complex. Table 5-1 shows possible use cases for checking out a group, and a report for listing all currently empty rooms for each data model.

Table 5-1. *Some Possible Use Cases for the Alternative Guest and Room Models*

	With Data Model in Figure 5-5	With Data Model in Figure 5-6
Check out a group	Update **date_out** for appropriate **Group** object.	Update **date_out** for appropriate **Group** object. Find all associated **Guest** objects and remove the *currently in* association with the **Room** object.
List all currently empty rooms	First find the occupied rooms: find all **Group** objects with **date_out** in the future. Find all the associated **Guest** objects for these groups, and the set of all **Room** objects associated with these guests. List the **room_number** for all **Room** objects *not* included in this set.	Find all **Room** objects that do not have an associated current **Guest** object.

It is clear that the reporting is simpler for a model such as that in Figure 5-6, while the maintenance is simpler for one like Figure 5-5. The problem with the model in Figure 5-6 is that if the updating required when checking out a group is not done correctly, we will end up with a database that has inconsistent information. While the model in Figure 5-6 appears easier to query, it is so at the expense of making the maintenance more difficult and therefore the reliability more likely to be compromised. As you shall see in the next section, it is best to avoid the situation where we have information stored more than once.

At this point we realize that neither of the models in Figures 5-5 or 5-6 is particularly good for the hostel problem if we want to keep historical data about room occupancy. The solution discussed in Chapter 4 allowed us to keep information about what groups had been to the hostel, who the guests were, and the current occupant of a room. That all worked well. Once we try to add the historical data about room occupancy, the model becomes difficult to manage. An alternative solution is suggested in the Testing Your Understanding section for Chapter 4.

Different Routes Between Classes

Using the model in Figure 5-6, we can find the current guest in a room by two routes: via the relationship *currently in* or by checking the **date_out** for each guest who has occupied the room. The problem here is that if the data are not carefully maintained, we might find that we come up with two different answers. For example, if a group is checked out but we did not remove all the *is currently in* associations (as in the use case in Table 5-1), the first route will give us the previous guest in the room, while the second route will show an empty room.

63

As argued in the previous section, the advantages in easy retrieval may appear to outweigh the associated data maintenance complications. What we should avoid at all costs is having alternative routes for a piece of information when there is no associated reduction in complexity.

Redundant Information

Having what should be the same piece of information available by two different routes can be referred to as *redundant information*. In the previous section, we had redundant information about the current occupant of a room. We could find the current occupant by inspecting the *is currently in* relation, or we could deduce the current occupant by looking at the check–out dates of the groups.

Let's have a look at Example 5-3, which is another case of redundant information.

EXAMPLE 5-3: STARTUP INCUBATOR

A startup incubator has employees who each work for one of a number of different small project groups. Each group and all its employees are housed in one particular room, with larger rooms housing several groups. We may require information such as where each employee is located, a particular employee's phone number, where to find a particular group, which employees work in each group, who is in each room, and so on. One possible data model is shown in Figure 5-7. Take a moment to understand the data model and the information it contains about the number of groups in a room and so on for this particular problem. The model has redundant information. Can you see what it is?

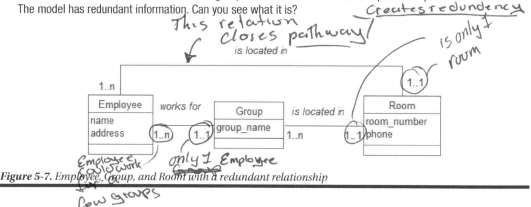

Figure 5-7. Employee, Group, and Room with a redundant relationship

With respect to Example 5-3, if we regularly want to find an employee's phone number, we might think that the top relationship in Figure 5-7 between **Employee** and **Room** would be a useful direct route. However, this same information is very easily available by an alternative route through **Group**. We can find the employee's (one only) group and then find that group's (one only) room. This is a very simple retrieval (it does not involve all the complications with dates that plagued the small hostel in Example 5-2).

However, the extra relationship is not just unnecessary, it is dangerous. With two routes for the same information, we risk getting two different answers unless the data is very carefully maintained. Whenever an employee changes groups or a group shifts rooms, there will be two relationship instances to update. Without very careful updating procedures, we could end up having that Jim is in Group A, which is in Room 12, while the other route may have Jim associated directly with Room 15. Redundant information is prone to inconsistencies and should always be removed.

64

> **Note** Whenever there is a closed path in a data model (as in Figure 5-7), it is worth checking carefully to ensure that none of the relationships are redundant.

Routes Providing Different Information

Not all closed paths necessarily mean redundant data. One of the routes may contain different information. Alter the problem in Example 5-3 slightly to allow an employee to work for more than one of the small project groups. This is shown in Figure 5-8. Can you deduce which room an employee is in now?

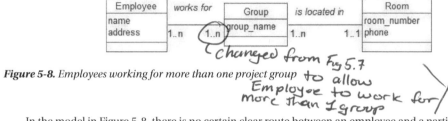

Figure 5-8. Employees working for more than one project group

In the model in Figure 5-8, there is no certain clear route between an employee and a particular room. For example, Group A may be in Room 12, Group B in Room 16, and Jim may work for both groups. Thus, Jim could be in either Room 12 or Room 16. Just narrowing the possibilities like that may be all the problem requires. If, however, each employee has a home room and we wish to record that information, we will need an additional relationship between employee and room as in Figure 5-9.

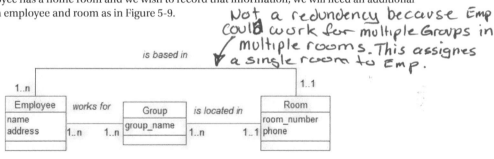

Figure 5-9. Different routes are providing different information.

It might seem that we have introduced another path that will give different answers to a question such as, "What room is Jim in?" Figure 5-9 allows us to have Jim based in a room different from that of any of the groups he works for. For real–life problems, this may be exactly what is required. The size of a room and the number of employees in a group are unlikely to always match. The important thing is to ensure that two routes do not contain what should be identical information so we do not introduce avoidable inconsistencies.

False Information from a Route (Fan Trap)

Not being able to deduce an employee's room from Figure 5-8 is an example of a more general problem. Take a look at Example 5-4.

EXAMPLE 5-4: LARGER ORGANIZATION

An organization has several divisions. Each of these divisions has many employees and is broken down into a number of groups. We might model this as in Figure 5-10. Have a look at the model. What can we deduce about which group or groups a particular employee is associated with?

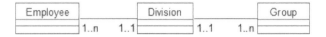

Figure 5-10. One (dangerous) way to model an organization

Figure 5-10 represents a very common problem often referred to as a *fan trap*. The danger here is to take a route between employee and group and infer something that was not intended. Figure 5-11 shows some possible objects consistent with the model in Figure 5-10.

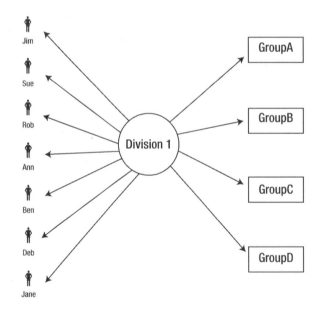

Figure 5-11. A fan trap

Consider employees Jim and Sue. It is not possible to infer anything about which groups Jim or Sue work for. It is only possible to get many combinations of a **Group** object and an **Employee** object that have a **Division** in common: Jim A, Jim B, Sue B, Jane D, and so on.[2] We must not mistake these combinations for the information we require—for example, which group or groups does Jane belong to?

The feature that alerts us to a fan trap is a class with two relationships with a Many cardinality at the outside ends. This leads to the fan shape in Figure 5-11.

---

[2] This situation is sometimes also referred to as a *lossy join*.

66

What can we do about it? If it is important for our system to be able to show the groups for which an employee works, we will need another relationship between **Group** and **Employee**, or we may need to model the problem quite differently (as shown in the next section).

Gaps in a Route Between Classes (Chasm Trap)

We might choose to model the relationships between divisions, groups, and employees in a hierarchical way as in Figure 5-12 (i.e., a division has groups and groups have employees). The optionality at one end of the employee–group relationship has not been specified. Think about the different possibilities.

Figure 5-12. *Another way of modeling an organization*

Figure 5-13 shows some example objects. We have a direct connection between an employee and a single group (Jim works for Group A) and another between a group and its one division (Group A is in Division 1). We can therefore make a confident and unique connection between Jim and Division 1.

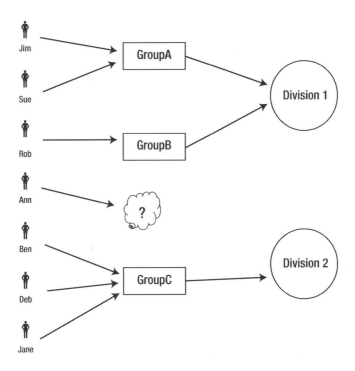

Figure 5-13. *A chasm trap*

67

So far, so good. However, in situations such as this, it is always useful to check that that connection is always there. What if Ann is not attached to a specific group? Maybe she is a general administrator for Division 1 and serves all groups. If an employee does not necessarily belong to a group, the model in Figure 5-12 does not provide a link between Ann and her division. To find the appropriate `Division` object, we need to know the `Group`, and Ann has no related `Group` object. If we need to know this information, we have a problem. This is sometimes referred to as a *chasm trap* (we can't get there from here).

This is yet another case where careful study of the data model provides quite interesting questions about the problem. For a model such as the one in Figure 5-12, we should always check for the exceptional case of an employee who may not be attached to any group.

How we solve the problem of a chasm trap depends on the situation we are modeling. One possibility is to add another relationship between division and employee so we can always make that connection. However, this extra relationship is going to cause redundant information. For many employees, we will have two routes for connecting them with a division: directly and via their group. This is the situation we had in Example 5-3 and can lead to inconsistent results for connecting employees and divisions. This is not recommended.

A different way to get around the problem in Example 5-4 is to introduce another group object (administration or ancillary staff). Ann could belong to this group, and we can then insist that every employee *must* be in a group. However, it may be that the problem needs to be remodeled entirely. It is often best to go back to the use cases and reconsider what information is the most important for the problem. It is never possible to capture every detail in a project with finite resources, so pragmatism becomes very important.

Relationships Between Objects of the Same Class

Let's return to our sports club from Example 5-1. Many clubs require a new member to be introduced or sponsored by an existing member. If it is necessary to store sponsorship information, a first attempt at a data model might be as shown in Figure 5-14.

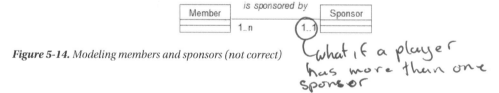

Figure 5-14. *Modeling members and sponsors (not correct)*

The problem with the model in Figure 5-14 is that (by definition) a sponsor is a member. The model will mean that if Jim sponsors a new member of the club, we will be storing two objects for him (one in the `Member` class and one in the `Sponsor` class), both probably containing the same information (until it inevitably becomes inconsistent). What is really happening here is that members sponsor each other. This can be represented by a *self relationship* as shown in Figure 5-15.

Figure 5-15. *Members sponsor other members*

68

The relationship in Figure 5-15 is read exactly the same as a relationship between two different classes. Reading clockwise, we have *a particular member may sponsor many members*, while counterclockwise we have *a particular member is sponsored by exactly one member*. As with all relationships, we have to change the verb depending on the direction (i.e., *sponsors* and *is sponsored by*). I have annotated Figure 5-15 to dispel any confusion about which way around we are going.

Nothing in this data model prevents members from sponsoring themselves. Such constraints need to be noted, most usefully by mentioning them in the appropriate use case (e.g., adding a member).

Self relationships appear in many situations. This is certainly true for data pertaining to genealogy or animal breeding. Consider the case in Figure 5-16 in which we record information about animals and their mothers (I am only leaving out fathers to keep the example simple!).

Figure 5-16. *Genealogical data about animals*

Reading clockwise, we have that *one animal may be the mother of several other animals*, and counterclockwise, that *each animal has at most one mother*. Why not *exactly* one mother? Every animal has to have a mum, does it not? This is where we have to be quite sure about the definitions of our classes. The class **Animal** represents those animals about which we are keeping data, not all animals. If we trace back the ancestry of a pure–bred dog for example, we may find his mother in our database, as well as her mother, but eventually we will come to a blank. You might argue that the additional generations should be added for completeness, but this could mean tracing back to the primeval slime. Our data model does not say that *some animals do not have mothers*, but merely that *some animals do not have mothers that are recorded in our database*.

As an aside, note that our **Animal** class will presumably contain animals of both sexes. Clearly if we establish an *is mother of* relationship between two **Animal** objects, the mother must be female. As it stands, there is nothing in the model to prevent male animals being recorded as mothers. This constraint could be expressed in the use case, but if this is a serious genealogical database, we may wish to treat males and females slightly differently. We will discuss ways to use techniques called *generalization* and *specialization* for situations such as this in Chapter 6.

Relationships Involving More Than Two Classes

In the examples so far, the information in which we have been interested generally relates to relationships involving two classes (e.g., which members are on which team, or which employee is in which group). Sometimes we have data that depend on objects of more than two classes. Let's reconsider a sports club. As well as keeping data about members and their current team, we might also want to keep information about games or matches between teams. Ignoring, for now, complications such as byes,[3] we can say that exactly two teams play in a match. A possible data model is shown in Figure 5-17.

---

[3] A *bye* sometimes occurs in a competition with an odd number of teams.

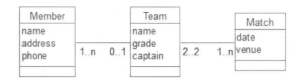

Figure 5-17. *Possible data model for members, teams, and matches*

The model in Figure 5-17 allows us to record a player's current or main team, the current members of a particular team, and the matches in which teams are involved. However, we cannot deduce that a particular player played in any given match (he may have been sick or injured). This is an example of the fan trap described earlier in the chapter. A team has many players and is involved in many matches, but we cannot say any more about which players were involved in particular matches. We could attempt to address this by adding a relationship between `Member` and `Match` as shown in Figure 5-18. Look carefully at the new data model. Can you see where there is a possibility that the data might become inconsistent?

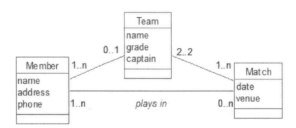

Figure 5-18. *Another model to represent members, teams, and matches*

From Figure 5-18, it is possible to have the following relationship instances:

- John plays for Team A.

- John plays in the match on Tuesday.

- The match on Tuesday is between Teams B and C.

If John plays for only one team (as the model indicates), then something weird is going on here.

Let's think through this problem with members, teams, and matches a bit further. If we want to keep track of who plays in which matches, our problem has some intricacies that the model does not adequately represent. If we are allowing for people being injured and not taking part, we also need to account for the situation in which someone from another team may need to fill in as a replacement. For example, John normally plays for Team A, but filled in for Team B on Tuesday because Scott was injured. Our scenario in the previous paragraph is not so weird—just a bit more complicated than we originally thought.

We still have a problem, however. We are happy that John normally plays for Team A and that he just happened to play in the match between Team B and Team C on Tuesday, but the model doesn't tell us which team he was playing for.

We need to step back, revisit the use cases, and figure out exactly what it is we want to know. If we want to know exactly which players played on each team for each match, then no combination of the relationships in Figure 5-18 will tell us that. The crucial point is that who played for which team in which match requires simultaneous knowledge of objects from three classes: which **Member**, which **Team**, and which **Match**. This is sometimes referred to as a *ternary relationship* (and, similarly, quaternary for four classes and so on).

When we have a case where the information we need requires simultaneous information from objects of three (or more) classes, we introduce a new class connected to all three classes as shown in Figure 5-19.

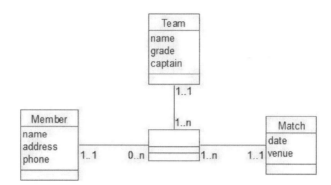

Figure 5-19. Members and the team for which they played in a particular match

We might be able to think of an appropriate name for this class; in this case **Appearance** would be sensible. If not, concatenating the other three class names will suffice (e.g., **Team/Member/Match**). This is not unlike introducing a new class in the Many–Many relationships we considered in Chapter 4. As in that case, the cardinality at each of the outer classes is 1.

Reading this model, we have something like this: each appearance involves one member, one team, and one match (e.g., Jim appeared for Team A in the match on Saturday the 12th); each member may have many appearances (Jim can appear in many matches, possibly for different teams); a team will have many players appearing in different matches; and a match will have many players appearing for each of the teams.

The new class may or may not have attributes. It may just be a holding place for valid combinations of **Member**, **Team**, and **Match** objects. If there are attributes for the new class, they must be something that involves all three classes. For example, what do we need to know about a particular player playing for a particular team in a particular match? Possibly the position. If we wanted to know that Jim played fullback for Team A in the match on Saturday the 12th, our new class is the place to record that information.

Figure 5-19 clearly has additional information that is impossible to deduce from Figure 5-18. What about vice versa? Can we re-create all the information in Figure 5-18 from 5-19? By looking at Figure 5-19, we can deduce all the teams a player played for, all the matches in which a player played, and the teams involved in each match. We do not need to add extra relationships between each pair of classes to figure out this information. In fact, it would be dangerous to do so as we would then have two routes for finding a piece of information and, as we have seen, that redundancy can lead to inconsistencies. However, there may be other information about each pair of classes that we would like to keep. For instance, in Figure 5-19 we know all the teams Jim played for but we don't know the team with which he regularly trains. Some binary relationships between each of the three classes may be required in addition to the relationships with the new class.

Whenever we have a pattern such as that in Figure 5-19, we should check whether the other binary relationships are necessary. If we have classes A, B, and C connected to a third class, for each pair of classes we should ask a question like, "Is there something I need to know about a relationship between A and B that is

71

independent of C?" For the preceding example, we could ask, "Is there something I need to know about player and team that is independent of the match?" The answer here would be, "Yes. I want to know the player's main team." We would therefore add a binary relationship to represent that information, as shown in Figure 5-20.

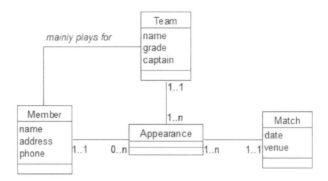

Figure 5-20. Including a binary relationship for information independent of one class

We need to ask a similar question for each of the other combinations; for example, "What do I need to know about a particular team and a particular match independent of the members?" The winning team maybe. "What do I need to know about a particular member and particular match independent of the teams?" Perhaps who was refereeing.

Summary

This chapter has described a miscellany of common modeling situations. Investigating these leads to a more precise understanding and representation of the real-life problem. These situations are summarized as follows:

- **Attribute, class, or relationship?**

  - Here are some examples of questions to help you decide. *Might I want to select objects based on the value of an attribute*? For example, might you want to select teams based on grade? If the answer is yes, consider introducing a class for that information (create a grade class).

  - *Am I likely now or in the future to store other data about this information?* For example, might I want to keep additional information about the captain: phone, address, and so on? If yes, consider introducing a class.

  - *Am I storing (or should I be storing) such information already?* For example, the information about a captain is the same or similar to information about members. Consider a relationship between existing classes.

- **More than one relationship between two classes:**

  - Consider more than one relationship between two classes if there is different information involving both classes. For example, a member might *play* for a team, *captain* a team, *manage* a team, and so on.

- **Consider self relationships:**

  - Objects of a class can be related to each other. For example, members *sponsor* other members, people *are parents of* other people.

- **Different routes between classes:**

  - Check wherever there is a closed loop to see whether the same information is being stored more than once.

  - Check to ensure you are not inferring more than you should from a route; that is, look out for fan traps where a class is related to two other classes and there is a cardinality of Many at both outer ends.

  - Check to ensure a path is available for all objects; that is, look out for chasm traps (are there optional relationships along the route?).

- **Information dependent on objects of more than two classes:**

  - Consider introducing a new class where you need to know about combinations of objects from three or more classes simultaneously; for example, which member played for which team in which match?

  - Any attributes in the new class must depend on a particular combination of objects from *each* of the participating classes; such as, what do I need to know about a particular *member* playing on a particular *team* in a particular *match*?

  - Consider what information might be pertinent to two objects from *pairs* of the contributing classes; for example, what do I need to know about a particular member and a particular team *independent* of any match?

TESTING YOUR UNDERSTANDING

Exercise 5-1.

The class in Figure 5-21 records information about a department and the manager's name. What other options are there for modeling information about the manager and location of a department?

Figure 5-21. Initial attempt at modeling the information about a department

Exercise 5-2.

A university wants to model information about the teaching of courses. A number of staff members may contribute to providing lectures, and one staff member is denoted as the course supervisor. Suggest an initial data model.

Exercise 5-3.

How would you model information about marriages- who marries whom and when? Think about all the different situations that could eventuate (for simplicity, do not worry at this stage about the gender of the participants).

Exercise 5-4.

An orchestra keeps information about its musicians, its repertoire and concerts. A partial data model is shown in Figure 5-22. The relationships store information such as that Joe Smith is required for Saturday's concert and that Beethoven's violin sonata is to be performed at Saturday's concert.

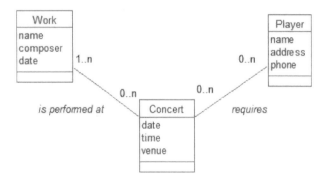

Figure 5-22. *A partial data model for an orchestra's repertoire and concerts*

What false information could be deduced from this initial model?
Amend the model so that it can maintain the following information correctly:

- Which players are involved in particular works in a concert

- The works being presented at a concert

- The fee a player receives for appearing in a particular concert

■ ■ ■

CHAPTER 6

Generalization and Specialization

As the data model begins to develop, situations will sometimes arise where we find that a class may not describe our possible objects as neatly as we might like. We might find that we have some objects for which some of the attributes do not really apply. For example, if we have a class to record information about all the people associated with a company, we might find that some have hourly pay rates while others have annual salaries. In many respects, much of the information about each of the employees is similar, but there are differences. We may also come across the case where we have started with two separate classes, for example **Lecturers** and **Students**, and then begin to realize that there is a great deal of information in common or that they are involved in the same relationships (who has parking permits, say). How do we handle these "same only different" cases in a pragmatic way?

Some questions that are useful to keep in mind are:

Do the two classes have enough in common to reconsider how they are defined?
Are some of the objects in a given class different enough from other objects to warrant reconsidering how they are defined?

Classes or Objects with Much in Common

Consider a company wishing to keep information about its employees. For all employees it needs to keep employee numbers, names, contact addresses, and job type, but depending on the type of job, the rest of the information might be different. Administrators might have a grade and technicians might have a date their certification needs to be renewed. Some workers might have a yearly salary, while others might have an hourly rate.

Let's just take a simple case of an outsourcing company keeping information about administrators and technicians. We could, as a start, consider having just one class, **Employee**, as shown in Figure 6-1. In Figure 6-2, we show some possible objects of that class.

Figure 6-1. Information about different types of workers kept in one class

number:	156	number:	188	number:	196	number:	208	number:	212
name:	Sue	name:	Bob	name:	Ann	name:	Jane	name:	Pat
job_type:	Admin	job_type:	Tech	job_type:	Tech	job_type:		job_type:	Admin
date:		date:	3/4/2012	date:		date:		date:	
grade:	A	grade:		grade:	A	grade:	B	grade:	

Figure 6-2. Some possible objects of the class Employee

What are we supposed to make of Ann? She is recorded as a technician, but instead of an expiry date, she has a grade. There is a bit of confusion here now. Is she both a technician and an administrator? If she is a technician, why doesn't she have an expiry date? Or (as is most likely) has there been some sort of data entry mess–up? A database that allows for obviously inconsistent or incomplete data to be entered is not going to deliver accurate or reliable information. We could have added some constraints to our use case description on maintaining the **Employee** data (e.g., if **job_type** = Tech, then **grade** must be empty and **date** must have a value), but this is quite messy and can only become more and more complicated as other job types are added. We could contemplate removing **job_type** altogether on the grounds that we can infer the type of job from the presence or absence of an expiration date or grade. We can deduce that Jane is an administrator even though the **job_type** field is empty. However, if we remove the **job_type** field, what can we deduce about Pat? At the moment, we know that she is an administrator whose grade is currently unknown or not required. Without the **job_type** field, we would know nothing.

The real question, of course, is, "Does it really matter whether we can enter inconsistent or incomplete data?" For some applications, it may not. However, if one of the objectives of the project is to be able to produce reliable statistics about the types of job and abilities of employees, clearly the simple class in Figure 6-1 is not very practical.

Specialization

The situation in the previous section is an example of *specialization*. In general, we have employees who share many characteristics, but depending on each person's job type, we may wish to keep different specialized data. Data modeling provides a mechanism for this idea through *sub-* and *superclasses*, an idea known as *inheritance*. Figure 6-3 shows a class, **Employee**, with two subclasses, sometimes called *inherited classes*, named **Administrator** and **Technician**.

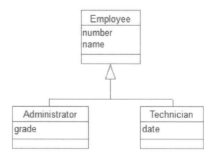

Figure 6-3. Subclasses to contain specialized information

The two classes beneath the arrow are derived from **Employee**, which means that in addition to any of their own attributes, they will also have all the attributes from the **Employee** class.

We now have three classes: objects of **Employee** will have a **number** and a **name** (and in general any other information that is relevant to all employees); objects of **Administrator** will have a **number**, **name**, and **grade**; and objects of **Technician** will have a **number**, **name**, and a **date**. Some possible objects are shown in Figure 6-4.

Administrator	Technician	Administrator	Administrator	Employee
number: 156	number: 188	number: 196	number: 212	number: 230
name: Sue	name: Bob	name: Ann	name: Pat	name: Jim
grade: A	date: 3/4/2012	grade: A	grade:	

Figure 6-4. Some objects consistent with the model in Figure 6-3

Each object is of one of the three classes: **Employee**, **Administrator**, or **Technician**. There is now no possibility of having a technician with a grade. It is, however, possible to have an employee such as Pat who is an administrator with an unknown grade. We also have an employee who is neither an administrator nor a technician (although we will see later in the chapter that this is not recommended).

With this model, we are able to keep accurate information about the different types of employees and the specialist data associated with their jobs. If we need to keep information about other types of employees, we can simply add more subclasses. For example, we might find we need to add another class to keep information about electricians and their registration numbers.

The ability to add new classes without disrupting the data kept about existing classes is very important for creating software that can evolve as situations change. In software engineering it is known as the Open Closed Principle: *Software entities (e.g. classes) should be open for extension and closed for modification.* Looking at Figure 6-3, this means that we should not alter the top class **Employee** once we start storing data. Any changes to that class will affect all the existing subclasses (**Technician** and **Administrator**) and that may have an impact on any applications that use them. However, we can extend the problem by adding additional subclasses (such as **Electrician**). This means that the top or parent class must be designed very carefully at the start; it should be as general as possible.

Generalization

A model using classes and subclasses is also useful when we start with two distinct classes and find that they have some behavior in common. Let's consider a database such as in Figure 6-5, with information about lecturers and students and the courses they teach or enroll in.

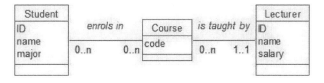

Figure 6-5. Lecturers and students as independent classes

77

The university may, as all universities do, have a parking problem and decide that each person is allowed one and only one designated parking space. If we wish to include this information in our model, we may try a solution as in Figure 6-6. However, we run into a real problem pretty soon. Can you see what it is?

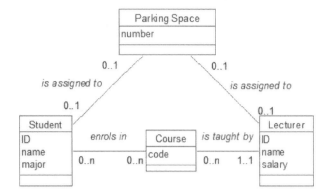

Figure 6-6. *Possible model for maintaining car parking information*

Reading the model from the bottom to the top, we have that students and lecturers can each have at most one parking space. That is fine. However, from the top to bottom, we have that a parking space could be assigned to a student, and the same space could be assigned to a lecturer. What the model doesn't show is that a single parking space cannot be assigned to both a student and lecturer simultaneously.

We have come across constraints on particular objects before, and we could specify these in the use cases for maintaining the data. However, we have a more elegant solution here. In many respects, our **Lecturer** and **Student** objects have the same behavior–they are assigned parking spaces. They also have attributes in common—they each have a name and an ID. We can capture this common data and behavior by creating a superclass, as in Figure 6-7.

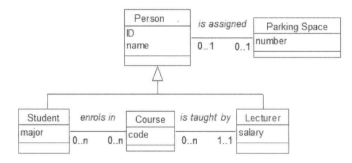

Figure 6-7. *Common behavior captured in a superclass*

In this model we have people, with IDs and names (and other common attributes), who can each be assigned a parking space. Students are people with a major who enroll in courses, whereas lecturers are people with a salary who teach courses. We do not have the problem now of extra tricky constraints because a parking space cannot be assigned to both a lecturer *and* a student; we just have that a parking space is assigned to one person.

Inheritance in Summary

Specialization and generalization in the examples we have looked at so far in this chapter are just two sides of the same coin. They both lead to the type of generic data model shown in Figure 6-8.

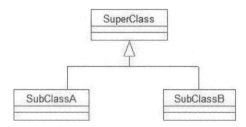

Figure 6-8. *A data model showing inheritance*

SubClassA and **SubClassB** are both specialized types of the class **SuperClass**. They will have all the properties of the **SuperClass** and in addition have their own specialized attributes and/or relationships with other classes.

Whenever you find yourself thinking things like, "But a parking space could be associated with a lecturer OR a student," or, "A booking could be for an individual OR a company," and so on, consider a superclass to capture the common behavior.

When you find yourself thinking, "Some objects will have a value for this attribute but not that one," or, "Only some objects of this class will have a relationship with an object of that class," you should consider creating some subclasses to capture that specialist behavior.

To check whether inheritance (subclasses and superclasses) is applicable to a given problem, you should ask the following questions. For example, to check whether **SubClassA** is really a subclass of **SuperClass** in Figure 6-8, ask:

> *Is an object of* **SubClassA** *a type of* **SuperClass**? *(always/sometimes/never)*
> *Is an object of* **SuperClass** *a type of* **SubClassA**? *(always/sometimes/never)*

If the answer to the first question is "always" and the answer to the second is "sometimes," the problem is a good candidate for an inheritance model. For example, we can check the validity of Figure 6-3 by asking:

> *Is an administrator a type of employee? (always)*
> *Is an employee a type of administrator? (sometimes)*

These answers mean that making **Administrator** a subclass of **Employee** is possible.

Asking the always/sometimes/never questions can help make sense of complicated problem descriptions. Say we have a complex employee hierarchy with administrators, agents, salespeople, and so on. Those two always/sometimes/never questions can sort things out. Let's say we discover that:

> *An agent is always a salesperson, and a salesperson is always an agent.*

We know that for this particular situation "salesperson" and "agent" are two different words for the same thing. We should have one class called either **Salesperson** or **Agent**.

However, say we have that:

A salesperson is always an agent, and an agent is sometimes a salesperson.

Here we have good grounds for considering a **Salesperson** class as a subclass of **Agent**.

When Inheritance Is Not a Good Idea

Inheritance in a data model is not as common as you might think at first. Humans are very good at categorizing things into hierarchies, and once people get a hold of the idea of inheritance in data modeling, there can be a temptation to use it everywhere. In the last section, I was careful to say that an affirmative answer to the question "Is A a type of B?" only meant that using inheritance *might* be a possible way of making sense of a problem. In this section, we will look at a couple of examples where inheritance is definitely not a good way to think about a problem.

Confusing Objects with Subclasses

Consider a database of dogs of different breeds. We may have a hierarchy of breeds and might at first sight think that inheritance is a possibility. Consider the following statements:

- A Corgi is a dog.

- Rover is a Corgi.

- Quin is a Labrador.

- A Labrador is a dog.

While the four statements are similar, they do not all suggest subclasses. Rover and Quin are not classes; they are *objects* of some class of dog. Corgi and Labrador, on the other hand, could possibly be subclasses of some super Dog class, but then again maybe not. Let's consider how we know whether something is an object or a class. Why is Rover probably an object and Corgi possibly a class?

A quick way to help decide whether something is a class or an object is to ask a question such as, "Am I likely to have several of <whatever> and am I interested in them as a group?" For example:

Am I likely to have several Corgis and am I interested in them as a group? Probably. Therefore Corgi is a potential class.
Might I have several Rovers and am I interested in them as a group? There might well be several dogs called Rover, but it is hard to think of why we would be interested in them as a group just because of their common name.

Corgis and Labradors are potential classes, whereas Quin and Rover are more likely to be objects of one of our dog classes. A possible hierarchy and some objects that are consistent with the preceding statements are shown in Figure 6-9.

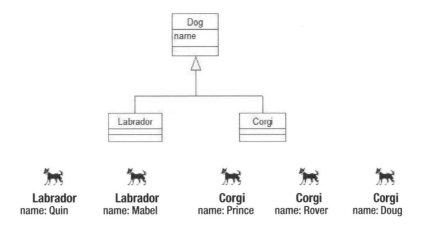

Figure 6-9. Some possible classes, subclasses, and objects of a dog data model

Confusing an Association with a Subclass

The model in Figure 6-9 may look fine for a start, but in fact we don't need inheritance to maintain simple information about the different breeds of our dogs. We are not keeping any different information about Labradors than we are about Corgis or any other breed (so far). We are merely noting that some of our dogs are Corgis and some are Labradors, and this can be done with a simple association between our **Dog** objects and objects of another class called **Breed** as shown in Figure 6-10 (assuming pure-bred dogs for now).

The model in Figure 6-10 is a much simpler way of representing our problem than the model in Figure 6-9. The resulting database will be much easier to maintain also. In Figure 6-9, if we add a new breed, we need to add a new *subclass*. For the model in Figure 6-10, we just need to add another *object* of our **Breed** class.

What if the problem changed to say that we want to keep the fees payable to the kennel club and that these are different for the different breeds (e.g., a Labrador will cost $100, a Corgi $80, and a Terrier $85)? Now that we have some different information about the breeds, should we reconsider specialized classes?

No. What we have here are just different *values* for an attribute, **fee**, which can easily be accommodated in the **Breed** class. We only need to consider specialized classes if we have different attributes or relationships (not just different values for an attribute).

When Is Inheritance Worth Considering?

We have seen that what looks like inheritance can often be represented more simply (and effectively) by simple relationships. At what point is it worth considering inheritance? Let's think of another scenario for our dog model.

Let's say the town council keeps a register of dogs. Some of these dogs are just your plain old family pet, while others might be show dogs with affiliations to kennel clubs. If (big if) the council wanted to keep this information, a model such as the one in Figure 6-11 might be worth considering.

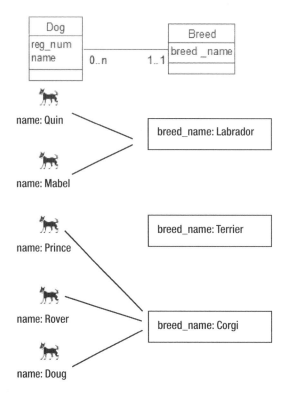

Figure 6-10. Each Dog object is associated with a breed.

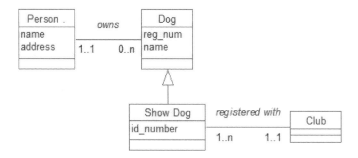

Figure 6-11. Possible model using inheritance to show different behavior

In Figure 6-11, we see that show dogs have not only additional attributes (e.g., an `id_number` to perhaps point to records of their genealogy), but also different associations (i.e., a show dog will be registered with a kennel club whereas an ordinary pet will not).

How else could we have modeled this? Well, we could have given all dogs an `id_number` attribute (that could be left unspecified for ordinary pets) and let all dogs have an optional relationship with a club as shown in Figure 6-12. Can you see any drawbacks to this model?

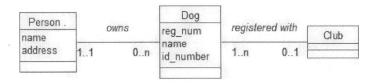

Figure 6-12. Possible model without using inheritance

It is possible to capture all the required information with the model in Figure 6-12, but it is not so easy to keep the data accurate. We run into much the same problems as we had with our model of **Employees** in Figures 6-1 and 6-2. What about dogs with no **id_number** that are associated with a club and vice versa? Are these show dogs, or has there just been a data entry mishap?

The decision of whether to use inheritance or not depends on how important the completeness and accuracy of the data are to the objective of the project. We get right back to the questions we considered in Chapter 3. What is the main objective? What is the scope? How important is the accuracy of this data? On the whole, when you are starting out on a problem, it is best to keep your solution as simple as possible. Inheritance provides an elegant solution to many problems involving specialization and generalization, but you should only use it when it is necessary.

Should the Superclass Have Objects?

In Figure 6-11, we had a class of dogs with show dogs as a subclass. The implication here is that your ordinary old pet will be an object of the superclass **Dog**, while show dogs will be objects of the subclass. This can lead to a few problems as the project evolves.

As we have seen, we should only be considering inheritance when we have objects with specialized data that needs to be accurately maintained. We need to make sure that the model we develop will be able to cope with changes or additions to the scope in the future.

Consider a library that sets up a small database to maintain information about books (catalog number, title, author). After some time it includes audio books in its collection. An audio book has all the same attributes as an ordinary book, but in addition it has a playing time. This seems like a reasonable candidate for setting up a specialized subclass, and we may arrive at a model as in Figure 6-13.

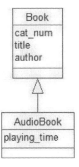

Figure 6-13. A specialized class for audio books

83

If we set up a database based on this model, we will probably have some objects of type **Book** (with a value for number, title, and author) and some objects of type **AudioBook** (with a value for number, title, author, and playing time). Some time later, the problem may change and we may want to keep some additional information about our regular books—say, number of pages. We now have a problem. Our audio books are objects of the superclass: if we add an attribute **page_num** to the parent **Book** class, it will be inherited by our **AudioBook** subclass objects, which is not what we want at all.

This problem can occur when a parent class of a data model has objects. It is generally advisable that any class which has subclasses should be an *abstract* class, meaning that it cannot have objects. The idea of an abstract class is to keep information that is common to its subclasses and which the objects of those classes can inherit. Following this advice we would have had an abstract class (say **Item**) at the top of our hierarchy with two subclasses, **Book** and **AudioBook**, as in Figure 6-14. This way we can make changes to each of our subclasses without affecting the other.

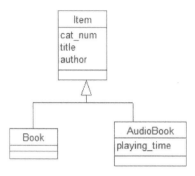

Figure 6-14. *Item as an abstract class*

It does not matter that **Book** might have no additional attributes originally. The class is there, ready for when we want to make a change. We can now add the number of pages to the **Book** class without it affecting the **AudioBook** class.

Objects That Belong to More Than One Subclass

In most of the examples in this chapter, the problems have been very simplified. In Figure 6-15, we have a model with **Lecturer** and **Student** represented as subclasses of a **Person** class, along with some objects of the two subclasses. We see that for this case our objects have to be either a lecturer or a student.

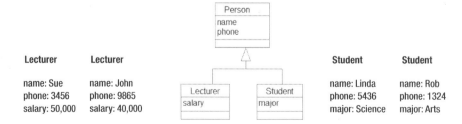

Figure 6-15. *Students and lecturers are distinct.*

84

Figure 6-15 copes with the simple case of lecturers and students being distinct. What is more likely, however, is that there is some overlap between the two. What if lecturer John is also doing some part–time study for an arts degree and student Linda is doing some part–time teaching to fund her fees? Where do we store John's major and Linda's salary?

We could make another two objects, an additional **Student** object for John and a **Lecturer** object for Linda, but there are problems with this approach. We would now have six **Person** objects in total when in reality there are only four people. Any counts or summaries of numbers of people will be inaccurate. An additional problem is that we would have two objects for Linda, and they will both have values for **name** and **phone**, causing problems when Linda's contact details change. They will have to be updated in two places.

One solution is to consider another class that inherits from both **Student** and **Lecturer**. Inheriting from two different parents is sometimes referred to as *multiple inheritance*. Objects of our new **Lecturer/Student** class will have attributes **name**, **phone**, **salary**, and **major** as in Figure 6-16.

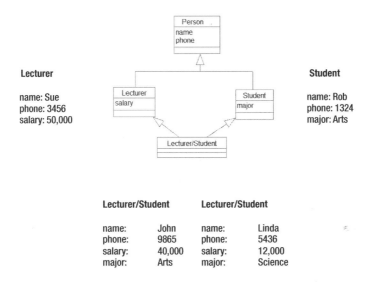

Figure 6-16. *Multiple inheritance to capture objects of two classes (not recommended)*

There are difficulties with the approach in Figure 6-16. The obvious problem, from a purely pragmatic design point of view, is that when more classes are added at the middle level, we will be in trouble. If we add new classes (e.g., **Administrator** and **Cleaner**) as additional subclasses of **Person**, we will need to add a whole slew of subclasses at the bottom level to cope with all the possible combinations. For example, administrators who do some lecturing, cleaners who do some study, poor students who do a whole raft of extra jobs to fund their studies, and so on. This approach very soon gets out of hand.

Our problem is that we have been thinking of students and lecturers as different types of people when in fact they are all just people doing different things. A better way to think of this type of scenario is not so much that there are different types of *people*, but that there are people who play many different *roles*. We can model these jobs or roles as a class with many different subclasses for the jobs about which we need to store different information. Rather than have subclasses of **People**, we can have another class (let's call it **Contract**) that has subclasses for the different roles we need to describe. Each person can then have many contracts as shown in the model in Figure 6-17.

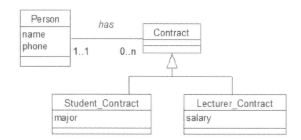

Figure 6-17. *People can have many roles (contracts)*

Some objects of a data model like Figure 6-17 and consistent with the scenario in Figure 6-16 are shown in Figure 6-18. We see that we very clearly have four people who are undertaking a number of different roles. A person can have more than one contract, and each contract is associated with a single person.

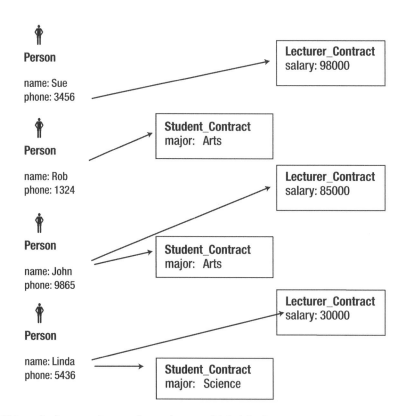

Figure 6-18. *Using roles (contracts) as an alternative to multiple inheritance*

The approach in Figure 6-17 is easy to adapt when new roles are added (e.g., administrator, cleaner). If we wish to include administrators with information specific to their contracts, we just add another subclass, `Administrator_Contract`, to our `Contract` class.

There is a slight problem, however. In Figure 6-17, we have that a person can be related to many contracts, but we don't have any constraints as to which type of contracts. The model does not prevent Linda being associated with several `Lecturer` contracts and/or several `Student` contracts. In reality, this may be what the problem actually requires. Linda may follow her arts degree with a science degree. John may be promoted and take out a new contract for $120,000. We can add some date attributes to the parent `Contract` class so the contracts can be recognized as being in succession or overlapping. Overall, the model in Figure 6-17 is very flexible and allows us to address many complications in a transparent manner.

However, we need to be sure the objectives of our problem require this sort of accuracy about people and the roles they undertake. If the objective is to keep reliable statistics about different types of employees, their pay, and their qualifications, then this sort of model is necessary to help us understand what is going on. If that information is of only secondary importance (i.e., our main objective is keeping student enrollments and results), then maybe we do not need to introduce subclasses to keep the specialized data about the other more minor roles that people might play.

Composites and Aggregates

Often we have objects that are made up of other objects: a forest is made up of trees or a building is made up of rooms. Some people use a special notation for this type of relationship, but I've never found it particularly helpful to do so.

When dealing with situations in which we have this type of composition or aggregation of objects, inheritance can become useful. Consider a building that has a number of rooms, as in Figure 6-19. Every year the building must undergo a safety check. Occasionally an individual room will need to be checked. We can have a `Check` class which records the date. Should the `Check` class be associated with the `Building` or the `Room` class, or both?

Figure 6-19. *A building has many rooms.*

For the purposes of this problem a `Room` and a `Building` have something in common. They both can be associated with safety checks. This therefore becomes a candidate for an inheritance solution. A first attempt is shown in Figure 6-20.

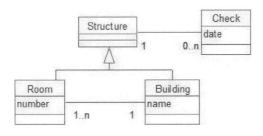

Figure 6-20. *Buildings and rooms are both types of structures that may have safety checks.*

87

Now we can store data about a single check that incorporates a building (and we know what rooms were included). However, if necessary the check can be associated with a single room. While this solution is fine, it can be made much more general by using a software pattern. There are a number of design patterns[1] that are useful for software developers. They mostly deal with behavior whereas our focus is on data. The solution in Figure 6-21 is based on the **Composite** pattern.

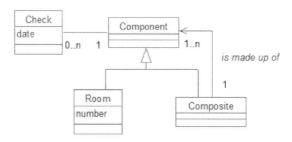

Figure 6-21. Using the Composite pattern. Checks are made on components, which may be a single room or a composite of other components.

The model in Figure 6-21 says that we have something (a component) on which a safety check can be made. That component may be an individual component (in this case a room) or a collection of other components. For instance, we can have a **Composite** object, which is a building that is made up of rooms. This would be analogous to Figure 6-20. However, our new model is more general because a **Composite** can be made up of other composites. For example: an industrial estate may be made up of buildings, each being made up of floors, which each contain rooms. With the **Composite** pattern in Figure 6-21, we can record safety checks at any of these levels (room, floor, building, etc.).

We will look at how to represent inheritance in a relational database in Chapter 7. In the meantime, the tables in Figure 6-22 show how the information might be recorded. The **Check** table shows that Component 3 was checked on 3/02/2012. From the **Composite** table we can deduce (by looking down the right hand column) that **Components** 40 and 60 belong in 3 and that **Components** 113, 115, and 117 belong in 40 or 60. The **Component** table records what all these entities are, so we know that the check on 3/02/2012 was on the Forbes Building, which contains a 4th and 6th floor, which in turn contain rooms F403, F409, and F632. On 10/02/2012 there was a check for 113 (Room F408) which has no subparts (does not appear in the right hand column of the **Composite** table).

ID	belongs_in		ID	name		date	component
2			3	Forbes Building		3/02/2012	3
3			2	Burns Building		9/02/2012	60
31	2		31	3rd Floor Burns		10/02/2012	113
40	3		40	4th Floor Forbes			
60	3		60	6th Floor Forbes			
113	40		113	F408			
115	40		115	F409			
117	60		117	F632			
121	30		121	B341			
Composite			Component			Check	

Figure 6-22. Database tables representing the Composite pattern

[1] Erich Gamma, Richard Helm, Ralph Johnson, and John Vlissides, *Design Patterns: Elements of Reusable Object-Oriented Software* (Indianapolis, IN: Addison and Wesley, 1994.)

It Isn't Easy

Inheritance offers some wonderfully elegant ways to model very complicated problems. However, getting a hierarchy of classes and subclasses that will cope with all the eventual data is very difficult. We have only touched on the *data* aspects of inheritance here in this chapter. Dealing with inherited classes becomes considerably more difficult if we need to add *behavior* (or methods) to our classes. Adding behavior, however, is outside the scope of the data-based problems we are considering in this book.

Even for just static data, we can still run into problems when we try to design an inheritance hierarchy. Consider the model in Figure 6-23.

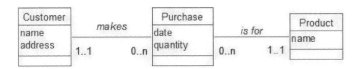

Figure 6-23. *An amateur biologist's model for keeping data about animals*

Dividing animals up into fish, mammals, birds, and so on may do quite well as we enter data about bears, dogs, sharks, and sparrows. But what happens when we come to whales? Whale doesn't fit at all into Figure 6-13's model. A whale is a mammal, but it also needs to be shown as living in sea water, similar to a fish. If a database has been implemented and lots of data entered, it can be very difficult to insert layers or move subclasses between layers. Getting it correct at the start is very important. Poorly thought-out inheritance can cause more problems than it solves, so use it very sparingly in database problems.

In Chapter 7, we will see how to capture the most important parts of these data models in a relational database.

Summary

Situations when inheritance is a possibility include the following:

- If different objects have mutually exclusive values for some attributes (e.g., administrators have grades but technicians have dates), consider specialized subclasses.

- When you think *this is like that except for...* consider subclasses.

- When two classes have a similar relationship with another class, consider a new generalized superclass (e.g., if both students and staff are assigned parking spaces, consider a generalized class for people).

Before you use inheritance, make sure that

- you have not confused objects with subclasses (e.g., Rover is probably an object, Dog or Cat could be classes).

- you have considered whether an association with a category class would be sufficient (e.g., Labrador and Corgi could be objects of a Breed class, and each dog could be associated with a breed).

- it is not just the value of an attribute that is different (e.g., don't consider inheritance because the fees for Labrador and Collie are different).

Other considerations:

- Classes that have subclasses should be abstract, which means they will never have any objects. This allows the problem to be more readily extended.

- Consider associations with roles when you come across the *my object is a member of both these classes* dilemma.

- Don't introduce the complexity of inheritance unless the specialized data in the subclasses is important to the main objectives of the project.

TESTING YOUR UNDERSTANDING

Exercise 6-1.

Consider the model in Figure 6-24 which describes purchases of a product by customers of a small mail order company selling toys. For simplicity, each purchase is for one or more of a single toy. Each transaction must have a customer so that he or she can be invoiced and the product delivered. The data will be used to prepare statistics about the different products sold, values of purchases, and the spending habits of customers.

Figure 6-24. Customers purchase products.

The company changes the way it does business to allow customers to walk in off the street and pay cash. No customer needs to be associated with a cash purchase. Discuss how effective the following changes to the data would be.

- Change the optionality at the customer end of the relationship to 0 so not all purchases need a customer.

- Leave the optionality as 1 but include a dummy customer object, with name CashCustomer.

- Create subclasses of `Customer`: `Cash_Customer` and `Account_Customer`.

- Create subclasses of `Purchase`: `Cash_Purchase` and `Account_Purchase.`

Exercise 6-2.

1. A farmer keeps information about the application of fertilizer (e.g. amount, date) to his crops. His farm is made up of large sections which are divided into fields. Usually an application of fertilizer is applied to an entire section, but occasionally it is to an individual field. How would you model this?

Exercise 6-3.

2. A volunteer library has staff, members, and books. It wants to know which books are on loan to whom, know how to contact the borrower, and charge fees for overdue books. Reference books cannot be borrowed. Members are fined $5 per day for overdue books, but staff do not receive fines. How might you model this situation? Some intial classes are shown in Figure 6-25.

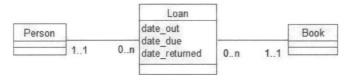

Figure 6-25. *People can borrow books.*

CHAPTER 7

■ ■ ■

From Data Model to Relational Database Design

Let's recap the story so far, in our endeavors to design a database. We started with use cases to describe the basic requirements of a problem and developed an initial data model. By looking carefully at the details of the model, we were able to develop questions to help understand further subtleties and complexities of the real–world problem. We then looked at a number of situations that occur in many models in the hope that these would be useful when difficult situations arose in other contexts.

The goal is not to attempt to get a perfect or complete model. The outcome we are seeking is agreement on a model that accurately reflects the essential requirements of the real–world problem. This will involve numerous iterations as the use cases adjust to reflect the improved understanding and the changing scope. Having arrived at a set of use cases and a data model with which everyone is comfortable, we can now move on to the third phase of the development process, as shown in the bottom–right square of Figure 7-1.

In this and the following chapters, we will look at how to design a database that could be implemented in a relational database product (e.g., MySQL, Microsoft Access, SQL Server, Oracle, etc.).

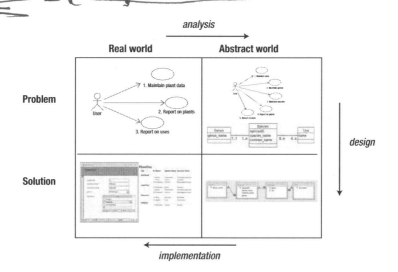

Figure 7-1. Database development process

93

Representing the Model

We have gone to a great deal of trouble to capture as much detail as possible in the data model. Much of this detail can be represented and enforced by standard techniques built into relational database management software. A good model, implemented using the standard techniques, allows us to capture many of the constraints implied by the relationships between classes without recourse to programming or complex interface design.

In this chapter, I will show you how many of the aspects of the data model can be captured by standard database functionality. To give you an idea of what is coming up, I have summarized the techniques in Table 7-1.

Table 7-1. *Techniques to Represent Aspects of the Data Model*

Feature in Model	Technique Used in Relational Database
Class	Add a table with a primary key.
Attribute	Add a field with an appropriate data type to the table.
Object	Add a row of data to the table.
1–Many relationship	Use a foreign key, i.e., a reference to a particular row (or object) in the table at the 1 end of the relationship.
Many–Many relationship	Add a new table with two foreign keys.
Optionality of 1 at the 1 end of a relationship	Make the value of the foreign key required.
Parent and child classes (inheritance)	Add a table for the parent class. Add tables for each child class with a primary key that is also a foreign key referencing the parent table (not an exact representation but OK).

All of the techniques described in Table 7-1 can be carried out in most database management products as part of the specification of the tables. More complex constraints may require some additional procedures or checking at data input time, but with a good model this can be minimized. By using the built-in facilities of the database product, the time required for implementation, maintenance, and expansion of the application is greatly reduced.

Representing Classes and Attributes

Consider Figure 7-2, which represents a small part of a data model for members and teams.

Figure 7-2. *Part of data model for members and teams*

The first step is to design a database table for each class. The attributes of the class will become the field or column names of the table, and when the data is added, each row, or record, in the table will represent an object. For example, as a start we would create a table called Member for the Member class in Figure 7-2. The table would have two fields or columns, one for a member's name and one for the address. We would then add a row to the table for each member object (e.g., John Smith, 83 SomePlace, Christchurch).

Creating a Table

All relational databases allow you to create a table using SQL, which is a language for creating, updating, and querying databases. First we need a database that stores all our tables. To create a table, we need to provide a name for the table and a name and domain for each of the columns. The domain specifies the set of values that is allowed for that particular column. We will talk a little more about domains later in this chapter. For many purposes it is sufficient to just specify a data type, for example a date (8/4/12), a piece of text or a set of characters ("Mary Smith"), an integer (467), or some other type of number (3.57). Particular database products provide different data types, and we will talk about suitable choices a little later on in the section "Choosing Data Types."

In addition to providing SQL as a way of creating a table, many databases provide a more graphical front end through which the user can provide information about the columns and their data types. Equivalent ways of creating a very simple Member table are shown in Listing 7-1 and Figures 7-3 and 7-4. Figure 7-3 shows the MySQLWorkbench front end, while Figure 7-4 shows the equivalent in MS Access. Both programs will generate SQL statements similar to those shown in Listing 7-1. Note that the data type for the two fields is called *Text* in Access and *VarChar* in SQL. These both just mean that the user will be able to enter any number of characters up to the maximum number stated (25 for name and 40 for address).

Listing 7-1. *Standard SQL Command to Create a Customer Table with Two Fields*

```
CREATE TABLE Member (
member_name VARCHAR(25),
member_address VARCHAR(40)
)
```

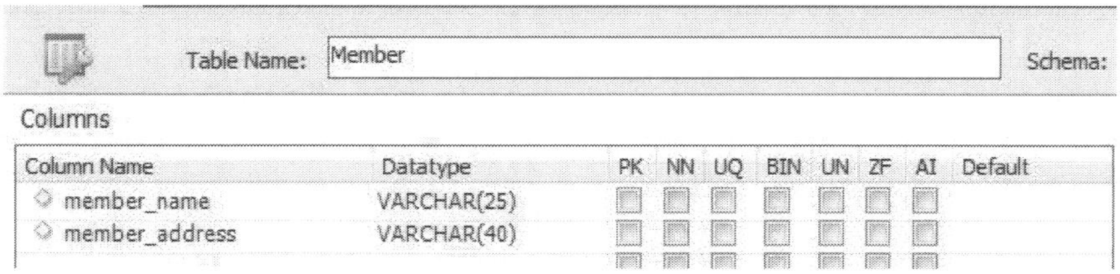

Figure 7-3. *Creating a Member table in MySQL Workbench*

95

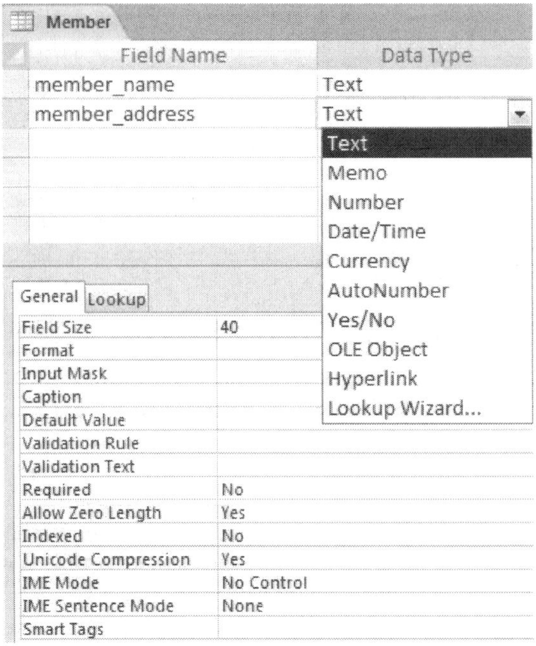

Figure 7-4. *Creating a Member table in Microsoft Access*

As you can see in Figures 7-3 and 7-4, there are many additional possible specifications for columns. We will come to some of those later. For now we have just declared the minimum requirements of a name and data type for each of the columns. Once the table has been created, we can enter data. In the case of the `Member` table, we would enter a row for each member object. Once again, this can be done with SQL commands as in Listing 7-2 or for many products through a table-like front end as shown for Access in Figure 7-5.

Listing 7-2. *SQL Command for Entering a Record into the Member Table*

```
INSERT INTO Member (name, address)
VALUES ('Green, Ruth' '36 Some Street, Christchurch' )
```

member_name	member_address
Green, Ruth	36 Some Street Christchurch

Figure 7-5. *Entering data through the MS Access interface*

Choosing Data Types

Each attribute in a class becomes a *field* or a column in a table. When we create the table, we need to provide a name for the field (e.g., name, address) and specify the type of data that will be stored in that field. Database products often offer a bewildering number of different data types, but they basically fall into the following groups:

Character types: These allow you to enter any combination of characters—numbers, letters, and punctuation. They are used for names, addresses, descriptions, and so on. You usually need to provide a maximum length for the data going into the field. In SQL, a type of VARCHAR(60) would allow you to enter any number of characters up to 60. In Access, the equivalent type is called Text. If you have very large amounts of text (notes, discussions, and so on), you might like to look at other types (e.g., Text in SQL Server or Memo in Access).

Integer types: These types are for entering numbers with no fractional part. They are great for ID numbers such as customer numbers and for anything that you can count. Database systems often provide different-sized integer types (long, short, byte, etc.) that have different maximum numbers that can be entered. Unless you have particular performance problems or extremely large amounts of data, you will probably be fine if you use the ordinary integer type (INT in SQL). Just check that the biggest number it can handle is large enough for your data.

Numbers with a fractional part: These are used for things that you measure (heights, weights, etc.) and also for numbers that result from calculations such as averages. Most of the time you will be just fine with what is called a *float* or *single* (depending on the product you are using). Other types exist if you need particularly accurate measurements or calculations. One situation when a float may not be suitable is when you need to record rather large amounts of money accurately. Many products now provide *money* or *currency* types for this situation, or you may find the type is called something like *fixed-length decimal*. These types enable you to have many significant figures so that you can accurately keep track of your billions, down to a fraction of a cent!

Dates: No prizes for guessing the type of data you can put in fields with these types. If your product has different date types, some may allow you to include times and others may allow you to access dates further into the past or future.

Why is it important to get the correct data type? You could argue that since you can put anything in a character field, you can have character fields for everything (and I've seen it done!). There are three main reasons why it is important to choose an appropriate data type for each of your fields:

Constraints on the values: A character field type has no constraints on what you can enter; however, most other fields do. Number fields won't allow you to accidentally mistype a number, say, by putting in an extra decimal point or a letter "O" instead of the number 0. Dates won't allow February 29 unless it is in a leap year, and so on. For this reason, phone numbers, which are likely to have extra symbols like ( ) for area codes, need to be stored in character rather than number fields.

97

Ordering: Different types of fields have different ways for comparing or ordering values. For example, character fields can be sorted alphabetically (A to Z), number fields numerically (small to large), and dates chronologically (older first). If you store numbers in character fields and then ask your product to sort them for you, you might get something like this: 10, 12, 123, 2, 200, 36. Dates in a character field might be sorted like this: August 1, 2012; February 1, 2012; May 4, 2012. Can you see why?

Calculations: Your database product can do arithmetic and perform other functions on your data, but only if it is the correct type. For example, it will be able to add, multiply, and average numbers; figure out how many days fall between two dates; and look for particular characters in a piece of text. You need to have the correct types in order to take advantage of this functionality. And getting back to phone numbers, you never want to subtract them, average them, or order them numerically, so they can and should generally be stored in a character field type.

Domains and Constraints

A domain is a set of values allowed for an attribute or field. For something like a product description it might be sufficient for the domain to be any set of characters up to some specified length. Other attributes might have more specific domains. For example, a gender attribute might only allow the values "M" or "F"; a day of the week might be constrained to the characters "Mon," "Tue," "Wed," "Thu," "Fri," "Sat," and "Sun"; possible marks for an exam might be whole numbers between 0 and 100.

Some database products (e.g., SQL Server) allow users to create their own domains or data types. For example, you might define the type ExamMark as an integer between 0 and 100. This user defined domain or type can then be used in all the tables in the database. Other products (e.g., Access) do not permit the creation of domains, but all products allow constraints to be declared on individual columns. For instance, we could declare gender as being a character type of length 1 with the constraint that it can only accept the values "M" or "F." The difference between a constraint and a domain is that the former has to be specified in every table whereas the latter only needs to be declared once in the database.

The SQL code for creating a table with a constraint on the values for a gender field is shown in Listing 7-3.

Listing 7-3. *SQL for Creating a Table with a Constraint*

```
CREATE TABLE Member (
member_name VARCHAR(25),
member_address VARCHAR(40),
gender VARCHAR(1) CHECK gender IN ('M', 'F')
)
```

One very important constraint is specifying whether a value is required or can be left empty. A field with nothing in it is said to be *null*, and when a table is created we can specify which fields are not allowed to have nulls. This is shown in SQL in Listing 7-4.

Listing 7-4. *SQL for Specifying That the Name Field Must Have Values*

```
CREATE TABLE Member (
member_name VARCHAR(20) NOT NULL,
member_address VARCHAR(45),
gender VARCHAR(1) CHECK gender IN ('M', 'F')
)
```

Looking at the code in Listing 7-4, it is reasonable to ask why we haven't insisted gender must always have a value as well. All members have a gender, after all. In general, there are two main reasons why we might need to put a null in a field: either the field doesn't apply for a particular record (a person may or may not have a driver's license number) or the field does apply, but at the moment we don't know the actual value. For the situation with gender then, clearly the value applies, but there could be situations where we do not know what it is. If we force a value to always be entered, we risk not being able to enter the record or having a distressed data entry operator taking a guess at a likely value.

Consider a university administrator entering details from a stack of student applications, a couple of which have left the box for gender empty. The university would much rather have the student's information entered incompletely than not at all. At least then they can extract some fees and contact the person about the gender at a later time. What about name–should that be allowed to be null? It is always a judgment call, but personally I think recording details about a nameless student is probably going to result in trouble somewhere down the line.

Even if you think a value is going to be essential for the accuracy of your data, do not underestimate the likelihood that disallowing nulls might cause an incorrect value to be entered. I find myself doing this all the time when filling in web forms for US sites that demand a value for a state. I live in New Zealand. We don't have states, so I just make something up. Some sites accept "XXX," while others demand a real US state; in those cases I use "Virginia." I don't know why. What I do know is that this situation drives me crazy, and that any statistics being gathered about the states of site visitors are going to be hopelessly inaccurate.

Checking Character Fields

Character fields are a bit different from other field types. With a character field, we can enter anything we like (if there are no other constraints), and so it is possible to enter several values into a field. Other fields such as numbers and dates only ever allow one value to be entered.

You have seen examples of storing several values in one character field in Figure 7-5. The member_name field as it stands could contain data about the first name, last name, possibly other names, initials, and titles. To find the record shown in Figure 7-5 is going to be very difficult. Will the user know whether to search for Mrs. Green, Mrs. Rose Green, Rose Green, Mrs. R. Green, or Ms. Green? It is also going to be difficult to sort the records sensibly. We usually want to order people by last names, and this is not going to be possible with the way we are recording the data in Figure 7-5. The way the address data is being recorded is going to make it difficult to select records by city or print nicely formatted address labels easily. Separating the data into fields as in Figure 7-6 makes the data much more useful. A good rule of thumb is that any data that you are likely to want to search for, sort by, or extract in some way should be in a field all by itself.

last_name	first_name	title	street_address	city	post_code
Turner	John	Mr	Flat 1, 6 Moa Street	Christchurch	8033
Green	Ruth	Mrs	36 Some Street	Christchurch	8041

Figure 7-6. *Improved fields to describe a customer*

If the accuracy of values in a field is really crucial to the project, maybe that particular piece of information should actually be in a class of its own. You might recall that we separated genus out of our Plant class (refer to the discussion of Figure 2-12) because its accuracy was important and we didn't want any misspellings. In the table in Figure 7-6 we might ask how important it is for the values in the city field to be accurately recorded. If accuracy is essential (e.g., we regularly want to target advertising to customers in a particular city), we may need two classes, City and Customer, with a 1–Many relationship between them. If we only want the address for sending general mail, accuracy isn't so important, as the postman can probably cope with the odd misspelling.

Primary Key

We have taken our model and for each class we have created a table. Each attribute in the class is represented by a field with a particular data type, and we can apply some constraints to the values we allow into a field. We have thus far overlooked one constraint that is so important that it gets a section all to itself. This involves choosing a *primary key* for the table. It is imperative that we can always find a particular object (or row or record in a table). This means that all records must be unique; otherwise, you can't distinguish between two that are identical.

Consider the consequences of two identical records: when a member pays his annual fee, we need to connect that payment to the member somehow. What if we have two identical rows in our Member table for Ruth Smith? How will we know which row is associated with a payment of fees? If we get it wrong, then one Mrs. Smith will be pretty upset when she receives another invoice. Every member needs to be able to be uniquely identified. There must never be two identical records in any of our tables.

Determining a Primary Key

A key is a field, or combination of fields, that is guaranteed to have a unique value for every record in the table. It is possible to learn quite a bit about a problem by considering which fields are likely to be possible keys. We will see later that there can be more than one set of fields that can have unique values in a table. We choose one of these to be the primary key and then use that to enable us to identify records uniquely.

Consider which fields could be keys for the following table where the names of the fields are given in parentheses after the table name:

Member (name, address, phone, birth_date)

How about name for a key? No; it is entirely possible that we may have two members with the same name, and we will need to be able to distinguish them. What about the combination (name, address)? This is more promising, but then dads have been known to name their sons after themselves, and it is not improbable that they may at various times of their lives share the same address and be members of the same club. Many organizations sometimes key their clients on the combination (name, birth_date), feeling this is unlikely to be duplicated. However, there are regular horror stories in the press of people who suddenly discover they have a namesake twin as they struggle to fend off bailiffs and police.

A potential key must be guaranteed to be unique for every possible record. In cases like our Member table, there is not much choice but to add a new attribute or field such as member_number and then assign all members their own unique numbers so we can distinguish them. This is sometimes called a *surrogate key*. In real life, we can always distinguish individuals, but when we look at the data we are storing about them, we may not be able to find a unique set of values. In many cases, privacy laws prevent information such as social security or tax numbers being used to identify people, so each business or organization is often compelled to provide its own personal identification number.

When we create a table in our database, we can specify the field which is to be the primary key of the table. The SQL to do this is shown in Listing 7-5. Most database products also usually provide you with an interface to help create a table and select the field(s) that make up the primary key.

Listing 7-5. *Specifying a Primary Key*

```
CREATE TABLE Member (
member_number INT PRIMARY KEY,
member_name VARCHAR (25)
)
```

With the primary key field specified, a constraint is put on the table that will ensure that every record must have a unique value for member_number. The user will never be able to put in two records with the same value for member_number, and so every member in our table can be uniquely distinguished. The constraint also ensures that the primary key field always has a value, so every record is certain to have a value for member_number.

It is possible to get the database to automatically generate unique values for fields like member_number. Depending on the product you are using, you will find a field type called identity, auto_increment, autonumber, or something similar. You can then specify some starting number and a step size, and every new row entered into the table will automatically be assigned the next available number.

Concatenated Keys

It isn't always necessary or even advisable to introduce a new automatically incrementing number field into a table to act as a primary key. With the case of members, there was no other way to ensure a unique field for every record, but often a unique field or combination of fields already exists in the table. When we have a combination of fields that can uniquely identify a record, this is referred to as a *concatenated* or *composite* key.Thinking about which combinations of fields are possible keys can help you discover and understand subtleties of the problem. Here is an example.

What is a possible key for the table in Figure 7-7, which is keeping information about students enrolling in courses?

student	course	year	grade
13887	COMP101	2011	B
17625	COMP101	2011	E
17625	COMP102	2012	A
18574	COMP102	2012	B

Figure 7-7. Enrollments table

student will not be suitable as a key, as a student will have a record for each of the courses in which he enrolls (we can see that the value 17625 appears in at least two records). Similarly, course will not do, as a course will have many enrollments each with its own record (the value COMP102 is duplicated).In fact, every column has duplicated values, so no single field is suitable as a key.

What about the combination (student, course)? In the few records shown in Figure 7-7, this combination is always unique, but we have to be sure this will *always* be the case for every record we may need to enter. We need to find out a bit more about the problem. Consider this dialog:

> *Analyst:* Could student 17625 enroll in COMP101 a second time to try and improve his grade?
>
> *Client:* Yes.

Now we see that student and course will *not* be a suitable key. As soon as the student tries to enroll in the course again, we will have another row with the same values for student number and course.

Let's try the combination (studentID, course, year):

> *Analyst:* Is it possible for a student to enroll in the same course again in the same year (say during the summer)?
>
> *Client:* It is for some subjects.
>
> *Analyst:* If a student did reenroll in the same subject in the summer, would you want to keep both her previous and her new grade?
>
> *Client:* Of course!

101

The combination (studentID, course, year) will not do as a key either because we will have to repeat the values of the three fields when a student enrolls in the same course later in the same year. Clearly, we need an additional attribute (semester maybe) to differentiate these enrollments. Thinking about a possible key has revealed a little more of the complexity of this problem and helped us spot a missing attribute or field.

Whenever we are checking the suitability of a combination of fields as a key, we need to find a question that checks that the combination will always be unique. In this case, we needed to ask questions such as the following:

> *Is a student ever likely to enroll in a course more than once?*
>
> *Yes. (*student, course*) is not a suitable key.*
>
> *Is it possible that a student will enroll in the same course more than once in a single year?*
>
> *Yes. (*student, course, year*) is not a suitable key.*
>
> *Is it possible that a student will enroll in the same course more than once in a single semester of a given year?*
>
> *No. (*student, course, year, semester*) is a possible key.*

Now look at the other fields in the table:

> *Is it possible that a student might need to have more than one grade for a given enrollment (e.g., an initial grade and a revised grade)?*
>
> *Maybe. (In that case, the problem is much more complicated than we thought.)*

Would it all have been easier if we had just abandoned looking for a concatenated key and added an automatically generated enrollment_number field that could be guaranteed to be always unique?

Enrollment (enrollment_number, student, course, semester, year, grade)

Consider the case where a student can only enroll in a course once a semester. The enrollment table now has two possible keys: enrollment_number and the combination (studentID, course, semester, year). What are the pros and cons of choosing one key over the other?

enrollment_number is shorter than the concatenated key, and you will see in Chapter 9 that this may be a consideration. However, if we make the combination of fields (student, course, semester, year) the key, the database will ensure that we never enter duplicate values (i.e., it will impose the constraint that a student cannot enroll in the course more than once a semester). This will effectively ensure enrollments do not get entered twice accidentally. If we choose the enrollment_number as the key, we will need to find another way to prevent such duplications.

An automatically generated number may be a sensible key, but it should not be included in a table because we can't be bothered thinking about alternatives. If we don't think about what values are suitable keys, we may miss discovering some subtleties of the problem.

Representing Relationships

So far we have represented each class as a table, each attribute as a field with a particular type, and decided on a field, or combination of fields with unique values, to be a primary key. We can now use this primary key to help us represent relationships between the classes in our model.

Let's consider our sports club example. A simple data model is shown in Figure 7-8 with some possible objects in Figure 7-9. A member may have *one* team that he currently plays for, and each team has exactly *one* captain.

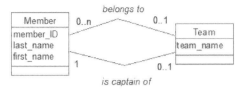

Figure 7-8. *Sports club data model*

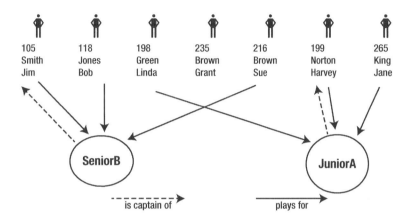

Figure 7-9. *Members, teams, and instances of the relationships between them*

First we design two tables to represent the classes and choose a primary key for each. We will adopt the convention of underlining the primary key fields.

- Member: (member_ID, last_name, first_name)

- Team: (team_name)

Each of the objects in Figure 7-9 will be a row in the appropriate table.

To represent the relationships *plays for* and *is captain of*, we need a way of specifying each of the lines between the objects in Figure 7-9. For example, we need to show that Bob Jones plays for SeniorB, and the captain of JuniorA is Harvey Norton.

As we have primary keys established, we can easily identify the row associated with each object (e.g., Harvey Norton is the row in the Member table where the primary key field member_ID has the value 199). To represent the relationship between the objects, we use these key values by way of a *foreign key* as described in the next section.

Foreign Keys

Figure 7-10 shows the two tables Member and Team again, but now we have added a field to show who is the captain of each team. What we have done is put a new field in the Team table (captain) that will contain the key value of the member who is its captain. This is a foreign key. A foreign key is a field(s) (in this case captain) that refers to the primary key field(s) in some other table (in this case it contains a value of the key field member_ID from the table Member). In this way, we establish the relationships between objects of different classes.

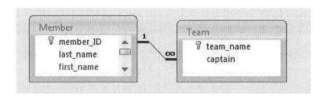

member_ID ▾	last_name ▾	first_name ▾
105	Smith	Jim
118	Jones	Bob
198	Green	Linda
199	Norton	Harvey
216	Brown	Sue
235	Brown	Grant
265	King	Jane

team_name ▾	captain ▾
JuniorA	199
SeniorB	105

Member table

Team table

Figure 7-10. *The Team table has a foreign key field (captain) referring to the Member table.*

The SQL statement for creating the table Team with a foreign key referring to the Member table is shown in Listing 7-6. Many products also provide a diagrammatic interface for specifying foreign keys. The interface for setting up a foreign key in Access is shown in Figure 7-11.

Listing 7-6. *SQL to Create a Team Table with a Foreign Key*

```
CREATE TABLE Team (
team_name VARCHAR(10) PRIMARY KEY,
captain INT FOREIGN KEY REFERENCES Member
)
```

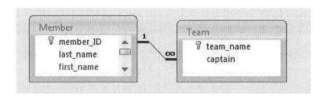

Figure 7-11. *Access interface for specifying captain is a foreign key referring to the Member table*

The two fields member_ID and captain will both have values from the same domain, that is, the set of MemberIDs. Formally, a foreign key and the primary key of the table it references must have the same domain. In most database products this is softened to requiring them to be the same data type or a compatible data type. The types of data that are regarded as compatible will depend on the database software being used (e.g., character fields of different lengths are compatible in some products, but not in others).

Referential Integrity

Arm-in-arm with the idea of a foreign key is the concept of *referential integrity*. This is a constraint that says that each *value* in a foreign key field (i.e., 199 and 105 in the Team table in Figure 7-10) must exist as values in the primary key field of the table being referred to (i.e., 199 and 105 must exist as values in the member_ID field in Member). This prevents us putting a nonexistent member (say, 765) as the captain of a team. It also means that we cannot remove members 199 and 105 from our member table while they are captains of teams. As soon as you set up a foreign key, this referential integrity constraint is automatically taken care of for you.

Representing 1–Many Relationships

In the previous sections, you have seen how it is possible to represent instances of a relationship in the data model by using a foreign key. In general, the process for a 1–Many relationship is as follows:

For a 1–Many relationship, the key field from the table representing the class at the 1 end is added as a foreign key in the table representing the class at the Many end.

We have already represented the relationship *is captain of* in Figure 7-8. Let's now use our general guideline to do the same thing for the relationship *plays for* between Member and Team.

The class at the 1 end is Team, so we take the primary key field from the Team table and add it as a new foreign key attribute in the Member table. We can give the field any name we like, but it should clearly indicate the relationship it is representing, for example current_team. This is shown in Figure 7-12.

member_ID ▾	last_name ▾	first_name ▾	current_team ▾
118	Jones	Bob	SeniorB
198	Green	Linda	JuniorA
199	Norton	Harvey	JuniorA
216	Brown	Sue	SeniorB
235	Brown	Grant	
265	King	Jane	JuniorA

team_name ▾	captain ▾
JuniorA	199
SeniorB	105

Member table

current_team is a foreign key referencing Team

Team table

captain is a foreign key referencing Member

Figure 7-12. Both relationships in sports club model represented by foreign keys

Referential integrity, which is a result of making the current_team field a foreign key, will ensure that the value entered in current_team can be found in the primary column (team_name) of the Team table. This ensures that members can only play for teams that already exist in the Team table.

Note that a foreign key field can be null. Grant Brown does not belong to a team, so there is no value in the foreign key field in his record. This is consistent with the optionality of the *plays for* relationship in the class diagram back in Figure 7-8. If the relationship was not optional, we would have to impose an additional constraint on the field to say that nulls were not permitted. If we wanted to ensure that every team had a captain (as the data model suggests), then as well as making the captain field in the Team table a foreign key, we would also specify that it cannot ever be null.

Let's look at another example of a 1–Many relationship–this time a self relationship. We will consider the case where a member sponsors other members who wish to obtain membership with the club. The relevant part of the data model is shown in Figure 7-13, and some objects and their relationships are shown in Figure 7-14.

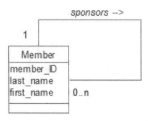

Figure 7-13. Self relationship: Member sponsors other members.

105

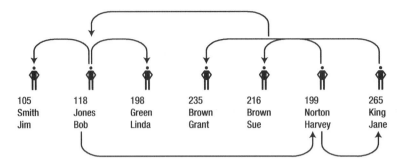

Figure 7-14. *Instances of members who sponsor each other*

This self relationship is a 1–Many relationship, and we do exactly the same as we do for any other 1–Many relationship. We take the key from the table representing the class at the 1 end (member_ID) and add it as a foreign key to the table representing the class at the Many end (Member). It makes no difference that it is the same table. We give the new foreign key field a name that describes the relationship, say *sponsor*, and the table will look like that in Figure 7-15.

member_ID	last_name	first_name	current_team	sponsor
105	Smith	Jim	SeniorB	118
118	Jones	Bob	SeniorB	216
198	Green	Linda	JuniorA	118
199	Norton	Harvey	JuniorA	118
216	Brown	Sue	SeniorB	265
235	Brown	Grant		199
265	King	Jane	JuniorA	199

Figure 7-15. *A foreign key (sponsor) representing a self relationship*

The table Member has a foreign key, sponsor, referencing its own table. Jim Smith is sponsored by member 118, who is Bob Jones. Unlike a primary key, there is no restriction that a foreign key such as sponsor must be unique. In Figure 7-15 we can see that 118 (Bob Jones) is sponsoring several members. Referential integrity ensures that a member can only be sponsored by someone who is already a member. There is a bit of a problem if the relationship is compulsory, which means we add a constraint not to allow nulls in the sponsor field. How do you ever get the first member into the database when there is no existing member to sponsor her? This isn't just a database problem, it is actually part of our problem description. All new members need a sponsor, but what about the founding members? Making the sponsor field required is probably not a good idea.

Representing Many–Many Relationships

You may remember from Chapter 4 that Many–Many relationships are not as common as you might at first expect. Often they are a sign that some information about the problem has been initially overlooked, and an intermediate class is required to store that information. They do, however, genuinely occur where we have objects that simultaneously belong in many categories. Figures 7-16 and 7-17 review the plant database from Chapter 2 where we had species of plants that were suitable for a variety of uses.

106

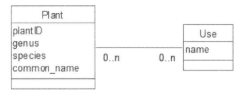

Figure 7-16. *Data model for plant database*

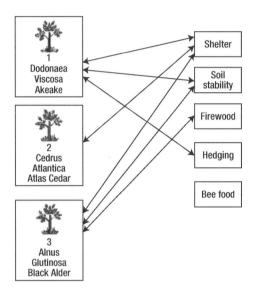

Figure 7-17. *Some examples of species and their uses*

How are we to represent all the instances of this relationship? Foreign keys will no longer do the trick, as we will never know how many uses a particular species will have, nor how many species will be related to a particular use. To deal with this in a relational database, we have to introduce a new intermediate class in our data model. You saw how to do this in Chapter 4 when we had some additional information that required a new class. In this Many–Many situation, the new intermediate class will not have any attributes, as there is nothing we wish to know about a particular combination of Species and Use. We use the new class (Species_Use) simply to store all the relevant pairings of Use and Species. As in Chapter 4, the new class connects to the existing classes with two 1–Many relationships as shown in Figure 7-18. We can interpret the diagram as: "Each Species_Use object (or pairing) consists of exactly one species and exactly one use."

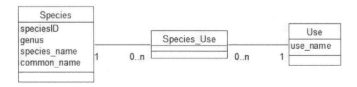

Figure 7-18. *Adding another class to represent a Many–Many relationship in a relational database*

The two 1–Many relationships can now be dealt with like any other 1–Many relationship. First we need to create a table, Species_Use, for our new class. Then for each of the 1–Many relationships, we add the primary key field from the table representing the class at the 1 end as a foreign key in the table representing the class at the Many end. This means adding two new foreign key attributes, species and use, to the Species_Use table. These foreign keys will reference the Species and Use tables, respectively. The resulting tables with some data are shown in Figure 7-19.

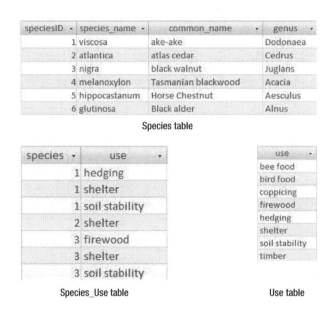

Species table

Species_Use table   Use table

Figure 7-19. *Representing a Many–Many relationship with an additional table with two foreign keys*

We now have to decide on a primary key for the new Species_Use table. The combination of the two foreign key fields (speciesID, use) will do the trick. This combining of foreign keys to form a primary key is often the case in the situation where an intermediate table has been introduced in a Many–Many relationship.

Representing 1–1 Relationships

In all of the previous sections, we have always ended up taking the primary key field at the 1 end of the relationship and using it as a foreign key in the table at the other end. If both ends of the relationship have a cardinality of 1, which way around should we do this?

Our example of members and teams had a 1–1 relationship: *is captain of*. That part of the data model is shown in Figure 7-20.

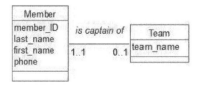

Figure 7-20. *Is captain of is a 1–1 relationship.*

108

The question is whether to put member_ID as a foreign key in the Team table or team_name as a foreign key in the Member table. The resulting tables for these alternatives are shown in Figure 7-21.

member_ID ▾	last_name ▾	first_name ▾	is_captain_of ▾
105	Smith	Jim	SeniorB
118	Jones	Bob	
198	Green	Linda	
199	Norton	Harvey	JuniorA
216	Brown	Sue	
235	Brown	Grant	
265	King	Jane	

OR

team_name ▾	captain ▾
JuniorA	199
SeniorB	105

Foreign key in Member table   Foreign key in Team table

Figure 7-21. *Alternative ways to represent the 1–1 relationship*

The same information is represented in both tables. We mustn't do both simultaneously, as we might end up with inconsistent data. For example, we could end up with Bob being captain of SeniorB according to the Member table, but Jim being the captain according to the Team table.

In the Member table in Figure 7-21, we have many empty values for the field is_captain_of because that end of the relationship is optional (a member doesn't have to be a captain and most members won't be). In general, you should put the foreign key in the table that has the compulsory association if there is one. A team *must* have a captain, so put the foreign key in the Team table.

Putting the foreign key in the Team table ensures that each team only has one captain, however there is nothing to prevent a member being captain of more than one team (e.g., there is nothing currently in the design of the Team table to prevent us putting 199 on more than one row). With the foreign key in the Member table we have the opposite situation: a person can only captain one team but we could have JuniorA appearing on several rows, and so effectively having several captains. We will see how to enforce both constraints with unique indexes in Chapter 9.

Representing Inheritance

Relational databases do not have the concept of inheritance built into them; however, it is possible to approximate the idea of inheritance.

As discussed in Chapter 6, inheritance is very useful to model tricky problems, but it should only be used when other more simple patterns cannot fully represent some essential complications. Figure 7-22 shows a simple case of inheritance in which lecturers and students inherit the attributes of a person and also have some specialized attributes of their own.

One way to capture the main aspects of inheritance in a relational database is to set up classes for each parent class and subclass and include a 1–1 relationship between each subclass and its parent as shown in Figure 7-23. The relationships (reading upward) say that a lecturer *is a* person and a student *is a* person, which is a natural way to think about the model.

The relationship between Student and Person in Figure 7-23 is compulsory at the top end because every student is a person, but optional at the bottom end because a person does not have to be a student. We can now set up tables as we did for the 1–1 relationship in the previous section. We choose to put the foreign key (personID) in the Student table (because a student has to be a person) and similarly for the Lecturer table. personID will also be the primary key of the Lecturer and the Student tables. We will end up with three tables as shown in Figure 7-24.

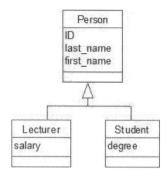

Figure 7-22. Simple model with inheritance

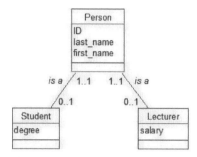

Figure 7-23. Inheritance approximated with 1–1 is a relationship

ID	last_name	first_name		personID	salary		personID	degree
101	Jones	Sue		101	75000		108	Arts
108	Brown	Lin		108	90000		110	Science
110	Li	Bo		110	12000		112	Arts
112	Green	Mike						

Person table   Lecturer table   Student table

Figure 7-24. Tables representing the model in Figure 7-23

What elements of the inheritance have we captured? Well, we have the contact details of each person in just one place–the Person table. We know who are lecturers and who are students, and we have the specialist attributes of each role neatly stored in the appropriate tables. As a special bonus, we have also managed to capture multiple inheritance! John and Linda feature in both the lecturer and the student tables.

What is different from true inheritance? In the model in Figure 7-23, we have just *one* object for Sue (a Lecturer object). In Figure 7-24, we have *two* rows (a row in the Person table and a row in the Lecturer table) with a relationship between them. Extending the model is also different in the two cases. If, at a later date, we require an additional subclass (e.g., Administrator), this can be added quite simply to the hierarchy in Figure 7-22. In Figure 7-23, we would need to add another class but in addition also create and maintain another relationship.

110

Summary

We have taken a data model and represented the main features using the functionality available in relational database products. Following is a summary of the steps:

1. For each class, create a table.

2. For each attribute, create a field and choose an appropriate data type. Consider whether some attributes (e.g., address) should be split into several fields.

3. Think about which fields should be required to have a value.

4. Consider what constraints need to be placed on the values of fields. Possibly create a new domain if your database product supports this.

5. Choose a field or combination of fields as the primary key. Ask careful questions to ensure that the key fields will always have unique values.

6. For each Many–Many relationship, insert a new intermediary class and two 1–Many relationships.

7. For each 1–Many relationship, take the primary key field(s) from the table representing the class at the 1 end and add this field(s) as a foreign key in the table representing the class at the Many end.

8. For a 1–1 relationship, put the foreign key in the table where it is most likely to have a value or where the attribute is most important.

9. For compulsory relationships, add a constraint to the foreign key fields that they must not be null.

10. For inheritance (as an approximation), alter the model to have a 1–1 *is a* relationship between the parent and each child class. Create tables and foreign keys as in point seven.

TESTING YOUR UNDERSTANDING

Exercise 7-1.

Figure 7-25 shows an initial data model for a small library. It is incomplete, so as you answer the questions below consider what else might need to be included.

a) Explain to the librarian what the initial data model means.

b) Design tables for a relational database which would capture the information represented by the model. Include primary and foreign keys and other appropriate constraints.

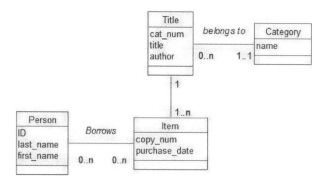

Figure 7-25. *Draft data model for a small library*

CHAPTER 8

Normalization

We are doing pretty well at designing a database. So far, you have learned how use cases and a data model can help you understand many of the complexities of the problem you are trying to represent. In the previous chapter, you saw how to represent the main parts of the data model in a relational database. To recap:

- Each class is represented by a table.

- Each attribute is represented by a field with a datatype and possible constraints.

- Each object becomes a row in a table.

- For each table, we determine a primary key, which is a field(s) that uniquely identifies each row.

- We use the primary key field(s) to represent relationships between classes by way of foreign keys.

At this stage, everything could be absolutely fine, but then again there may be some classes in our model (or tables in our database) that might still cause us problems. Normalization is a formal way of checking the fields to ensure they are in the right table or to see if perhaps we might need restructured or additional tables to help keep our data accurate. The initial idea of normalization was first proposed by E. F. Codd [1] in 1970 and has been a cornerstone of relational database design since then. Some readers of this book may be throwing up their hands in horror that I have left this important topic until Chapter 8. However, we have actually been normalizing our database right from Example 1-1 when we saw that two classes were needed to keep information about plants and their uses.

In this chapter, we will first look at why it is critical that all the attributes are in the right table and how normalization helps us make sure they are.

Update Anomalies

Let's have a look at a simple example where having the attributes in the wrong table can cause a number of problems in maintaining data. Let's say we have a database for maintaining information about many different aspects of a company. There may be several tables for maintaining customers, products, orders, suppliers, and so on, and there are also two tables as shown in Figure 8-1 about employees and some small projects to which they have been assigned. Can you see a problem lurking in the Assignment table?

---

[1] Edgar F. Codd, (June 1970). "A Relational Model of Data for Large Shared Data Banks." *Communications of the ACM*: 13(6): pp. 377–387.

113

empID ▾	last_name ▾	first_name ▾
1001	Smith	John
1005	Jones	Susan
1029	Li	Jane

emp ▾	project_num ▾	project_name ▾	contact ▾	hours ▾
1005	1	JenningsLtd	325-1234	8
1001	3	ABCPromo	142-3456	8
1005	3	ABCPromo	142-3456	14
1001	6	Smith&Co	365-8765	20

Employee   Assignment

Figure 8-1. *Tables with potential update problems*

A problem with the `Assignment` table is one that we encountered way back in Example 1-3, "Insect Data." We have repeated information about a project. The number, name, and contact can be repeated several times in this table if there is more than one employee working on the project. This will almost inevitably lead to some rows (for, say, project number 3) having inconsistent names or contact numbers at some stage. This is relatively easy to spot for the data in Figure 8-1, but often it can be less easy to see. If we hadn't had data for two employees working on project 3, we might not have even realized this was a possibility. Normalization gives us a formal way of checking for such situations before we get into trouble.

As well as the possibility of inconsistent data, there are other problems that the design of the `Assignment` table can cause. These are often collectively referred to as *update anomalies*. We will look at some of these other problems now.

Insertion Problems

You will recall that it is necessary to have a primary key for every table in our database. This is so we can uniquely identify each row and have a mechanism for relating rows in different tables. What is a possible primary key for the `Assignment` table in Figure 8-1? Just looking at the data in the table, we can see that there is no single field that is a potential primary key field. Every column has duplicated values. We need to look for a concatenated key, and the pair `emp` and `project_num` is possible. We need to confirm that each employee is associated with a project just once, and if that is the case, the pair of values for `emp` and `proj_num` is a suitable primary key.

However, we have a problem. If we want to keep information about a particular project but there is no employee yet working on it, we have no value for `emp`, which is one of the fields making up our primary key. If a field is essential to uniquely determine a particular row in our table, it makes no sense that it can be empty. As you may recall from the previous chapter, one of the constraints imposed by putting a primary key on a table is that the fields involved must always have a value. We cannot enter a record for which the value of `emp`, being part of the primary key, is empty. Therefore we have no way of recording information about any project before someone is working on it.

Deletion Problems

Here is another situation that might occur. Employee 1001 may finish working on the Smith&Co project. If this happens, we will remove that row from the `Assignment` table. What is a possible side effect of deleting this row? Well, if employee 1001 was the only person working on the project, every reference to Smith&Co will have gone, and we will have lost the project's contact number. By deleting information about employee 1001's involvement in a project, we have inappropriately lost information about the project.

114

Dealing With Update Anomalies

We have seen three different updating problems with the `Assignment` table in Figure 8-1: possible inconsistent data when repeated information is modified, problems inserting new records because part of the primary key may be empty, and accidental loss of information as a by-product of a deletion.

I'm sure you have spotted the solution to these problems ages ago. What we need is another table to record information about projects, as in Figure 8-2. With this design, we don't have a project's contact number recorded more than once, we can add a new project in the `Project` table even if no one is working on it, and we can delete an assignment (employee 1001 working on project 6) without accidentally losing information about the project.

empID	last_name	first_name
1001	Smith	John
1005	Jones	Susan
1029	Li	Jane

pro_num	proj_name	contact
1	JenningsLtd	325-1234
3	ABCPromo	142-2345
6	Smith&Co	365-8765

emp	project	hours
1005	1	8
1001	3	8
1005	3	14
1001	6	20

Employee   **Project**   **Assignment**

Figure 8-2. *Tables with update anomalies removed*

Chances are that the `Project` table would have surfaced in your original analysis of use cases and the data model. But how can you be sure you haven't missed anything? This is where the formal definition of a normalized table helps.

Functional Dependencies

Normalization helps us to determine whether our tables are structured in such a way as to avoid the update anomalies described in the previous section. Central to the definition of normalization is the idea of a *functional dependency*. Functional dependencies are a way of describing the interdependence of attributes or fields in our tables. With a definition of functional dependencies, we can provide a more formal definition of a primary key, explain what is meant by a normalized table, and discuss the different forms of normalization.

Definition of a Functional Dependency

A functional dependency is a statement that essentially says, "If I know the value for this attribute(s), I can uniquely tell you the value of some other attribute(s)." For example, we can say,

> If I know the value of an employee's ID number, I can tell you his last name with certainty.

Or equivalently,

> Employee's ID number functionally determines employee's last name.

Or in symbols,

`empID` $\rightarrow$ `last_name`

For the situation depicted in Figure 8-2, if I know an employee's ID is 1001, I can tell you that his last name is Smith. Does it work the other way round? If I know an employee's last name, can I uniquely tell you his employee ID number? From the data displayed in the tables, you might say, "Yes, you can." However, for a functional

115

dependency to hold, it must be true for any data that can ever be put in our tables. We know that in the long term it is possible we might have several employees called Smith, so that knowing the last name does not uniquely determine the ID. Or more formally, last_name does not functionally determine empID.

Let's try another example. For the database tables in Figure 8-2, do we have a functional dependency between an employee's ID number and a project to which he is assigned? If I know the employee's ID is 1001, I cannot tell you a *unique* project number. It could be project 3 or project 6, and so an employee's ID number does not functionally determine (or uniquely determine) a project number.

Determining the functional dependencies requires us to understand the intricacies of the specific situation. For the case of employees and projects we need to know whether an employee can be assigned to only one project or whether he can be assigned to many different projects. Does this sound familiar? Determining whether attributes functionally determine each other involves the same sort of questions we went through when trying to understand the data model in Chapter 4.

In terms of a data model with an Employee class and a Project class, we would ask, "Can an employee ever be associated with more than one project?"

If the answer is "No," we have a 1–Many relationship between employees and projects as in Figure 8-3a; otherwise, we have a Many–Many relationship as in Figure 8-3b.

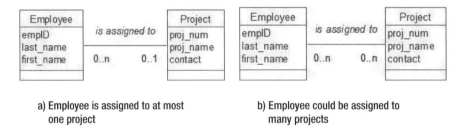

a) Employee is assigned to at most one project

b) Employee could be assigned to many projects

Figure 8-3. *Different relationships between Employee and Project*

In terms of functional dependencies, we have an analogous question: "If I know an employee's ID number, can I tell you a unique project number?"

If the answer is "Yes," empID →proj_num; otherwise, employee ID does not functionally determine the project number. Understanding the functional dependencies and understanding classes and their relationships are two different approaches to figuring out the intricacies of the problem we are trying to model.

Functional Dependencies and Primary Keys

Now that you know about functional dependencies, we have another way of thinking about what we mean by a primary key. If we know the values of the key fields of a table, we can find a unique row in the table. Once we have that row, then we know the value of all the other fields in that row. For example, if I know empID, I can find a unique row in the Employee table and so be able to determine the last_name and first_name. Or, in terms of functional dependencies:

empID → last_name, first_name

This leads us to a more formal way of defining a key:

The key fields functionally determine all the other fields in the table.

If I know the value of the key, I guarantee I can tell you the value of every other field in the row. This is why last_name cannot be a key field for our Employee table. If I know the last name of an employee is Smith, I cannot guarantee that I can find a single row and tell you the value for empID.

You have probably noticed that I've been using the term *key* rather than *primary key* in the last couple of paragraphs. There is a distinction between the two. Think about this. Is the pair of attributes (empID, last_name) a possible key for our Employee table? Our definition of a key is that if we know the value of the key fields, we can find a unique row. That is certainly the case if we know empID and last_name. However, I'm sure you can see that last_name is redundant. The pair of attributes (empID, last_name) is a key because empID is a key. If we know empID, we can find the row regardless of what additional information we have; we don't need to know last_name as well.

This idea of having fields in our key that are superfluous is the distinction between a key and a candidate for a primary key. To be considered as a primary key, there must be no unnecessary fields. More formally:

A primary key has no subset of the fields that is also a key.

Why is this important? Say each of our projects has one manager as shown in the snippet of the data model in Figure 8-4.

Figure 8-4. *A 1–Many relationship*

Remember how we represent a 1–Many relationship in our database. We take the primary key field(s) from the table at the 1 end (Employee) and put those field(s) as a foreign key in the Project table. If we had mistakenly used the pair (empID, last_name) as a primary key for the Employee table, we would get a Project table as shown in Figure 8-5. I'm sure you can see the information redundancy and potential for problems there.

pro_num ▾	proj_name ▾	contact ▾	manager_num ▾	manager_name ▾
1	JenningsLtd	325-1234	1005	Jones
3	ABCPromo	142-2345	1001	Smith
6	Smith&Co	365-8765	1001	Smith

foreign key fields

Figure 8-5. *Redundancy problems caused by not having a suitable primary key*

Now that you have an idea of what a functional dependency is and a more formal definition of a primary key, we can look at how normalization can help ensure that we have a good design for our tables.

117

Normal Forms

Tables that are "normalized" will generally avoid the updating problems we examined earlier in the chapter. There are several levels of normalization called *normal forms*, each addressing additional situations where problems may occur. In this section we will look at the normal forms that are defined using functional dependencies.

First Normal Form

First normal form is the most important, and essentially says that we should not try to cram several pieces of data into a single field. Our very first example of what can go wrong, Example 1-1, "The Plant Database," was a situation where this was a problem. In the plant database, we were keeping information about different plant species and the different uses for which they were suited. Some possible (but not recommended!) ways of keeping several uses for each plant are shown in Figure 8-6.

plantID	genus	species	common_name	uses
1	Dodonaea	viscosa	Akeake	soil stability, hedging, shelter
2	Cedrus	atlantica	Atlas cedar	shelter
3	Alnus	glutinosa	Black alder	firewood, soil stability, shelter
4	Eucalyptus	nichollii	Black peppermint gum	shelter, coppicing, bird food

plantID	genus	species	common_name	use1	use2	use3
1	Dodonaea	viscosa	Akeake	shelter	hedging	soil stability
2	Cedrus	atlantica	Atlas cedar	shelter		
3	Alnus	glutinosa	Black alder	soil stability	shelter	firewood
4	Eucalyptus	nichollii	Black peppermint gum	shelter	coppicing	bird food

Figure 8-6. Nonrecommended ways of keeping information about multiple uses

We saw in Example 1-1 the problems that eventuate from keeping the plant data in tables like those in Figure 8-6. For example, it can be difficult to find all the plants with particular uses (e.g., all the shelter plants).

Thinking back to our new definition of a primary key, let's reconsider the primary keys of the two tables in Figure 8-6. plantID is a primary key of both tables in the sense that it is different in every row. Does it functionally determine all the other attributes? If I know the value of plantID (e.g., plantID = 1), can I tell you a unique use? Well, in the top table I can tell you the character string in the uses field, and in the second table I can tell you what is in any particular one of the three columns, so in a very formal sense, yes, I can. However, if we are thinking about the meanings behind these fields, I can't give you any information about a unique use just by knowing the plant's ID. I can only tell you about a collection of uses for each plant.

The two tables are not in first normal form (except in a technical sense). They are both trying in a roundabout way to keep multiple values of use.

A table is not in first normal form if it is keeping multiple values for a piece of information.

Normalization has given us a formal way of determining that there is something wrong with the design of the tables in Figure 8-6. It also gives us a method for solving the problem.

If a table is not in first normal form, remove the multivalued information from the table. Create a new table with that information and the primary key of the original table.

For our plant database example, this means setting up two tables, as in Figure 8-7.

plantID	genus	species	common_name
1	Dodonaea	viscosa	Akeake
2	Cedrus	atlantica	Atlas cedar
3	Alnus	glutinosa	Black alder
4	Eucalyptus	nichollii	Black peppermint gum
5	Juglans	nigra	Black walnut

Plant

plant	use
1	soil stability
1	hedging
1	shelter
2	shelter
3	firewood
3	soil stability
3	shelter

PlantUse

Figure 8-7. Removing the multivalued field from unnormalized table to create an additional table

When we considered this problem by way of a data model, we decided that we actually had two classes, Plant and Use, with a Many–Many relationship between them. In Chapter 7, you saw that to represent a Many–Many relationship, we needed to add an intermediate table. If you go back and take a look at Figures 7-17 to 7-19, you will see that the new table is the same as the PlantUse table in Figure 8-7. We arrived at the same normalized solution, but via two different routes. As discussed in Example 1-1, normalized tables such as those in Figure 8-7 avoid the many problems associated with the original, unnormalized tables of Figure 8-6.

Second Normal Form

It is possible for a table in first normal form to still have updating problems. The Assignment table in Figure 8-8, which we discussed at the beginning of this chapter, is an example. It has the information about the names and contacts of projects repeated several times, with the result that eventually the information might become inconsistent. We also saw that there could be problems with inserting new records and losing information as a by-product of deleting certain records.

empID	project_num	project_name	contact	hours
1005	1	JenningsLtd	325-1234	8
1001	3	ABCPromo	142-3456	8
1005	3	ABCPromo	142-3456	14
1001	6	Smith&Co	365-8765	20

Figure 8-8. Assignment table with update anomalies

The definition of both first and second normal form requires us to know the primary key of the table we are assessing. The primary key of the Assignment table is the combination of the empID and proj_num fields. Is the table in first normal form? If I tell you an employee ID and a project number (e.g., 1005 and 1), can you tell me unique values for all the other non–key fields? Yes. The project name is Jennings Ltd, the contact is 325-1234, and the hours are 8. There are no multivalued fields in this table. We are not trying to squeeze several bits of information into one field anywhere. But there is still a problem with update anomalies.

119

The problem here is that while I can figure out the value of all the non–key fields by knowing the primary key, I don't actually need both fields of the primary key to do that. If I want to know the number of hours, I need to know the values of both empID and proj_num. However, if I want to know the contact number or the project name, I only need to know the value of the proj_num. Here is where our problem arises, and it leads us to the definition of second normal form.

> *A table is in second normal form if it is in first normal form AND we need ALL the fields in the key to determine the values of the non–key fields.*

We also have a way of fixing a table that is not in second normal form.

> *If a table is not in second normal form, remove those non–key fields that are not dependent on the whole of the primary key. Create another table with these fields and the part of the primary key on which they do depend.*

This means that we remove the non-key fields proj_name and contact from the Assignment table and put them in a new table with proj_num (the part of the key on which they do depend). This splitting up of an unnormalized table is often referred to as *decomposition*. So we could say the original Assignment table is decomposed into the two tables in second normal form, as shown in Figure 8-9.

empID ▾	project_num ▾	hours ▾
1005	1	8
1001	3	8
1005	3	14
1001	6	20

Assignment

pro_num ▾	proj_name ▾	contact ▾
1	JenningsLtd	325-1234
3	ABCPromo	142-2345
6	Smith&Co	365-8765

Project

Figure 8-9. *Assignment table decomposed into two tables*

Had we approached this from a data modeling perspective, we would have said we have two classes, Employee and Project, with a Many–Many relationship between them as in Figure 8-3b. As discussed in Chapter 7, to represent this relationship we need to add an intermediary table, and we would have come up with exactly the same tables (along with an Employee table), as in Figure 8-9.

Once again, we have arrived at the same solution via two routes: thinking about the classes and their relationships, or considering the functional dependencies and normalization.

Third Normal Form

You guessed it. Tables in second normal form can still cause us problems. This time, consider our Employee table with some added information about the department for which an employee works. Take a look at the table in Figure 8-10.

empID	last_name	first_name	dept_num	dep_name
1001	Smith	John	2	Marketing
1005	Jones	Susan	2	Marketing
1029	Li	Jane	1	Sales

Figure 8-10. Employee table with updating problems

What is the primary key for the Employee table in Figure 8-10? If an employee works for only one department, it is enough to know just the empID to find a particular row. Is the table in first normal form? Yes. If I know the value of empID (e.g., 1029), I can tell you a unique value for each of the other fields. Is the table in second normal form? Yes, the primary key is only one field now, so nothing can depend on "part" of the key. Are there still problems? Yes. The information about the department name is repeated on several rows and is liable to become inconsistent.

The situation in this table is that the name of the department is determined by more than one field. If I know that the value of the primary key field empID is 1001, I can tell you that the department name is Marketing. However, if I know that the value of dept_num is 2, I can also tell you that the department name is Marketing. There are two different fields determining what the value of the department name is. This is where the problem arises this time, and it leads to a definition for third normal form.

A table is in third normal form if it is in second normal form AND no non-key fields depend on a field(s) that is not the primary key.

As in the other normal forms, we also have a simple method for correcting a table that is not in third normal form.

If a table is not in third normal form, remove the non-key fields that are dependent on a field(s) that is not the primary key. Create another table with this field(s) and the field on which it does depend.

For the Employee table in Figure 8-10, this would mean removing the field dept_name from the original Employee table and putting it in a new table along with the field on which it depends (dept_num),v as shown in Figure 8-11. The field dept_num will be the primary key of our new table and will also remain in the Employee table as a foreign key.

empID	last_name	first_name	dept_num
1001	Smith	John	2
1005	Jones	Susan	2
1029	Li	Jane	1

Employee

dept_num	dep_name
1	Sales
2	Marketing
3	Research

Department

Figure 8-11. Employee table decomposed to two tables

121

Boyce–Codd Normal Form

This is the last normal form that involves functional dependencies. For most tables, it is equivalent to third normal form, but it is a slightly stronger statement for some tables where there is more than one possible combination of fields that could be used as a primary key. We are not going to consider those here. However, Boyce–Codd normal form is quite an elegant statement that encapsulates the first three normal forms.

A table is in Boyce-Codd normal form if every determinant could be a primary key.

Let's see how this works. Say I know that the value of a particular field (e.g., $proj\_num$) determines the value of another field (e.g., $proj\_name$). We say that $proj\_num$ is a *determinant* (it determines the value of something else). In any table where this is the case, then $proj\_num$ must be able to be the primary key.

Consider the Assignment table in Figure 8-8. $proj\_num$ determines $proj\_name$, but $proj\_num$ is not able to be a primary key (there can be several rows with the same value of $proj\_num$). In this case, Boyce-Codd normal form is a more general statement of second normal form—$proj\_num$ is a determinant, but it is not the whole key. In the Employee table in Figure 8-10, $dept\_num$ is a determinant, but it cannot be a primary key because it is not different in every row. In this case, Boyce-Codd normal form is a statement that includes third normal form.

One of the sweetest ways to sum up the normal forms we have discussed is from Bill Kent.[2] He summarizes the normal forms this way:

*A table is based on
the key,
the whole key,
and nothing but the key (so help me Codd)*

Just remembering this simple quotation can help you ensure all your tables are normalized to third normal form.

Data Models or Functional Dependencies?

In our discussions of the normal forms, based on functional dependencies, you have seen that in most of the examples we have arrived at the same set of tables as we did, in previous chapters, by considering classes and their relationships. What are the differences between the two approaches? In general, how should we go about our database design?

Essentially, we have two tools at our dipsosal, and we should use either or both when we find them helpful. This will depend on particular people and the particular problem we are trying to model. Whichever tool we use, the most essential thing is to understand the scope of the problem and the intricacies of the relationships between pieces of data. A detailed understanding requires us to ask very specific questions about the project. We can represent the answers with either part of a data model or by writing down a functional dependency. Sometimes one way just feels more natural than the other. Let's look at some examples.

For a particular problem, I may know I am going to require data about employees and projects, and I need to know more about the relationships between them.

From a data modeling perspective, I might ask, "Can an employee be associated with more than one project?"

I can use the answer to decide whether the relationship between the employee class and project class is 1–Many or Many-Many. To me, this feels like a natural way to think about and discuss the issue. From a functional dependency perspective, I would ask something like, "If I know the employee's ID number, can I know a unique project with which she is associated?"

---

[2] William Kent, "A Simple Guide to Five Normal Forms in Relational Database Theory," Communications of the ACM 26(2), Feb. 1983, 120-125.

If the answer is "Yes," I would represent this as the functional dependency

`empID → project`

To me, this latter way of describing this aspect of the problem doesn't feel natural. Other people might think quite differently. The two questions and the two ways of representing them (class diagram or functional dependency) contain pretty much the same information about the relationship between employees and projects.

Let's try another example. What about the relationship between salary and tax rate? From a functional dependency perspective, I would ask, "If I know the salary, can I uniquely determine the tax rate?"

To me, that feels like a good way to think about this aspect of the problem. If the answer is "Yes," I can represent it as the functional dependency

`salary → tax_rate`

From a data-modeling perspective, I'm not sure what question I would ask. I probably don't have a salary class or a tax rate class, so thinking about relationships between classes is not such a natural way to come to terms with this intricacy.

What would happen if we tried to do our whole database design in terms of functional dependencies and normalization? We could start out with one huge table with a field to hold every piece of information. This is sometimes referred to as the *universal relation*. We could make a list of all the functional dependencies that apply between all the different fields and then apply our normalization rules to gradually decompose our big table into a set of normalized tables. There are in fact algorithms that allow you to do exactly that automatically. However, putting all the rules about our database in terms of functional dependencies and treating all the pieces of information as independent fields of one big table is rarely a practical way to start.

When we first start thinking about a problem, it is natural to think in quite general terms. For example, we might know we have to keep data about people, and information about projects, and we mustn't forget the buildings. We might not have a clear idea at the start what data we want to keep about each of these things, so trying to capture this original information with functional dependencies is not going to be helpful. However, the very basic ideas about the project fall quite naturally into classes. A data model or class diagram will show us that we need classes for buildings, projects, and people, and will allow us to start thinking about the relationships. Do people work in a particular building? Do people work on more than one project? Do people have other relationships with projects (e.g., might they manage them as well as work on them)? Do people manage each other?

All these broad initial ideas about a project are easily captured by the data model. The data model also helps us to find out more detailed information as we question the cardinalities and optionalities of the relationships, or look for fan traps, or check to see whether some relationships are redundant.

Once we are satisfied that our class diagram captures the information correctly, we can then represent the diagram as a set of tables and primary and foreign keys as described in Chapter 7. At this point, it is then a good idea to look at each table and see whether it is normalized. We might have an `Employee` table with fields `empID`, `last_name`, `first_name`, `salary`, and `tax_rate`, with `empID` as the primary key. Now we might ask about the functional dependencies between `salary` and `tax_rate`. If there is a functional dependency, our table is not in third normal form (`tax_rate` depends on something other than the primary key) and it should not be in this table.

The data model is great for the big picture, and normalization is great for the finer details. Use both these tools to ensure that you get the best structure for your database.

Additional Considerations

We have looked at functional dependencies and the normal forms that are defined using them: first, second, third, and Boyce–Codd normal form. There are other dependencies that can exist between pieces of data and additional normal forms that protect against some problems that may occur. I am not going to describe these in any very formal way, but I will point out what aspects of data models they relate to.

Fourth and fifth normal forms deal with tables for which there are multi–valued dependencies. We have already seen a case where this can occur. Let's reconsider the sports team example from Chapter 5. We have players, matches, and teams. If I name a team, there are multiple values of match associated with that team, and similarly multiple associated players. Let's say we are particularly interested in matches—who plays in them and what teams are involved. We need to consider whether we should have the intermediate table (Appearance) and/or the other relationships in Figure 8-12.

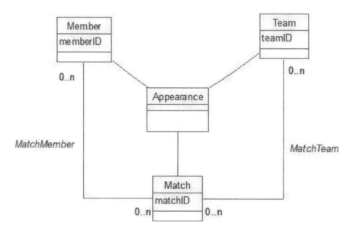

Figure 8-12. *What relationships are needed between Member, Team, and Match?*

If we represent the model in Figure 8-12 in a relational database, we would need tables for each of the classes Member, Team, Match, and Appearance. We would also need two additional tables to represent the Many–Many relationships between Match and Team, and between Match and Member. Figure 8-13 shows some data that could be in the tables.

Match ▾	Member ▾
MatchA	Jim
MatchA	Sue
MatchA	Hal
MatchA	Li

MatchMember

Match ▾	Team ▾
MatchA	Team1
MatchA	Team2
MatchB	Team1
MatchB	Team3

MatchTeam

Match ▾	Member ▾	Team ▾
MatchA	Jim	Team1
MatchA	Sue	Team1
MatchA	Hal	Team1
MatchA	Li	Team2

Appearance

Figure 8-13. *Sample data representing the relationships in Figure 8-12*

For each of the tables in Figure 8-13, the primary key is made up of all the fields. There are no non–key fields, and there are no functional dependencies. They are all therefore in Boyce–Codd normal form because there are no determinants that are not possible keys (there are no determinants!). The question is, "Do we need all three tables?" There is clearly some repeated information with the data as it stands. For example, the fact that Jim is involved in MatchA can be seen from both the MatchMember and the Appearance tables. When information is stored twice, there is always the danger of it becoming inconsistent. So what (if anything) do we need to get rid of?

A match has many members involved in it and many (two) teams taking part. The question we need to answer is, "Are these two sets of information independent for our problem?" If they are, we don't need (and

124

shouldn't have) the Appearance table. However, as we discussed in Chapter 5, it is likely that we will need to know which member played for which team in a particular match. We cannot work that out with just the data in the other two tables (nor even if we included a MemberTeam table). So for this situation where we need to know "who played for which team in which match," the Appearance table is necessary.

What about the other two tables in Figure 8-13? If we have the Appearance table, do we need these other two as well? Recapping the discussion in Chapter 5, the questions we need to ask are, "Do we want to know about matches and teams independent of the members involved?" and, "Do we want to know about members and matches independent of the teams?" Let's think about the first question. What happens when the original draw for the competition is determined? We will probably need to record in our database that Team1 and Team2 are scheduled to play in MatchA. If we only have the Appearance table, we cannot insert appropriate records. Why? Because as all the fields are part of the primary key, none can be empty, and we have nothing to put in the Member field. We want to record the fact that this match is scheduled, and we need to do that independently of the members involved. We may also have additional information to record about matches and teams that is independent of members. For example, we will probably need to record a score. Without a MatchTeam table, where would we store that? Which row in the Appearance table would it go in? Many of them. So yes, we do need the MatchTeam table if we want to store all this information. You can go through a similar thought process to decide whether the table MatchMember is also necessary.

These sorts of questions arise every time we have three (or more) classes that are interrelated in any way. Are there situations when we need to know about combinations of objects from all three classes? Do we have information about combinations of objects from two of the classes independent of the third? If we figure out the answers to these questions correctly, we can be confident that the final tables will adequately represent the problem.

Summary

If we have poorly structured tables in a database, we run the risk of having problems with updating data. These include:

- **Modification problems**: If information is repeated, it will become inconsistent if not updated everywhere.

- **Insertion problems**: If we don't have information for each of the primary key fields, we will not be able to enter a record

- **Deletion problems**: If we delete a record to remove a piece of information, we might as a consequence lose some additional information.

By understanding the concepts of functional dependencies, primary keys, and normalization, we can ensure that our tables are structured in such a way as to avoid the update problems described previously.

- A functional dependency exists between two sets of fields in a table: If field A functionally determines field B, this means that if I know the value for A, I can uniquely tell you a value for B.

- A primary key is a (minimal) set of field(s) that functionally determines all the other fields in the table.

- The first three normal forms can be summed up as

  A table is based on
  the key,
  the whole key,
  and nothing but the key

- A table in Boyce–Codd normal form is one in which every determinant could be a primary key.

- Where you have three or more interrelated classes, ask questions about what information, if any, you need to know that involves all three classes and what information involves two classes independent of the third.

When designing a relational database

- Create original use cases and a data model.

- Ask questions about the data model to improve understanding of the problem.

- Represent the data model with tables, primary keys, and foreign keys.

- Check that each table is suitably normalized.

TESTING YOUR UNDERSTANDING

Exercise 8-1.

Example 1-3 back in Chapter 1 is a good real–life example of unnormalized data. To recap: Farms are visited and a number of samples are taken from different fields. The number of each species (just Springtail and

FarmID	FarmName	Field	Date	Visit	SampleID	Insect	Count
1	HighGate	F2	12-Mar-11	14	3	Beetle	2
1	HighGate	F2	09-Feb-11	14	2	Beetle	4
1	HighGate	F1	09-Feb-11	14	1	Beetle	4
1	HighGate	F1	18-Mar-11	15	1	Springtail	5
1	HighGate	F2	09-Feb-11	14	3	Springtail	3
1	HighGate	F2	09-Feb-11	14	2	Springtail	5
1	HighGate	F1	09-Feb-11	14	1	Springtail	6
1	High-Gate	F1	18-Mar-11	15	1	Beetle	7
2	Greyton	F2	09-Feb-11	16	1	Beetle	2
2	Greyton	F1	09-Feb-11	16	2	Beetle	4
2	Greyton	F1	09-Feb-11	16	2	Springtail	5
2	Greyton	F2	09-Feb-11	16	1	Springtail	3

Figure 8-14. *Unnormalized version of insect data*

Beetle for now) in each sample is recorded. A version of the data is shown in Figure 8-14.

Consider the following questions:

a) What are some of the updating problems that could occur with the table in Figure 8-14?

b) Which of the following functional dependencies hold for the insect data?

- FarmID → FarmName?

- FarmID → Visit?

126

- $Visit \rightarrow Date?$

- $Date \rightarrow Visit?$

- $Visit \rightarrow FarmID?$

- $Sample \rightarrow Field?$

- $(Sample, VisitID) \rightarrow Field?$

- $(Sample, Insect) \rightarrow Count?$

c) $(VisitID, Sample, Insect) \rightarrow Count?$ $(VisitID, Sample, Insect)$ is suggested as an appropriate primary key. Can you determine all the other values from knowing the values of these three fields? Would it be a suitable primary key?

d) Using the fields in Part C as a primary key use the normalization rules to decompose the table in Figure 8-14 into a set of tables in third normal form.

127

CHAPTER 9

More on Keys and Constraints

In previous chapters, you have seen how to take a class diagram and represent it as a set of relational database tables. We looked at how to represent relationships between classes with primary and foreign keys and then applied the ideas of normalization to ensure the attributes were in the right tables. In this chapter, we take another look at some of these ideas and think about some alternative possibilities. In particular, we take a closer look at primary keys and how to choose them. We also take a look at how we can maintain referential integrity when data is being constantly updated.

Choosing a Primary Key

In the previous two chapters, I described how we need to choose a field or combination of fields to use as a primary key for a database table representing a class. The key fields will have unique values and so can be used to identify a particular row in a table. The primary key is also used to set up relationships between rows in different tables by way of a foreign key. Choosing a primary key is not always straightforward. For a person, combinations such as name and birth date are sometimes used as a key, but they cannot be guaranteed to be unique. You saw that introducing a customer number or using some sort of automatically generated ID number can ensure that we have a field that is unique for every row. Now let's have another look at this idea of ID numbers.

More About ID Numbers

A generated ID number does not solve all of our problems. If we have two rows in our table that are identical in every respect except for their ID, we are going to be in real trouble. Two John Smiths with the same birth date living at the same address are going to complicate matters whether they have different customer numbers or not. Are they the same person or are they different people? It would be intolerable if the only thing distinguishing one person from another was some generated ID. For one thing, who can ever remember all of their perhaps hundreds of different ID numbers? We always expect that a business will be able to find our customer number for us from information that differentiates us from everyone else.

So, does that mean that there will (or should) always be a possible key made up of some combination of the data kept about a customer? Probably yes. In that case, why do we need ID numbers? Wouldn't a primary key made up of all the fields in the table be OK?

One of the main reasons that ID numbers are necessary in many cases is that while there might always be some information that distinguishes one customer from another, it is likely that some of those values are constantly changing. If we decide that name, birth date, address, mother's maiden name, and so on will identify a customer, it is no use to us as a primary key in a table. Addresses are certain to change, names are likely to change, and this is where we have a problem. We use the primary key in order to make connections to rows in different tables. For example, we would use the Customer table primary key as a foreign key in the Order table to identify which customer placed a specific order. If we have to put a combination of names and addresses into our Order table as a foreign key, I'm sure you can imagine the sorts of problems we are likely to encounter associating orders with particular customers when they move to a new address. An ID number, however, will be constant. One order might be associated with customer 3602 for example, the information in the Customer table about customer 3602 can change as much as it likes. Jane Green can move and remarry as much as she pleases, and we can still keep track of her orders through her constant customer number.

When storing information about people in a database, an ID number is almost always necessary. People are generally fairly resistant to being described by a number, and yet they are likely to have a different one for every business they deal with. Universal ID numbers are resisted by many civil liberties groups for privacy reasons, although in many countries social security, tax, or driver license numbers have almost become default universal IDs. Many web sites now use an email address as a form of identification—although this can cause problems when you share a personal email address with a spouse or partner. (I know this!)

While ID numbers are essential, there are still problems with them. One problem arises when a person is assigned two ID numbers for the same organization. Consider being admitted to a hospital. You are ill, and your friends are asked for your name and address and whether you have ever been admitted before. The name they give may be different from your exact name. They call you Rob Brown, but your real name is Jacob Robert Brown, and they don't know that you were once admitted as a child with tonsillitis. A new patient is therefore entered into the database with a new number. Now there are real problems: Rob Brown has two patient numbers and two rows in the patient table. Allergies may be associated with one patient number, and treatments with the other. Anecdotally, at various times the number of patients associated with New Zealand hospitals has been about 25% more than the total population!

This can happen just as easily when a student enrolls at a university. One year she pre-enrolls but then decides to take a year off traveling instead. She doesn't realize that she has been assigned a student number. The next year when she enrolls, she ticks the *new student* box and is given another number. Come graduation year, the student finds that some subjects have been credited to one number and some to the other, and neither has enough credits to graduate (this really does happen!).

There is not much that can be done about these problems other than to have very careful procedures at data entry times. Existing customers or clients with similar names need to be brought to the data entry operator's attention so that checks can be made. The process cannot be automated though, because sometimes two different people will have identical names and even birth dates.

Candidate Keys

In the previous chapter, we used functional dependencies to help us define what we meant by a key.

The key fields functionally determine all the other fields in a table.

This means that if we know the value of the key fields, we can locate a single row in our table, and then we can see the values of all the other fields. We also talked about fields that were not necessary to make a set of fields a possible key. For example, if we have customerID as a key in a Customer table, then by our definition the combination customerID and customer_name would also be a key. Clearly, customer_name is superfluous, and in Chapter 8 we discussed how this extra field would cause problems if we used it as part of a foreign key. The term *candidate key* is used to describe a key with no unnecessary fields.

A candidate key is a key where no subset of the fields is also a key.

With this definition, we see that the combination customerID and customer_name is not a candidate key, as the subset customerID is a key on its own. There may be more than one candidate key in a table. For example, in the Customer table, we may also store the customer's tax or social security number.

Customer(customerID, customer_name, address, phone, birth_date, tax_number)

Now we have two candidate keys: customerID and tax_number. Both will be unique for every record, and (so long as every customer is able and prepared to supply a tax number) either would be sufficient to uniquely identify a record. In a situation such as this, you choose one of the candidate keys as the primary key for the table. What are the considerations for choosing a primary key from among two or more candidates?

An ID Number or a Concatenated Key?

Let's take a fresh look at the problem from way back in Chapter 1 about insect data (Example 1-3). This was an environmental project where researchers regularly visited farms and took samples of insects from different fields. Because I want to use the word "field" in its database sense, I'm going to use the Australasian synonym for a field on a farm, *paddock*.

Let's build up the class diagram and the associated tables slowly. To start, we need to keep information about each farm as well as about the paddocks on that farm. A possible class diagram is shown in Figure 9-1.

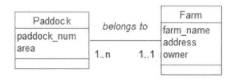

Figure 9-1. Farms and paddocks

What will be a suitable primary key for the table representing the Farm class? Over time the name and owner may change, and in any case one person may own several farms, so the value of owner may not be unique. The farm is not going to shift, but the address may well change when roads are altered or boundaries change. An ID number seems the safest bet.

What about paddocks? Each farmer probably has some numbering system for his own paddocks. Just considering the two classes in Figure 9-1, we could therefore set up two tables:

Farm(farmID, farm_name, address, owner)
Paddock(paddock_num, area)

To represent the relationship between Farm and Paddock, we include the primary key from the Farm table as a foreign key field in the Paddock table: Paddock(paddock_num, area, farm), where farm is a foreign key the value of which will be the farmID of the corresponding farm.

Now we have a decision to make. Is the paddock number a unique number over all paddocks, or is it just unique within a farm? The two possibilities are shown in Figure 9-2. In Figure 9-2a, the primary key would be paddock_num, and in Figure 9-2b, the primary key would be the combination (farm, paddock_num).

131

paddock_num ▾	area ▾	farm ▾
336	30	18
337	23	18
345	25	17
346	25	17
347	35	17

farm ▾	paddock_num ▾	area ▾
18	1	30
18	2	23
17	2	25
17	3	25
17	4	35

a. Primary key paddock_num   b. Primary key farm and paddock_num

Figure 9-2. *Simple and concatenated primary keys for the Paddock table*

In Figure 9-2a, we only need the one field as a primary key; however as the project grows, the numbers for a paddock will get large, and they don't mean very much. In the second option, the numbers for paddock_num are no longer unique (they restart from 1 for each farm), and we need two fields to identify a paddock. However, paddock (17, 2) means more to the owner of farm 17 than paddock 345. At this stage, the choice doesn't matter too much.

This relationship between farm and paddock (a 1–Many with a compulsory 1 end) is sometimes referred to as an *ownership* relation. The paddock *must* have an associated farm, or looking at it the other way around, the farm *owns* the paddock. When we get a long line of 1–Many ownership relationships, the issue of the size of the foreign key becomes more pressing. Consider some more of the insect data model as shown in Figure 9-3. The model describes a somewhat simplified version of the problem we considered before. Each visit has to be associated with a paddock, and each sample has to be associated with a particular visit.

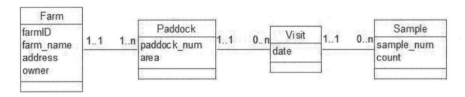

Figure 9-3. *Several 1–Many ownership relationships*

For each of the 1–Many relationships, we need to include the primary key from the 1 end as a foreign key in the Many end. Let's assume that a paddock can only be visited once on any given date. One possible set of tables for the preceding model could be as follows:

Farm(<u>farmID</u>, farm_name, address, owner)

Paddock(<u>farmID</u>, <u>paddock_num</u>, area), with farmID being a foreign key referring to Farm

Visit(<u>date</u>, <u>farm</u>, <u>paddock</u>), with (farm, paddock) being a foreign key referring to Paddock

Sample(<u>date</u>, <u>farm</u>, <u>paddock</u>, <u>sample_num</u>, count), with (date, farm, paddock) being a foreign key referring to Visit

In this set of tables, we are assuming paddocks are numbered from 1 within each farm and samples are numbered from 1 within each visit. The Visit table doesn't need to have an ID because the combination (date, farm, paddock) is unique for this problem.

The Sample table is now looking quite cumbersome because the foreign key referring to the Visit table is a combination of three fields. This table is going to have the most rows eventually, so in addition to it just looking

132

ugly, there could also be a size consideration. Had we used the alternative in Figure 9-2a of a single key for Paddock, the foreign keys in the Visit and Sample tables would be a little smaller, but at the expense of having less-intuitive identifications for paddocks.

What other options do we have? Introducing a visitID makes some sense. Visits will probably be in a chronological order so that the ID number will mean something. Visit 458 will probably be the one that occurred after visit 457, whereas paddock 458 has no obvious relationship to paddock 457.

A happy compromise might be the following set of tables:

Farm(farmID, farm_name, address, owner)

Paddock(farmID, paddock_num, area) with farmID being a foreign key referring to Farm

Visit(visitID, date, farm, paddock) with (farm, paddock) being a foreign key referring to Paddock

Sample(visit, sample_num, count) with visit being a foreign key referring to Visit

The paddocks are numbered within farms, the visits are numbered chronologically, and the samples are numbered within a visit. All our introduced ID numbers therefore have some meaning, and the sample table is considerably smaller than in the previous design. In summary, choosing a primary key may not be straightforward. There are times when an automatically generated ID number will be necessary but won't solve all our problems. We might like to consider a primary key that is a concatenation of ID numbers (e.g., numbering paddocks within farms or samples within visits). There will always be a trade-off between concatenated ID numbers that might be more meaningful and having potentially cumbersome foreign keys in other related tables. There are always going to be alternative ways to choose a primary key, and as with most design issues, there is no hard-and-fast set of rules to say which choice is best.

Unique Constraints

Let's take another look at our Visit table, shown in Figure 9-4. We have two candidate keys: visitID and the combination (date, farm, paddock). For the reasons discussed in the previous section, we choose visitID as the primary key. Do we lose anything by making this choice?

visitID	date	farm	paddock
23	1/03/2011	18	1
24	1/03/2011	18	2
25	1/04/2011	17	3
26	1/04/2011	17	4

Figure 9-4. Visit table with a generated visitID

If the (date, farm, paddock) combination is not a primary key, we have lost the constraint that each row must have unique values for this combination of fields. This means we could mistakenly insert two rows for a visit to paddock 3, farm 17, on 1/04/2011. We still want to maintain the uniqueness of this combination, and we can do this by setting up a unique constraint.

Listing 9-1 shows the SQL to create the Visit table with a unique constraint to ensure that the combination (date, farm, paddock) is not duplicated in the table.

133

Listing 9-1. *SQL to Create the Visit Table with a Unique Constraint*

```
CREATE TABLE Visit (
visitID INT PRIMARY KEY,
date DATE,
farm INT,
paddock INT ,
FOREIGN KEY (farm, paddock) REFERENCES Paddock
UNIQUE (date, farm, paddock) )
```

Unique constraints are also a way to enforce a 1–1 relationship between tables. Consider the class diagram for sports teams in Figure 9-5, where each team has a member as its captain.

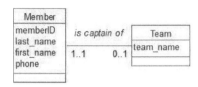

Figure 9-5. *A 1–1 relationship between Team and Member*

When we set up the classes in Figure 9-5 in a relational database, the 1–1 relationship will be represented by a foreign key in the Team table as shown in Figure 9-6.

team_name	captain
SeniorA	203
SeniorB	156
Wed Social	203

Figure 9-6. *Team table*

Each team can have only one captain (because we only have one `captain` field); however, we have yet to discuss a way of ensuring that each member can captain only one team as required by the 1–1 relationship. In Figure 9-6, note that member 203 is the captain of more than one team. We can prevent this from happening by adding a unique constraint on the `captain` field in the Team table. This will prevent a value being entered into the `captain` field in more than one row. The SQL to create the Team table with a unique constraint on the `captain` field is shown in Listing 9-2.

Listing 9-2. *Ensuring a 1–1 Captain Relationship Between Member and Team*

```
CREATE TABLE Team (
team_name VARCHAR(20) PRIMARY KEY,
captain INT UNIQUE FOREIGN KEY REFERENCES Member)
```

Unique constraints are able to help us with a couple of design issues: enforcing a 1–1 relationship and maintaining uniqueness for a candidate key that has not been chosen as a primary key.

Using Constraints Instead of Category Classes

Much of our discussion about classes and their corresponding tables in a relational database has involved introducing new classes and tables in order to keep data accurate and consistent. Now we are going to have a look at when you might decide not to add additional classes and why. Let's think about members of a club and their membership type (e.g., Senior, Junior, or Social). If we include membership type as a field in the Member table, we can have problems with consistency as can be shown by the misspelling in the first row of the table in Figure 9-7.

memberID ▾	last_name ▾	first_name ▾	type ▾
156	Jones	Graeme	senor
187	Green	Chris	Junior
203	Wang	James	Senior

Figure 9-7. Keeping membership type as a field in the Member table

If we are interested in creating reports that group all the members of different types (e.g., all the Seniors, and all the Juniors, etc.), we are going to run into trouble with the table in Figure 9-7 where we have different spellings of the types. Our solution in previous chapters was to create an additional class (table) to keep the different membership types and set up a 1–Many relationship as shown in Figure 9-8.

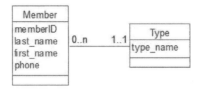

Figure 9-8. Representing membership type with a class

We can now have objects of the Type class or rows in a Type table to represent each of our types: Junior, Senior, and so on. This ensures that we have consistency in naming the different types. Take a look at the tables in Figure 9-9. The Type table seems a bit superfluous.

memberID ▾	last_name ▾	first_name ▾	type ▾	type_name ▾
156	Jones	Graeme	Senior	Senior
187	Green	Chris	Junior	Junior
203	Wang	James	Senior	Social

Member   Type

Figure 9-9. Membership type is a separate table

All the additional Type table is achieving is to ensure the consistency of the entries in the type field of the Member table. We can achieve the same thing by putting a check constraint on the type field. We discussed constraints on fields in Chapter 7. Figure 9-10 shows how easily this can be done in a product like Access, and Listing 9-3 shows the equivalent SQL.

135

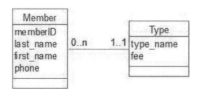

Figure 9-10. *Membership type with a constraint*

Listing 9-3. *Placing a Constraint on a Field*

```
CREATE TABLE Member (
memberID INT PRIMARY KEY,
last_name VARCHAR(20),
first_name VARCHAR(20),
type VARCHAR(20) CHECK type IN ('Senior', 'Junior', 'Social'))
```

Which should we prefer: a table with a constraint on a field (Figure 9-10) or one with a reference to another table (Figure 9-9)? In Figure 9-10, we have a constraint built into the design of the table. If additional membership types are added at a later date, the definition of the constraint would have to be changed. This is something that needs to be done by a system manager or at least someone trusted to alter the design. On the positive side, we have one fewer table in our database.

In Figure 9-9, we have the additional complexity of an extra table. However, if another membership type is required, it can be added simply as a new row in the Type table. This is just a data entry job and doesn't involve any change to the design of the database. If the types are going to be fairly constant, the constraint is simpler, whereas the reference to another table makes it easy for a user to add different types.

There is one case in which the extra table will always be the appropriate choice. This is when there are (or may later be) some additional attributes belonging to the Type class. For example, if we wish to keep a fee for each different membership type, the only way we can do this is via a Type class as shown in Figure 9-11.

Figure 9-11. *An extra class is needed if there are additional attributes.*

In summary, when we have a piece of data that acts like a category (e.g., membership type), we sometimes have a choice as to whether we store this as a simple field in a table and keep the values consistent by way of a constraint or validation rule, or we have a separate table of categories to which we refer. If the number of categories is likely to increase, the second option is better, as this then becomes a simple matter of adding additional rows to the category table rather than changing the constraint on the parent table. If there are or are likely to be other attributes associated with the category, the additional table is the only option. If neither of these situations applies, it is worth thinking about whether a simple field with a constraint may be more appropriate.

Deleting Referenced Records

You have seen how we can use foreign keys to represent relationships between two tables. Have another look at our model of teams and members in Figure 9-5. We can represent the relationship *is captain of* with a foreign key (captain) in the Team table, as shown in Figure 9-12.

team_name ▾	captain ▾
SeniorA	203
SeniorB	156

memberID ▾	last_name ▾	first_name ▾	type ▾
156	Jones	Graeme	Senior
187	Green	Chris	Junior
203	Wang	James	Senior

Team   Member

Figure 9-12. *Teams and members*

A foreign key ensures that we have referential integrity. Recall from Chapter 7 that referential integrity prevents us from having a value in the foreign key field captain if the value does not exist in the primary key field memberID in the Member table. This ensures that all of our captains are members for which we have already recorded names and other details. Unlike a primary key, a foreign key field is not necessarily mandatory, and the captain field may be empty (i.e., referential integrity does not make it necessary for every team to have a captain). We can of course impose that extra constraint if we want to, by specifying that the captain field must be NOT NULL.

So far we have only looked at referential integrity from the point of view of adding new teams and captains. However, we also have the situation of deleting members from the Member table. If we attempt to delete member 156, for example, we shall have a problem with the referential integrity in the Team table. The captain of SeniorB will no longer exist in the Member table.

There are three ways to deal with this situation. Database software products vary in their ability to provide each of these options, but all will provide the first, as follows:

Disallow delete: You cannot delete a row that is being referenced. For example, the deletion of member 156 will not be allowed while it is being referenced by the Team table. If we want to delete member 156, we will first have to remove the reference to him in the Team table and then delete him from the Member table.

Nullify delete: If member 156 is deleted, the field that is referencing it, captain, will be nullified (made empty). This essentially is saying that if a captain of a team leaves the club, that team has no captain—which is probably quite sensible in this situation.

Cascade delete: If a row is deleted, all the rows referencing it will be deleted also (and the rows referencing them, and on and on). In this case, deleting member 156 would mean that the team SeniorB would be deleted. This is clearly not desirable.

137

When we set up a field as a foreign key, we can specify what should occur when there is an attempt to delete the row to which it refers. Listing 9-4 shows the SQL statement for specifying a "nullify delete" for the foreign key `captain` when we create the Team table. If you do not specify an option, the default is generally "disallow delete."

Listing 9-4. *Specifying a Deletion Option on a Foreign Key*

```
CREATE TABLE Team (
team_name VARCHAR(20),
captain INT FOREIGN KEY REFERENCES Member ON DELETE NULLIFY )
```

Depending on the particular problem, we can choose the deletion option that is most appropriate. For the team and member situation, a "nullify delete" seems sensible for the foreign key `captain`. We want to be able to delete members, and it makes sense that if member 156 leaves, there will be a vacancy for the captain of the SeniorB team. Our model as it stands in Figure 9-5 doesn't allow this, however. It says every team must have a captain. Maybe it is worth reconsidering this. While in the normal course of events we expect all our teams to have captains, we are going to come across cases where people unexpectedly leave or resign. What do we want to happen to the data we are keeping in these cases? If we insist that every team has a captain (by making that field required), we will have to find a new captain before we can delete the old captain from our membership list. Perhaps this is what we want to do, or maybe that will be too restrictive. We talked in previous chapters about the consequences of making fields required. Thinking about deletions from the database may make us reconsider the relationship *is captain of* and whether or not it should be optional.

Let's consider a different situation, of orders and products, as in Figure 9-13.

order_num ▾	date ▾	customer ▾	product ▾	quantity ▾
10034	1/Mar/11	1345	809	4
10035	1/Mar/11	1562	975	3
10036	2/Mar/11	1345	996	1

Order

product_num ▾	name ▾	price ▾
809	teddy	10.50
810	doll	15.75
811	cart	23.80

Product

Figure 9-13. *Orders and products: What happens if we delete a product?*

What happens if we no longer stock product 809? If we delete this row in the `Product` table, our referential integrity will be compromised as order number 10034 refers to it. What are our choices? A "nullify delete" means having nothing in the foreign key `product` field in the `Order` table. This makes no sense. We would have that there was once an order for four of some product—but we don't know what that product was and we have no way of finding the price. Clearly, this is not going to be useful. A "cascade delete" would mean that all the orders for product 809 would be deleted. This doesn't seem sensible either, as a business is going to need to keep track of all its orders to determine profits, tax, and so on. Our only choice in this case, then, is the "disallow delete" option. If there is an order for the product, we can't delete that product from the `Product` table.

It is important that we keep discontinued products in the table, but we will want to be able to distinguish them from current products. For a case like this, we might decide to add an additional field to our `Product` table (say `current`) to distinguish current products from discontinued ones. We have a new problem now. How do we prevent new orders from being entered for discontinued products? This is starting to get outside the scope of this book. Many database applications allow you to put additional constraints on a table by way of *triggers*. A trigger is a procedure that is fired by a change to a table (e.g., adding or updating a row) and will carry out specified actions. In this case, the trigger would check whether a potential new row in the `Order` table was for a discontinued product, and if so prevent that row from being permanently added to the table. Constraints such as only allowing orders for current products can also be implemented through the interface of the database, and we will look at the benefits and drawbacks of this in Chapter 11.

When might a "cascade delete" be a good choice? It is a fairly brutal solution, and you should be very careful about setting it up. If we have enrollments for a subject, and then that subject is cancelled, it is perhaps reasonable to expect that all the enrollments for it should be deleted also. We have to be careful, though, that there aren't historical enrollments from previous years. Deleting information does not happen as often as you might expect. Products and subjects may be discontinued, but if we have historical orders or enrollments for subjects which have since been discontinued, we need to keep the information. In these cases, the "disallow delete" option is the best bet. When customers and orders do outlive their usefulness, it is more usual to archive the important, or summarized, information and store it elsewhere rather than deleting it entirely. Use the "cascade delete" option with caution.

Having said all that, we might think that the safest option is to never delete anything. It is possible to set up tables so that no rows can ever be deleted. However, while this might seem like a good idea, we will always need to delete records that have been entered into a table by mistake. Say we accidentally enter the same customer twice (with a different customer number), for example. We need to get that extra record out of the table as quickly as possible before it causes us all sorts of problems.

Summary

In this chapter, we have looked at some issues involved with choosing appropriate primary keys and for ensuring referential integrity is maintained when we update the data in our tables. Some of the important points to remember are the following:

- We often need to introduce a generated ID number to ensure we have a field, with stable and unique values, that we can use as a primary key. This is particularly true for people, where identifying information such as names and addresses are likely to change.

- Be aware that mistakes in data entry means it is possible to have a person in your database twice with two different ID numbers. Try to avoid this!

- Where a primary key is made up of several concatenated fields, it is worth considering a generated ID number to reduce the size of the foreign keys referencing the table.

- Where a generated ID has been introduced, constraints should be used to retain the uniqueness of the combinations of fields that have been replaced as a primary key.

- Unique constraints can be used to enforce a 1–1 relationship.

- A constraint on the value of a field may be more appropriate than a relationship to another (very simple) table.

- You have three options when you wish to delete a row that it is being referenced by a foreign key:

  - Disallow the deletion.

  - Make the field referencing the deleted row NULL ("nullify delete").

  - Remove all rows that reference the deleted row ("cascade delete").

TESTING YOUR UNDERSTANDING

Exercise 9-1

The ever–useful "customer orders product" example again—there is always something new to discover. Design the table that will represent the Order class in Figure 9-14. Consider constraints, primary and foreign keys, and updating rules.

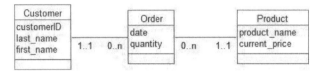

Figure 9-14. *Model for customers placing orders*

Exercise 9-2

A car sales yard needs to keep information about makes and models of cars that are available, and also the registrations of the individual cars they have in stock. For example, Ford Siestas are available in sedans and hatchbacks, and they currently have a blue sedan with registration TC545 in stock. For some models you might be able to choose automatic or manual transmission and some come with different capacities (e.g., 1.5 l or 2.0 l). Think about the options available for setting up tables for this situation.

CHAPTER 10

■ ■ ■

Query Basics

We have spent a considerable amount of effort designing our database in order to make sure the data can be stored in a consistent and accurate way. In this chapter, we are going to look at how to get information back out again. The data will be stored in many separate tables, and depending on the questions we are asking, we will need to combine data from those tables in a number of different ways. This chapter is just a brief introduction to the art of querying. For further information you might be interested in looking at my book *Beginning SQL Queries: From Novice to Professional*.[1]

Simple Queries on One Table

Let's start with looking at just one table. We'll use the Student table, a small part of which is shown in Figure 10-1, to illustrate some of the main types of queries that are possible.

studentID	last_name	first_name	first_enrolled	city	degree
12654	Green	Linda	2010	Auckland	Science
13887	Smith	John	2010	Christchurch	Arts
17625	King	Steven	2011	Christchurch	Arts
18574	Smith	James	2011	Christchurch	Science
19876	Smith	Alison	2010	Auckland	Commerce

Figure 10-1. A small part of the Student table

Over time, the Student table is likely to accumulate hundreds of thousands of records, and in reality there are going to be several more columns to record birth dates, phone numbers, immigration status, and so on. It is manageable subsets of this information that are going to be relevant for users. We should look back at the original use cases for the project to see what sort of questions people are going to ask about the data. The registrar might want a list of all students starting their studies this year; the alumni manager might want a list of current and past students living in Christchurch; a dean might want lists of students enrolling this year in an Arts degree; the management might need the numbers of enrollments in the last ten years to determine trends. All that information can be gleaned from this one table. To do this, we can use the basic relational operations *select* and *project*, along with ordering and aggregating functions.

---

[1] Clare Churcher, *Beginning SQL Queries: From Novice to Professional* (Apress, 2008)

The Project Operation

The project operation allows us to specify which columns of the table we would like to retrieve. If we want a list of names, we don't really want to see all the other information about each student. If we just want to see the ID number and the names of every student, we project (or retrieve) just the first three columns. Listing 10-1 shows how to achieve this with an SQL command. The first line says which columns are required and the second line says from which table they are to be retrieved.

Listing 10-1. *SQL for Projecting Three Columns from the Student Table*

```
SELECT studentID, first_name, last_name
FROM Student
```

The result of the query in Listing 10-1 will be a new set of rows with just the three fields or columns we have specified. The project operation is one of the simplest of the operations on a table, but even for this simple process we have to think carefully about what we are doing. Every row in a table is guaranteed to be unique because we always have a primary key. However, if the primary key is not one of the columns we specify in our query, the rows resulting from a project operation may not be unique. What should we do about the duplicate rows? The answer depends entirely on what your query is to be used for.

Consider a couple of examples of queries that would produce duplicates from the small sample of data in the Student table in Figure 10-1. Say the alumni manager is organizing a dinner and wants a list from which to produce name tags for all the guests. He projects first_name and last_name from the Student table, and there are two rows with John Smith. Does he need them both? He certainly does, as two distinct people with the same name are going to be turning up for the dinner. Now consider that the alumni manager wants to set up alumni branches and so would like a list of all the cities that students come from. He projects city from the Student table and gets several rows with Christchurch. Does he want them all? No. He just wants to know the set of cities.

So, sometimes we want the duplicate rows in a query and other times we don't. By default, an SQL statement such as the one in Listing 10-1 will retrieve duplicates. If you don't want the duplicates, you can use the keyword DISTINCT as in Listing 10-2.

Listing 10-2. *Specifying Only Unique Records Be Retrieved*

```
SELECT DISTINCT city
FROM Student
```

The Select Operation

The other thing that we want to do with a single table is to retrieve just some of the rows. For example, we may want to retrieve information about those students who are doing a science degree or just those students who first enrolled in 2011. Retrieving a subset of the rows is known as a *select* operation. We need to specify how we will determine which rows we want. We do this by specifying a test condition that, for each row, is either true or false. To find all the science students, we would specify the condition degree = 'Science', while to find all the students entering the university in 2011, the condition would be year = 2011. The condition is checked for each row in turn, and if it is true, then that row is included in the set being retrieved. We can build up more complicated conditions by using operators such as AND, OR, and NOT. For example, if we want just the science students enrolling in 2011, the condition would be degree = 'Science' and year = 2011. If we wanted a list of all commerce and arts students (but not any other degree), the condition would be degree = 'Arts' OR degree = 'Commerce'

A select operation is specified in an SQL statement, by using the keyword WHERE followed by the appropriate condition as shown in Listing 10-3. The * in the first line means retrieve *all* the columns or fields for the selected rows.

Listing 10-3. *Specifying Which Rows Are to Be Retrieved*

```
SELECT *
FROM Student
WHERE degree = 'Science' and year = 2011
```

One small but important point to bear in mind is that if a field (e.g., degree) has no value, then the truth of a statement such as degree = 'Science' is unknown. SQL queries only return those rows for which the condition statement is *known* to be true. If we retrieve rows for degree = 'Science' and then retrieve rows for degree <> 'Science' we will miss the rows that have no value in degree because we do not know the value (it might be Science and it might not). To find those fields which are empty we can use the expression where degree is NULL.

Most queries will require a combination of the select and project operations. In this case, the rows are first selected according to the condition, and then the specified columns are retrieved. Rather than seeing all the information about each of our selected students as in Listing 10-3, we may just want to see their ID numbers and names. Listing 10-4 shows the select and project operations being combined in an SQL statement.

Listing 10-4. *Specifying Which Rows and Columns Are to Be Retrieved*

```
SELECT studentID, first_name, last_name
FROM Student
WHERE degree = 'Science' and year = 2011
```

Note that the fields involved in the condition (degree and year) do not have to appear in the columns being projected.

Aggregates

The other types of information that we might want to retrieve from our Student table are counts, averages, and totals. For example, we might want to know the number of students that have ever enrolled, the number enrolled in each degree, or the number enrolled each year for the last ten years. If we had more columns in the Student table, we might want to total fees or average ages, and so on.

SQL provides a number of different functions for counting, and for aggregating numeric data (e.g., COUNT, AVG, SUM, MAX, MIN). We will now look at how to do a couple of different queries.

If we just want a simple count of how many students have ever enrolled at the university, we can issue an SQL statement such as the one in Listing 10-5.

Listing 10-5. *Selecting a Single Count*

```
SELECT COUNT(*)
FROM Student
```

COUNT(*) simply means count each record. This will return us just one number, which is the number of rows in the table. Had we wanted to find the largest studentID, we would have issued a similar statement, but specifying the field for which we want to find the maximum value, as in Listing 10-6.

Listing 10-6. *Finding the Maximum Value of a Field*

```
SELECT MAX(studentID)
FROM Student
```

We can specify a particular field in a COUNT statement. What do you think will be returned if we ask for COUNT(studentID) or COUNT(city)? In both these cases, we will probably get the same answer (the number of

143

rows), as most versions of SQL will default to just counting all the rows with a value in that field. This is probably what we want if we ask to count the student IDs, but when we ask for a count of the cities, we are really asking for how many distinct cities appear in the table. This can be achieved by adding the keyword DISTINCT in the COUNT function as in Listing 10-7.

Listing 10-7. *Counting the Number of Distinct Cities*

```
SELECT COUNT(DISTINCT city)
FROM Student
```

Each of these aggregate statements can be combined with a select operation to first of all retrieve a subset of the rows. We can do this by adding a WHERE clause to specify the rows to which we want to apply the aggregate. For example, to find the number of students that have ever enrolled in a science degree, we would use the statement in Listing 10-8. We can think of this as first retrieving the appropriate rows and then counting them.

Listing 10-8. *Counting a Subset of the Rows*

```
SELECT COUNT(*)
FROM Student
WHERE degree = 'Science'
```

One particularly powerful feature of aggregating in SQL is being able to group subsets of rows and then count the rows in each subset. For example, Listing 10-8 returns the number of students who have enrolled in science. It is likely that we might want numbers of students in science, arts, and other degrees as well. Rather than having to issue several commands, one for each degree, we can combine this into a single statement as in Listing 10-9.

Listing 10-9. *Retrieving Counts for Each Degree*

```
SELECT degree, COUNT(*)
FROM Student
GROUP BY degree
```

I like to think of the query in Listing 10-9 as working like this: Go and get all the rows in the Student table, group all the ones for each degree together, count the rows in each subset, and then write out the degree and the count (as specified on the first line). The result would be something like Figure 10-2.

degree	count
Arts	24087
Science	37986
Commerce	38065

Figure 10-2. *Result of a grouped aggregate query as in Listing 10-9*

Once again, all these aggregate queries can be combined with a WHERE clause to retrieve just a subset of the rows before we do the grouping and counting. This means we can answer a multitude of requests such as retrieve the numbers of students enrolling in science in each of the last ten years, retrieve the number of students from each city, retrieve the number of science students that have come from each city, and so on.

Ordering

When we retrieve a subset of rows and columns from a table, we might want to see them in a particular order. For example, if we want a list of the names of all students first enrolling in 2011, it is likely that we would prefer to see them ordered by name rather than in a random order. The SQL phrase ORDER BY allows us to specify the order in which the rows are presented. Listing 10-10 shows the SQL statement that retrieves a subset of the rows and then orders them: first by last_name and then, for rows with the same value of last_name, by first_name.

Listing 10-10. Retrieving a Subset of Rows and Columns in a Specified Order

```
SELECT last_name, first_name, studentID
FROM Student
WHERE year = 2011
ORDER BY last_name, first_name
```

Queries with Two or More Tables

The last section gave an overview of some of the queries we can carry out on a single table. Most of our queries will require information from several tables in our database.

There are a number of different relational operations that we can use to combine tables, and we will look at some of them in this section. One really elegant feature of relational database operations is that when we carry out operations on one or more tables, we can think of the result as a new table. This new table does not exist permanently in the database, but conceptually it is convenient to think of it as a virtual table that exists for the time of the query. All the operations that we used in the previous section (projecting columns, selecting rows, aggregating, and ordering) can then be applied to the new virtual table. We can also take a virtual table that results from combining two tables and then combine that with another real table, and then another. So with a few quite simple operations, we can easily build up queries that involve a number of tables that will satisfy quite complex questions. Let's first look at some of the operations that combine tables.

The Join Operation

The most common operation to combine two tables is the *inner join*. Consider the Student and Enrollment tables in Figure 10-3.

studentID	last_name	first_name	first_enrolled
12654	Green	Linda	2010
13887	Smith	John	2010
17625	King	Steven	2011
18574	Smith	James	2011
19876	Smith	Alison	2010

Student

studentID	course	year	grade
17625	COMP101	2010	A
13887	COMP101	2010	B
19765	COMP101	2011	B
17625	COMP102	2010	E
13887	COMP102	2011	A
17625	COMP102	2011	C
18574	COMP102	2011	B

Enrollment

Figure 10-3. Parts of the Student and Enrollment tables

If we want to answer a question such as "Who was enrolled in COMP102 in 2011?" we need data from both tables. If we were answering this question by just looking at the tables, we would first find the rows from the Enrollment table that satisfy the condition course = 'COMP102' AND year = 2011. We would then need to look at the Student table to find the corresponding names. An inner join allows us to combine the two tables so that all the required information appears together. For this query, we are interested in rows from the Student table and rows from the Enrollment table where the value of the studentID is the same in each. This will be the join condition. Let's look at the SQL statement in Listing 10-11 and then consider what it means.

145

Listing 10-11. *SQL Statement to Join Two Tables*

```
SELECT *
FROM Student INNER JOIN Enrollment ON Student.studentID = Enrollment.studentID
```

It is useful to think of an inner join operation as making a new virtual table that will have all the columns from both original tables. We fill this table up with every combination of rows from each table and then retain those that satisfy the condition Student.studentID = Enrollment.studentID (i.e., where the values of studentID are the same in each table). Figure 10-4 shows part of the resulting set of rows.

S.studentID ▾	last_name ▾	first_name ▾	first_enrolled ▾	E.studentID ▾	course ▾	year ▾	grade ▾
13887	Smith	John	2010	13887	COMP101	2010	B
13887	Smith	John	2010	13887	COMP102	2011	A
17625	King	Steven	2011	17625	COMP101	2010	A
17625	King	Steven	2011	17625	COMP102	2010	E
17625	King	Steven	2011	17625	COMP102	2011	C
18574	Smith	James	2011	18574	COMP102	2011	B

Figure 10-4. *Rows resulting from joining Student and Enrollment on studentID*

In Figure 10-4, the first four columns are from the Student table, and the second four columns are from the Enrollment table. We only see the combinations of rows from each table where the studentID is the same. Now that we have this virtual table, we can apply all the single table operations to it. We can select just those rows for enrollments in COMP102 for 2011 with a WHERE clause and then project or retrieve just the IDs and names of the students. The SQL statement to do this is shown in Listing 10-12 and the resulting rows in Figure 10-5.

Listing 10-12. *SQL Statement to Retrieve IDs and Names of Students in COMP102 in 2011*

```
SELECT Student.studentID, last_name, first_name
FROM Student INNER JOIN Enrollment ON Student.studentID = Enrollment.studentID
WHERE course = 'COMP102' AND year = 2011
```

studentID ▾	last_name ▾	first_name ▾
13887	Smith	John
17625	King	Steven
18574	Smith	James

Figure 10-5. *Rows resulting from combining join with select and project operations*

This is just a very cursory explanation of an inner join, but I'm sure you can see how you can keep joining the resulting virtual table to another table and then another to build up ever more complex queries.

One last point that is worth mentioning in this basic introduction to joins is what happens when we join two tables such as those in Figure 10-6.

courseID ▾	examiner ▾
COMP101	1001
COMP102	1018
COMP205	
COMP303	1018

personID ▾	last_name ▾	first_name ▾
1001	Jones	Jim
1018	Li	Henry
1100	Harrow	Jenny

Course   Lecturer

Figure 10-6. *Course and Lecturer tables*

146

If we want a list of courses with the names of the examiner, we might first try an inner join where examiner in the Course table is equal to personID in the Lecturer table. If we were to do this, then the resulting rows would be those shown in Figure 10-7.

courseID ▾	examiner ▾	personID ▾	last_name ▾	first_name ▾
COMP101	1001	1001	Jones	Jim
COMP102	1018	1018	Li	Henry
COMP303	1018	1018	Li	Henry

Figure 10-7. Result of inner join between Course and Lecturer tables

The rows in Figure 10-7 may not be what we were expecting if we thought we were going to see a row for each course. The inner join returns combinations of rows from the two tables where examiner = personID and this will never be true where the examiner field is Null. The course COMP205 is missing from the resulting table because it does not have an examiner. If the question is more accurately worded as "Retrieve *all* the courses and, *for those courses that have one*, the examiner as well," we can use what is called an *outer join* as shown in Listing 10-13.

Listing 10-13. Outer Join to Retrieve All Courses Along with Examiners

```
SELECT *
FROM Course LEFT OUTER JOIN Lecturer ON examiner = personID
```

The result of this query, shown in Figure 10-8, is the same as for the inner join, but in addition, any rows in the left–hand table (Course) with nothing in the join field (examiner) will appear as well.

courseID ▾	examiner ▾	personID ▾	last_name ▾	first_name ▾
COMP101	1001	1001	Jones	Jim
COMP102	1018	1018	Li	Henry
COMP205				
COMP303	1018	1018	Li	Henry

Figure 10-8. Result of outer join to retrieve all the courses

Which way around you put your tables in the join statement doesn't matter, so Course LEFT OUTER JOIN Lecturer is equivalent to Lecturer RIGHT OUTER JOIN Course. Standard SQL also supports a full outer join, which means that every row from both tables will be represented in the result. Lecturer FULL OUTER JOIN Course will retrieve all the lecturers (even if they don't examine a course) and all the courses (even if they don't have an examiner). While a full outer join is part of standard SQL, not all systems support it explicitly (MS Access doesn't). However, we can always achieve the same result by combining two outer joins with a *union* operation (which I describe in the next section).

Set Operations

While joins are probably the most often used operation for combining information from several tables, there are a number of other operations. A join can be used between any two tables. Set operations are used on two tables (or virtual tables) that have the same number and type of columns. They are used for queries such as "Retrieve the rows that appear in both these tables" or "Retrieve the rows that are in this table but not that one." We can use the Enrollment table in Figure 10-9 to illustrate these ideas.

147

studentID	course	year	grade
13887	COMP101	2010	B
13887	COMP102	2011	A
17625	COMP101	2010	A
17625	COMP102	2010	E
17625	COMP102	2011	C
18574	COMP102	2011	B
19765	COMP101	2011	B

Figure 10-9. Enrollment table

Here are some queries we might like to carry out:

- Retrieve the ID numbers of all students who have done *both* COMP101 *and* COMP102.

- Retrieve the ID numbers of all students who have done *either* COMP101 *or* COMP102.

- Retrieve the ID numbers of all students who have done COMP101 *but not* COMP102.

First we need two queries that will return the IDs of students who have done COMP101 and COMP102, respectively. These queries and the virtual tables they produce are shown in Figure 10-10.

SELECT distinct studentID
FROM Enrolment
WHERE course=('COMP101'

SELECT distinct studentID
FROM Enrolment
WHERE course=('COMP102'

Figure 10-10. Results of queries to select students who have done particular papers

A little reordering and overlaying of the two virtual tables as shown in Figure 10-11 can help us see what rows will satisfy each of our questions.

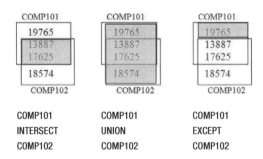

Figure 10-11. Using set operations to find answers to questions about enrollments

The three set operations shown in Figure 10-11 show us those students who have done *both* subjects (intersect), *either* subject (union), and COMP101 *but not* COMP102 (except). Oracle uses the key word MINUS instead of EXCEPT. Listing 10-14 shows the SQL to retrieve the union of the two sets of studentIDs starting from the original real tables.

Listing 10-14. *The studentIDs for Those Students Who Have Done Either COMP101 or COMP102*

```
SELECT distinct studentID FROM Enrollment WHERE course = 'COMP101'
UNION
SELECT distinct studentID FROM Enrollment WHERE course = 'COMP102'
```

In principle, in SQL we can replace the keyword UNION in Listing 10-11 with the keywords INTERSECT and EXCEPT to obtain the other set operations. In practice, not all database systems provide these latter two keywords. This is because it is possible to obtain the same results using some other SQL statements. How this is done is getting beyond this introduction, but can be found in my SQL Queries book. The important thing is to know that your relational database system will allow you to write an SQL statement to retrieve rows equivalent to each of the set operations in Figure 10-11.

How Indexes Can Help

Many queries will require joining a number of tables, extracting particular rows and columns, and possibly presenting the result in a specified order. As tables become large, these operations will clearly become more time consuming. Indexes are a way of enabling particular rows in a database table to be found quickly.

■ **Note** This is a very brief introduction to how indexes can help in query execution. If you are responsible for creating indexes on large databases, you'll want to read more on the topic. Books such as *Expert Indexing in Oracle Database 11 g* (Apress, 2012) and *Expert Performance Indexing for SQL Server 2012* (Apress, 2012) can help.

Depending on your database software, you may find that a number of indexes are put on your tables by default. There are also several considerations for planning useful indexes:

- Whether you are updating or retrieving data;
- Whether you are retrieving very general or very specific data;
- The relative sizes of tables involved in joins;
- The sizes of the rows in the table;
- A myriad of other imponderables.

I am not attempting to address these issues here. Hopefully this chapter will make you aware of what indexes can do, so that you can begin to learn more and also have a useful discussion with your database administrator.

Indexes and Simple Queries

Let's start by looking at simple queries on a single table such as the Enrollment table in Figure 10-12. We will want to retrieve different subsets of the rows for different purposes.

studentID	course	year	grade
18887	COMP101	2010	B
18887	COMP102	2011	A
17625	COMP101	2010	A
17625	COMP102	2010	E
17625	COMP102	2011	C
18887	COMP103	2011	B
19765	COMP101	2011	B

Figure 10-12. A small part of a potentially very large table

It is likely that we will want to access this table by course (in order to retrieve the students enrolled in a particular class) and at other times by studentID (to get a student record). Indexes help us to do both these tasks efficiently. A database index acts very much like an index that you would find in the back of a book. For example, if you have an index on names, it would store all the values of the name field in alphabetical order and also store a pointer or reference to the full record elsewhere. The reference is like storing a page number in a book index. Figure 10-13 shows how you can envisage indexes on the Enrollment table.

Figure 10-13. Two indexes on the Enrollment table

If we want a class list for COMP101, the system can quickly search the course index to find the COMP101 entries. The index also contains a reference to the full row in the Enrollment table so the system can quickly locate the rest of the information. Alternatively, if we need a record of student 17625's progress, we can use the student index to quickly access the appropriate records for that student.

Listing 10-15 shows the SQL statements to create the two indexes on the student and course fields of the Enrollment table.

Listing 10-15. Creating Two Indexes on the Enrollment Table

```
CREATE INDEX IDX_student ON Enrollment (studentID)
CREATE INDEX IDX_course ON Enrollment (course)
```

Let's look at another example using the Student table in Figure 10-14.

studentID ▾	last_name ▾	first_name ▾	first_enrolled ▾	city ▾	degree ▾
12654	Green	Linda	2010	Auckland	Science
13887	Smith	John	2010	Christchurch	Arts
17625	King	Steven	2011	Christchurch	Arts
18574	Smith	James	2011	Christchurch	Science
19876	Smith	Alison	2010	Auckland	Commerce

Figure 10-14. Student table

In the Student table, the primary key field is studentID. When we specify a field as a primary key, most databases will automatically create an index for that field. The index will be specified as being *unique*, meaning that only one entry for each value can be included. This index is how the primary key constraint is physically implemented. When we add a new row to the table, the system quickly searches the index to see whether the primary key value is already there, and if so it rejects the new row.

With the Student table, two things that we will regularly want to do are find a particular student by name and retrieve students in alphabetical order. As the table is likely to have several thousands of entries, we do not want to have to scan the entire table looking for a particular student's name, so some sort of index involving names will be useful. If we are just looking for a particular student, an index on the field last_name will speed things up, as all the Smiths will be together, and there will be fewer records to scan to find the one we want. To improve access further, we can set up a compound index in which the last names are ordered, and where there are duplicate last names the entries are ordered by first name. This index can be used to access the records of the table very quickly if they are required to be in alphabetical order. The SQL for creating a compound index is shown in Listing 10-16.

Listing 10-16. Creating a Compound Index on the Student Table

```
CREATE INDEX IDX_fullName ON Student (last_name, first_name)
```

Another likely candidate for an index in the Student table might be the degree field. This is likely to be a foreign key referencing another table, Degree, which contains information about the different degrees. One reason for an index on a foreign key field is to speed updates for the table to which it refers. For example, if a row in the Degree table is marked for deletion it is necessary to see if it is being referred to by the Student table. As the Student table is likely to become large, it could be slow to find any rows referencing the Degree table if there is no index on the degree field. Foreign key fields are also often involved in join conditions and appropriate indexes may help find matching rows in this situation also.

In summary, indexes can help us speed up select queries where we want to find a particular set of records (e.g., all the rows for student 17625 in the Enrollment table) or to find a particular record (e.g., for a student given her names). They are also sometimes useful for speeding up queries with an ORDER BY clause, and indexes on foreign keys can speed the updating of referenced tables and the execution of joins.

Disadvantages of Indexes

Clearly, indexes are very useful for speeding up queries. However, before we get too carried away and start indexing all our columns, we need to consider any disadvantages.

Let's look at what happens with our Enrollment table and its two indexes, one on studentID and one on course. This table is likely to be huge, and these two indexes are going to speed up the retrieval of specific rows for a student record or a class list. But what happens when we add a new row to the table? The system will have to add the actual row, but it will also have to update the two indexes. This will involve finding the correct place in each index, inserting an entry and adding a reference to the new row. A similar process will be necessary if rows are deleted. Database systems are actually pretty clever about how they manage indexes, but nevertheless there is a performance cost.

A database administrator needs to carefully weigh the reduced performance in updating records compared with the increased performance of retrieving records. In the enrollment case, the retrieval is likely to be happening every day, whereas new enrollments are probably only entered at the beginning of each semester. The increased performance in retrieval will probably outweigh any loss of performance in data maintenance. However, what about the situation at a supermarket checkout? Every time a purchase is made, an entry may be made into a database table. With thousands of updates an hour, this needs to be as efficient as possible. Maintaining a couple of indexes on this table might considerably reduce performance if they had to be updated with every purchase. By contrast, retrieving information from the table (such as totals and summaries) can probably be done overnight or at less busy times when speed is not such an issue.

Types of Indexes

The indexes we have been discussing so far have all been what are called *nonclustered* indexes. A nonclustered index is where we keep the values from just one (or a couple) of the fields in order, along with a reference to the full row, which is kept elsewhere. Nonclustered indexes can be specified as being unique, which means none of the entries can be duplicated. When we declare a field as having a unique constraint, as we did in the last chapter, it is likely the system will construct a unique nonclustered index to manage that constraint. A table should always have at least one unique index, and that will be on its primary key field; this is how the system ensures that the value of the primary key is different for every row. A table can also have several other nonclustered indexes if that seems sensible.

Another type of index is a *clustered index*. A clustered index affects how the complete records or rows are physically stored on disk. When we ask the database system to find records for us, it retrieves an area of disk that will usually contain several records. If records that we are often likely to want at the same time are physically stored together, this will speed things up. For example, if we regularly want to fetch customer information in order of name, storing all the records in that order on the disk might be useful. Clearly, we can only have one clustered index on a table. If we don't specify a clustered index, rows that have been added at the same time are likely to be stored near each other, but we can't rely on that. A clustered index contains all the data in the table, while a nonclustered index contains only the indexing fields and a reference to the table. This means that after finding the required value in the index there is some overhead in looking up the rest of the information in the table.

Which fields to index and which type of index to use are not easy questions to answer. Different arrangements of indexes will be more suitable depending on the type of queries or updating procedures being undertaken at any given time. Large database products will usually provide a query analyzer that will show you how indexes are being used in a given query and estimate the time it will take. If a particular query is causing performance problems, you can use the analyzer tools to experiment with different index types to determine the best arrangement for that query. This arrangement, sadly, may be suboptimal for other queries or updating procedures that you require. After all, database design is an art rather than an exact science!

Views

In our discussion of queries so far, we have thought of them as one-off questions that we might like to ask the database. Many queries, however, will be ones that we want to carry out regularly—for example, retrieving order information to construct an invoice or product information for printing a catalog. *Views* are a way of saving the specifications of queries so that they can be reused.

Creating Views

To create a view, we simply issue the statement for the query we want and preface it with the words "CREATE VIEW ... AS." Listing 10-17 shows the SQL statement to create a view that joins the Customer and Order tables. Cust_Ord is just a name given to the view so that we can refer to it.

Listing 10-17. *Creating a View Joining the Customer and Order Tables*

```
CREATE VIEW Cust_Ord AS
SELECT * FROM Customer INNER JOIN Order ON custID = customer
```

When we run or open the view, the system will carry out the join and return the results as a single virtual table, which it will call Cust_Ord. We can treat that table as we would any other table, combining it with other tables in new queries and so on. It does not physically exist, however. If the data in the underlying tables changes, so will the resulting rows in the view.

Part of the design of a database includes providing a set of views that will be helpful to the users. Referring back to the original use cases will be the best guide as to the views that will be most important.

Uses for Views

Clearly, views are useful for retrieving data from the database. You will see in the next chapter how to use views as a basis for reports such as invoices or price lists. Views can also sometimes be used for entering data. If we have a customer who places an order for a product, we need to enter a new row in the Order table, find the customer number from Customer table, and probably look up the product number and price in a Product table. Accessing all these tables individually is not going to be efficient, and in the next chapter you will see how to use views underneath forms in order to manage data entry and maintenance.

Another use for views is providing some security for our data. Consider an Employee table. It will have information that everyone will need such as offices and phone numbers. It will also have quite private information such as salaries that only managers should be able to see. There is also the issue of updating information. A secretary might be able to change a phone number but not a salary.

A complete discussion of security issues is well beyond the scope of this book, but it is useful to see how views can be used to manage who can see and do what. For example, we can set up two views on our Employee table. One will display employee names and phone numbers, and the other will include salaries. These are shown in Listing 10-18.

Listing 10-18. *Two Views of the Employee Table*

```
CREATE VIEW Phone_view AS
SELECT empID, last_name, first_name, phone from Employee;

CREATE VIEW Manager_view
AS SELECT empID, last_name, first_name, phone, salary from Employee;
```

When a table or a view is created, it is owned by the person who created it. This will typically be some sort of data administrator. By default, he will be the only one to be able to see or update the table or view. The owner of the table or view can grant permission to other users or groups of users to read, update, or delete from the table or view as appropriate.

Typically, the users of the database will be placed into groups that will have different security levels or rights. There will always be a Public group, which will consist of all the users, and for controlling who can view or update different data, we might consider groups such as Managers and/or Secretaries.

We would like everyone to be able to view the names and phone numbers, so we can grant everyone (the Public group) permission to retrieve or select information from the Phone_view. We only want managers to be able to see the salaries, so we grant only that group permission to see rows from the Manager_view. The SQL to give these permissions is shown in Listing 10-19.

Listing 10-19. *Granting Different Groups Read Access to Different Views*

```
GRANT SELECT on Phone_view
TO Public
GRANT SELECT on Manager_view
TO Managers
```

There are a number of different types of permissions that can be granted to individual database users or groups of users. Listing 10-20 shows how we can allow the Secretaries group to update the information in our view of employees and phone numbers.

Listing 10-20. *Granting a Group of Users the Right to Update Data Through a View*

```
GRANT UPDATE on Phone_view
TO Secretaries
```

Summary

This chapter has provided a very brief introduction to how queries can be used to retrieve information from a database.

- We can retrieve different subsets of data from our database using a number of different relational database operations. These include the following:

    - Retrieving a subset of rows from a table or view

    - Retrieving a subset of columns from a table or view

    - Combining two tables or views with a join

    - Performing set operations (intersect, union, and difference) on tables or views with the same columns

- Indexes can help speed up queries. You should consider indexes on fields that are involved in select or join conditions in your queries or are used regularly for ordering data. Indexing a foreign key can be beneficial in many situations. Remember that indexes can speed up retrieval but may slow down the updating of data.

- Views are a way of storing the specification of a query so you can reuse it. Views are useful as a basis for forms and reports and can help with controlling access for different groups of users.

TESTING YOUR UNDERSTANDING

Exercise 10-1

Figure 10-15 shows a data model describing the meal delivery problem considered in Chapter 3. It shows the available meals and which ones appear in each order.

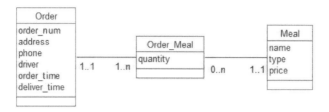

Figure 10-15. *Data model for meal delivery*

Some of the requirements identified by the client include the following:

a) Determine the cost of a specific order.

b) Prepare a list of undelivered orders.

c) Determine the income from different types of meals in a given month.

Determine the queries that would provide the required information. (Caution: after such a brief introduction to queries it is not reasonable to expect that a novice would be able to write down the queries in full, but do think about what joins might be required, which rows need to be selected, and so on.) To help you think about the problem, Figure 10-16 shows the database tables and some possible data. In the Order_Meal table, order and meal are foreign keys to the Orders and Meals tables respectively.

order_num	address	phone	driver	order_time	deliver_time
231	16 Lincoln Road	3475621	Billie	3/02/2012 2:34:00 p.m.	3/02/2012 3:03:00 p.m.
232	3a Breezes Road	3896834	Billie	3/02/2012 2:38:00 p.m.	
233	22 Waimea Tce	8563209	Jane	3/02/2012 2:56:00 p.m.	

Orders

name	type	price
Butter Chicken	Indian	8.95
Lamb Korma	Indian	8.95
MeatLovers	Pizza	15.99

Meals

order	meal	quantity
231	Butter Chicken	2
232	Lamb Korma	1
232	MeatLovers	1

Order_Meal

Figure 10-16. *Tables for meal delivery*

CHAPTER 11

■ ■ ■

User Interface

Right back at the beginning of this book, we looked at defining our database problem in terms of what different users of the database would need to do. We specified these requirements in terms of use cases, and most fell into one of two categories: tasks a user would need to carry out to enter data efficiently and tasks for retrieving information in the form of different reports.

In the intervening chapters, we have mostly been concerned with separating our data into several normalized tables in order to ensure the data is kept in a way that will allow the construction of different reports as the database evolves. This separation of data also ensures that it is kept in an accurate and consistent manner.

In Chapter 10, we looked at how queries and views allow us to gather together information from several tables in a number of different ways. In this chapter, we take a brief look at how to design forms and reports that will satisfy the original use cases. These can be added as a front end to your database to provide a convenient, friendly, and efficient way for users to interact with the data.

Input Forms

Figure 11-1 shows some possible use cases for our (very tiny) university database. Use cases 1 through 3 involve data entry, and use cases 4 and 5 are reporting tasks.

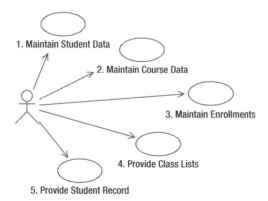

Figure 11-1. Use cases for the university database

A simple data model for satisfying the use cases in Figure 11-1 is shown in Figure 11-2, along with some representative data in Figure 11-3.

Figure 11-2. *Simple data model for the university database*

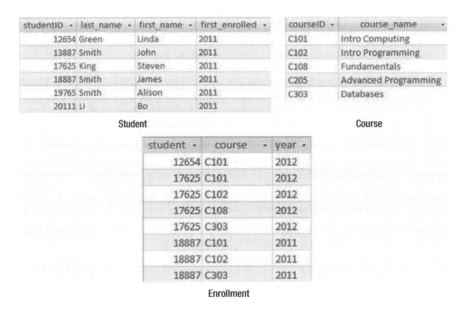

Figure 11-3. *A small portion of the data in the university database*

Data Entry Forms Based on a Single Table

Let's look at use case 1 first. This is a task likely to be carried out when a student first enters the university and at infrequent times when her contact information or other details change. The data entry involves interacting with just one table, the Student table in Figure 11-3. Form–generating software that may come with your database system usually offers a number of different ways to input data to a single table. One way is to design a form that shows several records in a grid (similar to the tables in Figure 11-3). This is useful in cases where each record only has a few fields that can all fit across a screen. In reality, our Student table is going to have many more fields than we have shown. Where there are many fields, it is preferable to have just one record displayed per form. An example is shown in Figure 11-4.

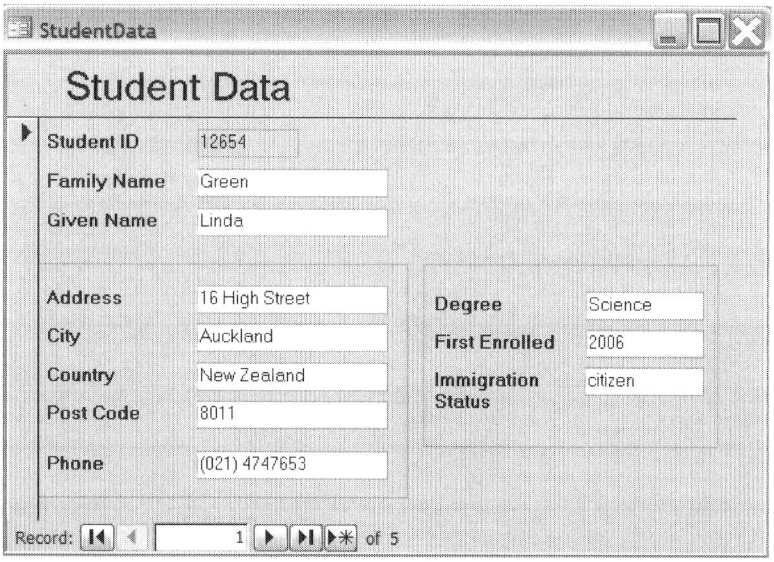

Figure 11-4. Form to update a single student's details

The form in Figure 11-4 was produced using the default options from the MS Access Form Design Wizard with a few alterations. I've added a title, relocated and resized some of the fields, and added some borders to keep similar fields together. A proper graphic designer would do an infinitely superior job! The default form provides navigation buttons along the bottom to move between records or to add a new one, and there are also built–in search features that enable you to move quickly to records matching a value you might type into a field. We would create a similar form for entering course data.

Data Entry Forms Based on Several Tables

The use case for entering enrollment data requires a bit more thought. On the face of it, we only need to enter information into the Enrollment table, but in practice we need to see corresponding information in the other two tables. Let's say that James Smith is an existing student wanting to enroll in three subjects in 2012. We need a convenient way to add something like the bottom three rows shown in the Enrollment table in Figure 11-3. If typing into a form based only on the Enrollment table, the data entry operator would have to type the year and the studentID three times (once on each row), and there is no feedback to let him know that 18887 is actually the correct number for James Smith. Typing each of the course codes may also lead to errors.

Referential integrity between the tables will ensure each enrollment is for an existing student and an existing course. However, the data entry operator will only get an error message after he tries to enter an enrollment record for a nonexistent student or course. Fortunately, forms based on views allow us to make the process much more efficient and less prone to error.

We can create a view with the relevant information from all three tables. Listing 11-1 shows the SQL to join the three tables and Figure 11-5 shows the resulting data.

Listing 11-1. SQL to create a view which joins the Enrollment, Student, and Course tables

```
CREATE VIEW all_info as
SELECT * FROM
(Course INNER JOIN Enrollment on courseID = course)
INNER JOIN Student on studentID = student
```

courseID	course_name	student	course	year	studentID	last_name	first_name	first_enrolled
C101	Intro Computing	12654	C101	2012	12654	Green	Linda	2011
C108	Fundamentals	17625	C108	2012	17625	King	Steven	2011
C102	Intro Programming	17625	C102	2012	17625	King	Steven	2011
C101	Intro Computing	17625	C101	2012	17625	King	Steven	2011
C102	Intro Programming	18887	C102	2011	18887	Smith	James	2011
C303	Databases	18887	C303	2011	18887	Smith	James	2011
C101	Intro Computing	18887	C101	2011	18887	Smith	James	2011
C102	Intro Programming	19765	C102	2012	19765	Smith	Alison	2011
C101	Intro Computing	19765	C101	2011	19765	Smith	Alison	2011
C108	Fundamentals	19765	C108	2011	19765	Smith	Alison	2011
C101	Intro Computing	20111	C101	2011	20111	Li	Bo	2011

Figure 11-5. Some data resulting from joining the Enrollment table with the Student and Course tables

We can base a form on the view in Figure 11-5 and then apply some conditions and formatting to the fields to produce something like Figure 11-6.

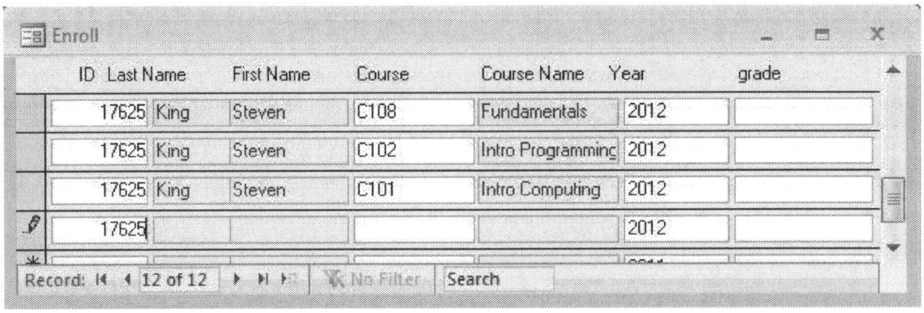

Figure 11-6. Form based on view in Figure 11-5

The data entry operator enters the details into the white boxes, but as the studentID and courseID are entered, the corresponding names will appear, providing some feedback to the user. It is also possible to constrain what the user is allowed to do. In the form in Figure 11-6, the properties of the three name fields have been changed to read-only so that the user can see, but not accidentally change, the values. Graying out the background makes it clear to the users that these three fields are just for information. Default values can also make forms more efficient to use. At the beginning of any particular year, it is probable that only enrollments for that year will be entered, so specifying a default value in the year field will speed data entry. Form generators allow forms such as that in Figure11-6 to be quickly developed. Web software such as Expression Web or Dreamweaver allows similar forms to be generated which allow access to a database through web browsers. How else could we improve the form for enrollment entry? Have another look at the data model in Figure 11-2. Both the Student class and the Course class have a 1–Many relationship with the Enrollment class. Each student has many enrollments, as does each course. From the point of view of data entry, which of these is most relevant?

160

At the beginning of the year, it is likely that a student will turn up in the registrar's office and want to make all his enrollments at one time. It makes sense to let our form reflect this 1–Many relationship between a student and his enrollments.

The form in Figure 11-7 is a combination of two forms. The top part is a form based on fields from the Student table. The bottom part is a subform set out in a similar way to the one in Figure 11-6 but based on a view joining the Enrollment and Course tables. The two forms are related so that we only see enrollments for the student displayed at the top. Now once a particular student's record is located, the data entry operator can enter all the enrollments in one place.

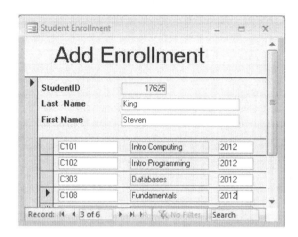

Figure 11-7. Form based on Student with a subform based on a join between Enrollment and Course

Constraints on a Form

The next obvious addition to help with data entry is to allow a user to choose from a list of available choices rather than having to type them in. For example, in the enrollment form in Figure 11-7, referential integrity requires that the course codes entered into the Enrollment table must be ones that already exist in the Course table. If the user enters a code that does not exist, he will get an error message from the underlying database system. Rather than have that happen, we can present the user with a drop–down list of allowed courses. In Figure 11-8, we have changed the text box for the course code to a list box. We then specify that the list box is to display the primary key values from the Course table.

We can also use a list box for other constraints. A likely situation is that in our table of course data, we might specify that particular subjects are or are not being offered, as in Figure 11-9.

When entering new enrollments in the Enrollment table, we want to restrict the value of course to just those courses from the Course table with Y in the offered field. How are we to do this? A check constraint as described in Chapter 9 won't do. Check constraints are based on values in the table we are updating. Here we are updating one table, Enrollment, but we need to check something about a row in a different table, Course. Referential integrity won't help because that only requires the course code to exist in the Course table and would therefore allow C205. We can use a list box as in Figure 11-8 to help with this problem. Instead of populating the list box with all values from the Course table, we can populate it with values from a view that selects just those courses that are offered. The SQL to create such a view is shown in Listing 11-2.

161

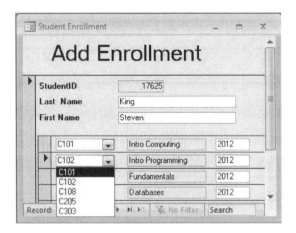

Figure 11-8. A list box to allow the user to select a subject

courseID	course_name	offered
C101	Intro Computing	Y
C102	Intro Programming	Y
C108	Fundamentals	Y
C205	Advanced Programming	N
C303	Databases	Y

Figure 11-9. Course table with field for whether a course is being offered

Listing 11-2. A Query that Will Select the Codes of Offered Courses

```
CREATE VIEW OfferedCourses AS
SELECT courseID FROM Course
WHERE offered = 'Y'
```

Now if we restrict the user to just those values in the list box populated with this query, we have effectively applied our constraint. Be aware that this constraint only takes effect for this particular form. If we update the Enrollment table in any other way, the constraint will not be in place. The only way to ensure that a constraint will always be in place is to put it directly on the table. This can be by a check constraint or, for constraints across more than one table, by a trigger as discussed in Chapter 10.

There is a place for constraints that take effect only on some forms. Our enrollment example is one of them. The offered field is relevant for the current year. There will be many rows in our Enrollment table from previous years for courses that are no longer offered. We may need to retrospectively update some of those rows, so we don't actually want the constraint on the table. We just want to restrict *new* rows to courses being offered in the current year. A data entry form is a good place to apply that constraint. This is the same as the problem discussed in Chapter 9 involving how to prevent orders being placed for items that are no longer in stock. The same solution will work there, too. In effect, we have a set of permanent constraints applied to our database tables through the table design. In addition, we can have other constraints on our forms that apply only in certain situations.

Restricting Access to a Form

Forms offer designers a great deal of versatility on what they can allow users to do. Most form design software will allow you to specify whether the form can be used just for viewing the data, or for updating or deleting records. You can also specify that certain fields on a form cannot be changed. For example, in Figure 11-8 we would probably not want a user who is meant to be entering enrollments to change a student's ID number or change the name of a course. However, we do want him to be able to see these values for confirmation that he has the correct records. Allowing read–only access to the ID and course name fields will prevent accidental changes to that data.

Because the forms are based on views or tables, we can also restrict *who* can see or update the data through the form. We can do this by granting different permissions to the underlying views to different groups of users as described in Chapter 10. We might grant a responsible group, such as administrators, update permission to our view, while allowing less–reliable groups such as academics read permission only.

Reports

Use cases 4 and 5 in the diagram in Figure 11-1 are both concerned with output. They require useful, easy–to–read reports based on the data in our tables. Reports are probably the most visible part of a database for a casual user. Our university database needs to be able to provide class lists and student records; a business would need to provide product lists, invoices, and summaries of sales. All of these reports are based on a subset of the data, such as invoices for unpaid transactions for a particular client, summaries of sales for the last month, enrollments for a particular course, and so on.

Many database systems provide report–generating software, and there are also independent products such as Crystal Reports. Most software uses the same principles for designing reports, so we will take a look at the basic elements.

Basing Reports on Views

Most informative reports are going to need data from more than one table. If we are interested in the details of enrollment information, we will likely want to see a student's name as well as her ID, and the course name along with its code. Clearly, we are going to need a view joining these three tables. Be careful here. It is probable that we will want to see all the courses and all the students, even those with no enrollments. As we discussed in the last chapter, this requires outer joins as in Listing 11-3.

Listing 11-3. *A View to Retrieve Information About Enrollments*

```
CREATE EnrollView AS
SELECT courseID course_name, studentID, last_name, first_name, year
FROM (Course FULL OUTER JOIN Enrollment ON courseID = course)
FULL OUTER JOIN Student ON studentID = student
```

Some of the rows retrieved when the view in Listing 11-3 is run are shown in Figure 11-10.

163

courseID	course_name	studentID	last_name	first_name	year
C101	Intro Computing	17625	King	Steven	2012
C101	Intro Computing	18887	Smith	James	2011
C101	Intro Computing	12654	Green	Linda	2012
C101	Intro Computing	20111	Li	Bo	2011
C102	Intro Programming	17625	King	Steven	2012
C102	Intro Programming	18887	Smith	James	2011
C303	Databases	18887	Smith	James	2011
C303	Databases	17625	King	Steven	2012
C205	Advanced Programming				
C108	Fundamentals	17625	King	Steven	2012
		13887	Smith	John	

Figure 11-10. Result of a view on Enrollment outer joined with Student and Course

Note that the outer joins mean we have a row for courses with no enrollments (C205) and also for students with no enrollments (John Smith). Now that we have this underlying view, we can create a host of different reports based on it.

Main Parts of a Report

Report generators generally have the following parts:

Report header: Text appearing at the top of the report, typically a title and date

Page header: Text appearing at the top of each page, such as column headings

Detail: The values you want to see from each row in the query or table on which the report is based

Page footer: Text appearing at the bottom of each page, typically page numbers

Report footer: Text appearing at the end of the report, often overall summaries

Figure 11-11 shows a report with a report header and page header, and with all the fields being displayed in the detail area (one for each row in the query result). In the report design, we can specify the order in which the detail rows are displayed (in this case by StudentID), and the report software will do all the necessary formatting to deal with page breaks and so on.

The report in Figure 11-12 isn't of much use at the moment, but there are a couple of simple things we can do to improve it. Often it is useful to put a select condition on the rows we want to see (e.g., the rows for a particular course). We could include this in the underlying view, but that would mean changing the view each time we want a list for a particular course. It is more useful to build these criteria into the design of the report so that each time we run the report we can specify the condition. Depending on what tool you are using, there will be different ways of doing this.

Enrollment Data

courseID	course_name	studentID	last_name	first_name	year
C205	Advanced Programming				
C101	Intro Computing	12654	Green	Linda	2012
		13887	Smith	John	
C108	Fundamentals	17625	King	Steven	2012
C303	Databases	17625	King	Steven	2012
C102	Intro Programming	17625	King	Steven	2012
C101	Intro Computing	17625	King	Steven	2012
C303	Databases	18887	Smith	James	2011
C102	Intro Programming	18887	Smith	James	2011
C101	Intro Computing	18887	Smith	James	2011
C101	Intro Computing	20111	Li	Bo	2011

Figure 11-11. Basic report based on EnrollView

Grouping and Summarizing

It is possible to adapt our basic report in Figure 11-11 in order to satisfy the use cases more effectively. The basic report provides all the information we need, but it is just not structured appropriately. Using the *grouping* features of a report generator can provide the appropriate structure. For a class list, we want to see all the enrollments for each class grouped together, whereas for a student record, we want the enrollments grouped by student. This is essentially reflecting the two 1–Many relationships in our data model—a student has many enrollments, and a course has many enrollments. Our model allows us to report from either point of view as required.

When we apply grouping, the report generator allows us to add a group header and footer for information relevant to that group. What happens is this: if we group by courseID, the rows in the view (as shown back in Figure 11-10) will be sorted in order of courseID. When the report writes out each row, it will insert a footer and header each time the value of courseID changes. Figure 11-12 shows two reports, both based on EnrollView: one is grouped on studentID, the other on courseID and then year.

In the student record report, we have a group header displaying each student's studentID, last name, and first name, while the detail displays the course data. In the class list report, the first group header has the course information, the next group header has the year, and finally the detail contains the student information. In the class list, we also have a group footer that summarizes the number of students in that course. This is done with a calculated field that will have a formula, something like = Count(*). We can restrict these two reports to only presenting data for a specified course, student, or year if we wish.

We have now satisfied the requirements of our two reporting use cases. A number of other reports are also possible. For example, we can choose to suppress the detail section of a report, in which case we will just see the header and/or footer of each group. A report grouped on courseID with the detail suppressed and a report footer for the overall count would look like Figure 11-13.

165

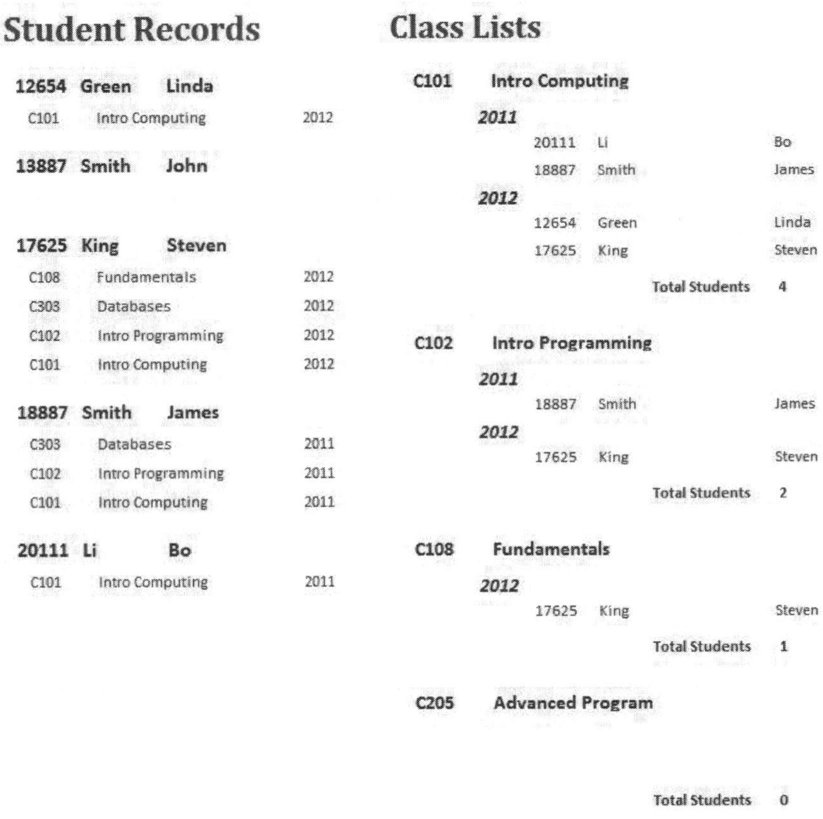

Student Records

12654 Green   Linda

C101   Intro Computing   2012

13887 Smith   John

17625 King   Steven

C108   Fundamentals   2012
C303   Databases   2012
C102   Intro Programming   2012
C101   Intro Computing   2012

18887 Smith   James

C303   Databases   2011
C102   Intro Programming   2011
C101   Intro Computing   2011

20111 Li   Bo

C101   Intro Computing   2011

Class Lists

C101   Intro Computing

2011

    20111   Li   Bo
    18887   Smith   James

2012

    12654   Green   Linda
    17625   King   Steven

            Total Students   4

C102   Intro Programming

2011

    18887   Smith   James

2012

    17625   King   Steven

            Total Students   2

C108   Fundamentals

2012

    17625   King   Steven

            Total Students   1

C205   Advanced Program

            Total Students   0

Report grouped by student   Report grouped by course and year

Figure 11-12. Parts of two reports based on EnrollView with different grouping

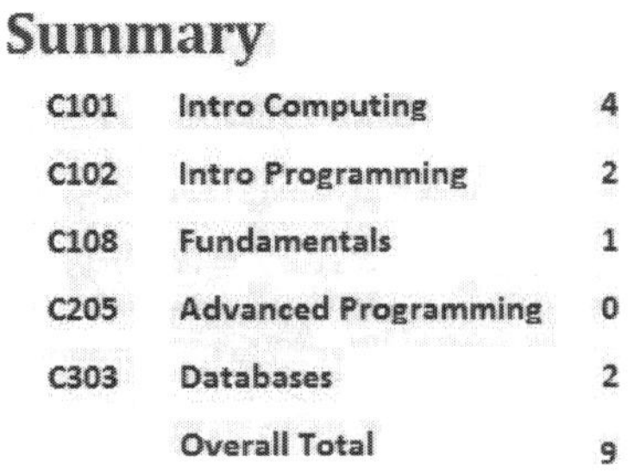

Summary

C101   **Intro Computing**   4

C102   **Intro Programming**   2

C108   **Fundamentals**   1

C205   **Advanced Programming**   0

C303   **Databases**   2

        Overall Total   9

Figure 11-13. A summary report grouped by course

166

We can see that there are numerous very useful reports that can all be based on our one view of the enrollment data. All these reports can have a select condition placed on them so that the user can limit them to particular years, particular subsets of courses, or an individual student. Part of our database design should be to provide a set of reports that will satisfy the use cases agreed upon in the early stages of the design.

Summary

Part of the design of a useful database is to provide a convenient interface for users to enter data and retrieve information. The original use cases will be a good indication of what is required.

- Forms and reports allow convenient ways to enter data into the database and to see well–presented output.

- Both forms and reports are usually based on views.

- By controlling the permissions granted to the views, we can restrict the access of groups of users to specific forms and reports.

- Subforms are a way to conveniently input data involved in a 1–Many relationship (e.g., a student has many enrollments).

- On forms, list boxes allow users to select from a set of values. By populating a list box from a view, additional constraints can be applied to data being entered through that form.

- By using different grouping, several very different reports can be constructed on a single view. These can be used to satisfy the output use cases identified in the requirements.

- Reports can include summary data such as totals, subtotals, counts, and so on.

- Reports can be designed to further refine the subset of data each time a report is run.

TESTING YOUR UNDERSTANDING

Exercise 11-1

In Exercise 3-1 we looked at the problem of a school recording pupil absences. The initial use cases are shown in Figure 11-14, and a first data model in Figure 11-15. Design some forms to satisfy the data entry requirements (use cases 1–3) and reports to satisfy the output use cases (4 and 5).

167

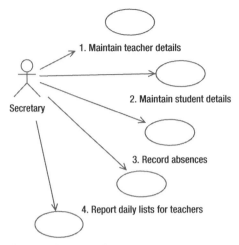

Figure 11-14. Use cases for recording and reporting school absences

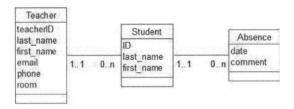

Figure 11-15. Data model for recording school absences

CHAPTER 12

Other Implementations

In the first few chapters of this book, we focused on obtaining a set of use cases and a data model that accurately represented the scope of a problem and the interrelation of the different data items. Chapters 7 through 9 showed how we could take the data model and represent it in a relational database as a set of normalized tables with the relationships implemented by foreign keys. The previous two chapters showed how we could efficiently enter data into these tables and use queries to extract meaningful information and reports.

Now we will have a brief look at other ways to represent the data model. We will look at object-oriented databases, spreadsheets (for simple data models), and XML as ways to represent data models.

Object–Oriented Implementation

Our data models are *object oriented*. This means that we look at the data and relationships in terms of specific objects, as in this description of a 1–Many relationship: "One object of the Customer class can be associated with many objects of the Order class." A programmer in object-oriented (OO) languages such as Java, VB .NET, or C# can create and manipulate objects directly. OO languages also have additional features that are not present in most relational database software. These features include the ability to have complex types for attributes (an object or a collection of objects) and the ability to store methods describing the behavior of an object as part of the class definition. Another advantage of an OO language is that it is able to directly implement and maintain classes and subclasses and so make full use of inheritance. One thing that is sometimes missing in OO languages is a way of saving and retrieving objects to and from persistent storage in a transparent manner. OO databases provide a way of seamlessly creating objects, storing them to disk, and then finding them again. The design of OO programs is a huge topic, so here I merely outline some of the main techniques in capturing the essential elements of a data model.

Classes and Objects

Unlike relational databases, OO programming languages support the idea of classes and objects directly. Classes are a definition or a template for how objects are going to be constructed. For example, a Customer class will specify the attributes that each Customer object will have (e.g., a name, an address, etc.). Each Customer object will be created according to the definition of the class and will have its own values for each of the attributes. Classes are just an abstract idea, but the objects themselves are independent entities. By contrast, in a relational database we think in terms of tables. We construct a table to represent each class, and the objects are represented by rows. We perform operations such as joins and unions on tables, not rows. Whereas operations within a relational database are firmly based on tables, in an OO environment the emphasis is on objects (hence "object oriented").

The difference between OO languages and relational databases is particularly marked when we consider inheritance. In Chapter 6 we saw how the ideas of specialization and generalization could help us model particular situations where we had classes that had much in common. In Figure 12-1, we have a data model which captures the similarities between students and lecturers in a parent `Person` class.

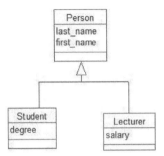

Figure 12-1. *Data model with inheritance*

Figure 12-2 shows how we attempt to capture the main features of this data model with tables in a relational database.

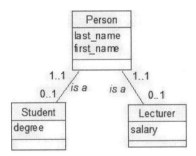

Figure 12-2. *Inheritance represented with 1–1 relationships*

The representation in Figure 12-2 requires three tables. Each student will be represented by two rows: one in the `Person` table and one in the `Student` table. If we want all the information about a particular student, we need to join the `Student` and `Person` tables in order to retrieve both the degree and the names. In an OO environment, if we create an object of either the `Student` or `Lecturer` class, it will have all the relevant attributes embedded in that object. We do not need to look up any other object or refer to any other class to retrieve the required information. This is depicted in Figure 12-3.

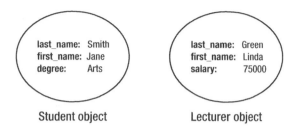

Figure 12-3. *A student and lecturer object in an OO environment*

In an OO environment, each object is a separate entity with its own unique object identification (OID). Because each object has its own identification, there is no requirement that the values of its attributes be unique. Put another way, from an implementation point of view, there is no need to provide the equivalent of a primary key that we needed in a relational database. For example, the two objects in Figure 12-4 can each be identified by the system via their unique OID, even though the values of their attributes are the same. However, the OID is not necessarily available, nor is it meaningful to the user. The program can distinguish the objects, but can the user?

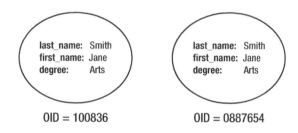

Figure 12-4. *Two distinct objects; but can the user tell them apart?*

In reality there will be some information that will differentiate the two different students (e.g., an address or birth date). Although it is not essential, a unique identifier such as a student ID number is probably still useful for helping users refer to particular people. Referring to student 128675 is easier than referring to the Jane Smith who lives in Beckenham.

Complex Types and Methods

In most relational systems, we generally use attributes of a simple type (e.g., number, text, date, etc.). In an object-oriented environment, we can have more complex attributes.

Consider the issue of addresses and names. In Chapter 7, we argued that a single address field was inadequate, and we introduced individual fields such as `street`, `city`, `post_code`, and `country`. We did a similar thing for names by introducing fields such as `title`, `first_name`, `last_name`, `initials`, and so on. This made it possible to effectively search or sort the rows by country or last name, and to format addresses properly in reports. In a relational database, these fields are all independent; without creating a new table, there is no simple way to say *these fields should all be kept together in some way because they form an address*. Creating a new table to hold the address attributes would not really achieve much, as we would need to create joins each time we needed all the information about a person and his address. Little is really achieved for that extra overhead.

171

In an object–oriented environment, we can define a class, `Address`, with its own attributes (`street`, `city`, `country`, `postcode`) and then in a `Customer` class we can have an attribute, `address`, which refers to an `Address` object. Figure 12-5 illustrates this idea for addresses and names.

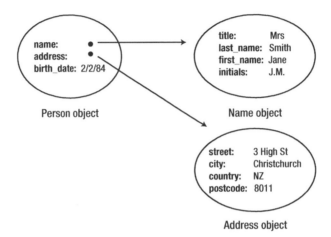

Figure 12-5. A Person object can refer to an Address object and a Name object.

In the `Person` class, we have three attributes: name and address, which are references to objects of our new Name and Address classes, and `birth_date` which is a simple date type. One of the main advantages of having these new classes is that we are able to declare methods or sets of instructions that can be carried out on the attributes. Let's look at a simple example for the Name class. In Figure 12-6, we have a class diagram as before, but now we have some methods in the bottom rectangle.

Name
last_name first_name initials title
formal_name() full_name()

Figure 12-6. The Name class with two methods

The method `formal_name()` might instruct the program to print out `title`, `initials`, and `last_name` (e.g., Mr. J. A. Wilson), while `full_name()` might print out first_name, last_name (e.g., John Wilson). In a relational database, these types of instruction would be kept with particular reports or forms. Every time we needed a new report, we would have to reissue the instructions. In an OO environment, these instructions are kept with the data. Everywhere we use a Name object, we just need to ask for `full_name`, and the instructions are available.

172

Collections of Objects

OO environments have the concept of *collections* (or sets or lists) of objects. In much the same way that a Student table is a way of managing all the rows in a relational database, in an OO environment we can set up many different collections of objects. There is probably a built-in collection for every object in a particular class (all Student objects, for example), but we can also create our own collections. We might have collections called AllStudents, CurrentStudents, Lecturers, People, and so on. Each of these collections will contain a set of references to individual objects. Figure 12-7 shows how you can visualize collections and objects. Particular objects may be referred to by more than one collection (e.g., a Lecturer object might be referred to by the People collection and also by the Lecturers collection).

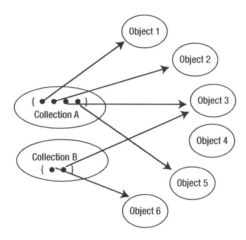

Figure 12-7. *Collections referring to objects*

Collections are important for representing relationships between objects, as you will see in the following section. Collections can also be used to help ensure that objects have some attribute(s) that have unique values so that they can be distinguished by the user. There is no such concept as a primary key in an OO environment, but we can use collections to enforce a similar uniqueness constraint. Typically, there will be different types of collections from which we can choose. A useful type of collection is one that can be keyed on a particular attribute or combination of attributes. A collection, say AllStudents, keyed on studentID, will be set up in such a way as to be very efficient at locating a particular object when given an ID number. A collection keyed on last_name will be efficient at finding a particular object based on a name. Finding particular objects in a keyed collection is very similar to finding rows in a table that has an index on it. As in the relational model, we can specify that a particular keyed collection may only have unique values of the key. If we have a collection, AllStudents, uniquely keyed on studentID, and we ensure that all our Student objects are added to this collection, we have effectively enforced the constraint that no two Student objects have the same value for studentID. This ensures that all our objects have an attribute (or set of attributes) that make them identifiable to the user.

Representing Relationships

References to objects and collections of objects can be used to represent the relationships in a data model. Consider the model in Figure 12-8, in which a customer can have many orders and each order is for exactly one customer.

Figure 12-8. *Data model for a relationship between customer and orders*

We will have two classes, Customer and Order. Each customer will have its own object, and each order will have its own object. What about the relationship between these two objects? Let's look at the 1 end of the relationship. Every order has one associated Customer object. Because we are able to have complex types as attributes in a class, we can have an attribute in each Order, which is a reference to the appropriate Customer object. This is illustrated in Figure 12-9.

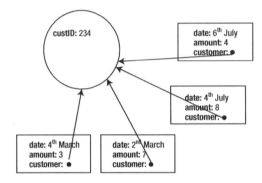

Figure 12-9. *Each Order object contains a reference to a Customer object.*

This reference in the Order object is not so unlike the idea of a foreign key in the relational model; it is different in the sense that with a foreign key the reference is to the table, and the application will have to find the associated row. In the OO environment, the reference is directly to the relevant Customer object.

Now let's think about the Many end of the relationship. Each Customer object has many Order objects, and we can set up this association directly also. We can include a collection of Order references as an attribute in the Customer class as shown in Figure 12-10.

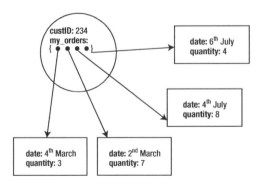

Figure 12-10. *A Customer object has a collection of references to its associated Order objects.*

174

We can choose to include the reference to a `Customer` in the `Order` class (Figure 12-9), the collection of `Orders` in the `Customer` class (Figure 12-10), or both. The decision will depend on which way we want to *navigate* between classes. The use cases will be our guide. If we want to know what orders a particular customer has placed, we need to navigate from `Customer` to `Orders` through the collection of `Order` objects. If we have an uncollected order and we want to know the name of the customer, we need to navigate from `Order` to `Customer` through the reference to the `Customer` object.

How is this different from a relational database? In a relational database, each row in the `Order` table has a foreign key, `customer`, referring to the `Customer` table, but we do not have a direct connection between specific rows. If we want information from both `Customer` and `Order` tables, we need to join the two tables and create a new virtual table. That table is quite symmetric, and we are able to find customers for particular orders and orders for particular customers from this one virtual table. This is very useful. Recall from the previous chapter how we were able to create two very different reports, a student record and a class list, both from a single virtual table.

By contrast, in an OO environment, we have to explicitly provide both paths if we think we will need them. If we don't have the collection in `Customer`, then we cannot easily find a particular customer's orders. If we don't have the reference to a customer in the `Order` objects, we would have no straightforward way of finding the appropriate customer. However, the direct links we can provide are very efficient for navigating between objects.

Given that we can represent a Many end of a relationship with a collection of objects, Many–Many relationships can be represented directly. This is in contrast to the relational model, where we had to create a new intermediate table to handle Many–Many relationships. For example, in the model in Figure 12-11, the Many–Many relationship between plants and uses can be represented by having a collection of `Use` objects associated with each `Plant` object and a collection of `Plant` objects associated with each `Use` object. The association between objects is direct; we do not need an additional table, nor do we need to perform two joins as in the relational model.

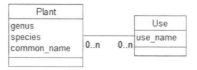

Figure 12-11. *A Many-Many relationship*

You may have spotted the potential problem with all this. Take the example about customers and orders. If we choose to include both the reference and the collection as shown in Figures 12-9 and 12-10, we are potentially storing information about an association between objects twice. A particular order will be in a customer's collection of orders, and a customer reference will be kept with the order. There is potential now for inconsistencies to arise. Order A may be in customer Smith's collection, but the Order A object may refer to customer Green. How this is managed depends on the software you are using. More about that in the next section.

OO Environments

There are numerous development platforms that use object–oriented concepts. Many modern programming languages (e.g., VB .NET, C#, Java, C++, Python) are based on classes and objects. However, it is not necessarily easy to use these languages to maintain data. While they provide all the concepts we have discussed so far, the problem comes when you try to store the data permanently. When you enter a row into a relational database, the software automatically takes care of saving it to disk so that it will be available after the software and the computer are shut down and restarted. This is *permanent*, or *persistent*, data. Other variables—intermediate results of calculations and so on—are not saved in this way and are known as *transient* data.

175

In OO programming languages, the programmer usually has to specifically save and retrieve the data about objects, and this is not necessarily a trivial matter. Specially designed OO database systems (e.g., Cache from Intersystems[1] and JADE[2]) can handle the storage and retrieval of objects transparently. A system like JADE allows you to take your data model and define a hierarchy of classes. The relationships between objects in the classes can be specified and are automatically maintained. For example, the problem mentioned in the previous section about inconsistent references between Order and Customer objects would not arise. If an order is removed from a customer's collection, the reference to that customer in the Order object will be automatically updated.

A good object–oriented database product provides a great many advantages. It can employ the full power of inheritance, manage complex types, store methods with the data, and provide very efficient links between related objects. However (there is always a however), one of the most powerful aspects of the relational model is the set of operations that we can perform on tables to retrieve complex subsets of data, as described in Chapter 10: joins, unions, intersections, and so on. The SQL commands to carry out these operations are relatively straightforward and are an integral part of any relational database system. However, the operations are all defined on tables and have no direct counterpart in an OO system. There is much work in progress to develop a set of standards for object–oriented databases and to develop OO database query languages[3].

One compromise between a full OO database and a relational database is an OO programming language connecting to a relational database. Objects are converted to rows in a table, and then the full data management power of the relational database can be used for storage and retrieval. Within the programming language, it is then possible to communicate with the database and insert and retrieve data using SQL. Tools such as Hibernate[4] facilitate this process of object relational mapping. In doing the transfer between objects and tables, however, we can lose many of the specific OO advantages with respect to our data objects.

Implementing a Data Model in a Spreadsheet

Spreadsheets are perhaps one of the most versatile of the applications widely available on the desktop. There are many products to choose from, including Microsoft Excel, Open Office, and Google Docs. The popularity of spreadsheets stems from the ability to open a sheet and start entering numbers and equations immediately— there is no need to declare variables or design tables.

For those people who have some data and who need to find statistical or calculated results quickly, a spreadsheet is wonderful. Spreadsheets have amazing power readily available in the form of an abundance of functions and features. However, they can also be quite dangerous. Anyone who contemplates using a spreadsheet for performing important calculations should visit one of the web sites[5] that discuss the many and varied mistakes and errors that plague most spreadsheets.

Spreadsheets are great for performing calculations but are less suited to storing data that may need to be extracted in a variety of ways. To query and report on data easily, the required information usually needs to be on one sheet. This is a bit like keeping all the data for a problem in one database table. We showed some examples of the problems of doing this in Chapter 1. The rest of the book has essentially been about how to avoid these problems by splitting our data into classes or normalized tables. However, spreadsheets are such a popular tool that it is worth looking at how to use them to represent a small data model effectively.

Where there are many classes with complex relationships, a spreadsheet will not be able to capture the complexities accurately and in a maintainable way. For problems that have only a few classes, , (mostly category type classes) it is sometimes possible to capture quite a substantial amount of the complexity of a data model with a properly designed spreadsheet.

---

[1] http://www.intersystems.com/cache/index.html

[2] http://www.jadeworld.com/

3 http://www.odbms.org/

[4] http://www.hibernate.org/

[5] http://study.lincoln.ac.nz/spreadsheet, http://panko.shidler.hawaii.edu/SSR/index

Consider a small business that is keeping data about the transactions of its customers in a spreadsheet. You might imagine that a first attempt at a spreadsheet would look something like Figure 12-12.

	A	B	C	D	E	F	G	H
1	order_num	custID	name	address	date	product	price	quantity
2	1001				3-Dec	56789	250	6
3	1002	1231	Smith	PO Box Z-547	5-Dec	56789	250	7
4	1003	1231	Smith	PO Box z-548	12-Dec	76253	375	10
5	1004	1354	Robson	PO Box 541	17-Dec	65789	250	4
6	1005	1657			19-Dec	65789	250	5

Figure 12-12. Spreadsheet for (very) simple orders from customers for products

By now, you should be able to see the potential problems in such a solution. Data is repeated (e.g., the address of a customer and price of a product) with the potential to become inconsistent as in rows 3 and 4. Orders can be entered without an associated customer (row 2), and as far as we can see here there is no check on whether a valid product code has been entered (is there really a product 76253?).

A suitable data model for the preceding situation (assuming orders are just for a single product) is shown in Figure 12-13. By separating the information about customers and products into separate classes, we can ensure that transactions are always for valid customers and products, and that the associated names, addresses, and prices are consistent.

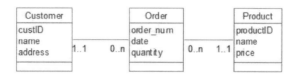

Figure 12-13. Data model for customers ordering products

In a spreadsheet, the main focus for our calculations and analyses is going to be the orders. We will want to sort them by date, total the amounts, search for them by customer, and so on. To do this, all the information has to be on one sheet as in Figure 12-12. How do we maintain some control over the consistency and accuracy of the data?

The data model in Figure 12-13 has two 1–Many relationships, so let's first look at how to represent those in a spreadsheet.

1–Many Relationships

To represent a data model involving 1–Many relationships as in Figure 12-13, we first set up a separate sheet for each class at the 1 end. Figure 12-14 shows a sheet containing the information about customers with the data given a range name (all_Customers). There would be another sheet with information about products. The separate customer sheet enables rows to be added or updated independently of other information (orders and products).

Figure 12-14. Sheet with information about customers with the range name all_Customers

We then create a third sheet for the class at the Many end (orders) where we will accumulate all the information we need. Rather than type in all the information about each customer, we can enter the customer ID and display the matching data from the customer sheet. This can be done with a function called VLOOKUP.

Listing 12-1. VLookup Function

```
=VLOOKUP(1672,all_Customers,2,FALSE)
```

The formula in Listing 12-1 takes the value (e.g. 1672) and finds it in the range all_Customers (Figure 12-14); the parameter "2" means return the associated value in the second column of that range (the name - Li). The "FALSE" means if the value isn't in the table, return an error message. Listing 12-1 is valid in Excel, Google Docs, and (if the commas are replaced by semicolons) Open Office.

Figure 12-15 shows the results from the VLOOKUP function in column C. Columns D and G also contain functions to look up data from the appropriate sheets. The problem with the inconsistent address for Mr. Smith (Figure 12-12) has been resolved and we have a warning that there is a problem on row 6 in that there is no customer 1657 in all_Customers.

Figure 12-15. Order sheet with lookups to customer and product details

The custID column in Figure 12-15 is acting somewhat like a foreign key in a relational table. Unlike a foreign key, though, there is nothing so far to stop us from entering a value in column B that is not represented in the customer sheet (row 6), but if we use *exact match* lookups (including the parameter "FALSE" as in Listing 12-1), we get a very clear signal with the error message #N/A (not available) that there is a problem.

Spreadsheet products also offer data validation tools so that we can have control over the customer numbers we enter into column B. We can specify that the values in column B on our order sheet must come from the list of values in the ID column of the customer sheet. The way this is done in Google Docs is shown in Figure 12-16. We have named the range of cells containing the customer numbers on the customer sheet custIDs.

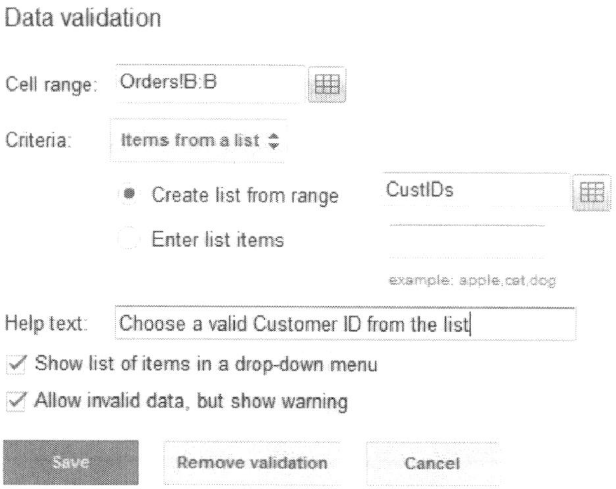

Data validation

Cell range: Orders!B:B

Criteria: Items from a list ◆

     ● Create list from range   CustIDs

     ○ Enter list items

                       example: apple,cat,dog

Help text: Choose a valid Customer ID from the list|

☑ Show list of items in a drop-down menu

☑ Allow invalid data, but show warning

[Save]   [Remove validation]   [Cancel]

Figure 12-16. *Google Docs validation tool*

In addition to restricting the values we can enter into the column, validation tools also provide a convenient list box of the valid values to help data entry, as shown in Figure 12-17.

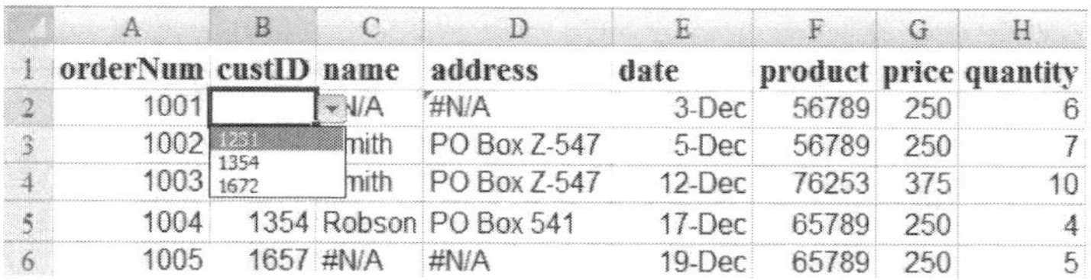

	A	B	C	D	E	F	G	H
1	orderNum	custID	name	address	date	product	price	quantity
2	1001		N/A	#N/A	3-Dec	56789	250	6
3	1002	1251	mith	PO Box Z-547	5-Dec	56789	250	7
4	1003	1354 1672	mith	PO Box Z-547	12-Dec	76253	375	10
5	1004	1354	Robson	PO Box 541	17-Dec	65789	250	4
6	1005	1657	#N/A	#N/A	19-Dec	65789	250	5

Figure 12-17. *Using data validation tools to restrict values in a column*

Using a data validation on column B in Figure 12-17 has given us a type of referential integrity at the point where data is entered or updated on the order sheet. The lookup functions themselves act a bit like joins. The order sheet in Figure 12-15 has brought together data from the customer and product sheets in a manner quite similar to an outer join between three tables in a relational database. This method of dealing with relationships rapidly gets out of hand where there are lots of different classes in our model, but it is not a bad approximation for small problems.

We have managed to separate the data for our three classes so as to avoid inconsistencies, used data validation to simulate referential integrity to a degree, and used lookups to perform something similar to a join. So we have some control over the accuracy of the data. We can use sorting and filtering tools to do the equivalent of selecting rows, and we can hide columns to simulate projecting columns. Spreadsheets also offer a huge range of analysis features. What we don't have is the ability to easily perform complex queries that require other relational operations, such as, *which customers have ordered both product 76253 and 56789?*

179

Many–Many Relationships

Let's now have a look at Many–Many relationships in a spreadsheet. This situation often arises where we have categories, and we will take one last look at our plant example data model shown in Figure 12-18.

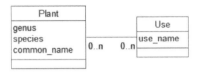

Figure 12-18. *A Many-Many relationship representing plants with many uses*

There are a number of different ways you can store multiple values for uses in a spreadsheet. We will look at some of the advantages and disadvantages of three different methods: repeated columns, categories as columns, and normalized ranges.

Figure 12-19 shows a common way that people store multivalued categories in a spreadsheet (and often in a database!): repeated columns.

	A	B	C	D	E	F
1	genus	species	common_name	use1	use2	use3
2	Dodonaea	viscosa	akeake	shelter	hedging	soil stability
3	Cedrus	atlantica	atlas cedar	shelter		
4	Alnus	glutinosa	black alder	soil stability	shelter	firewood

Figure 12-19. *Representing multiple values of use in repeated columns*

The reason this way of storing the data is so popular is that it is in a format the user finds useful. The user probably initially thought of the data in terms of plants and their uses, and this format displays each plant with all its uses on one line. (This can be difficult output to achieve from normalized database tables.) We have already discussed in Chapter 1 some of the problems of storing the data this way, but by using some spreadsheet functionality, we can reduce some of the problems. One issue was ensuring that the entries in columns D through F had consistent spelling. This can be achieved in a spreadsheet by using the data validation feature and insisting that values in those columns come from a list of possible uses stored on another sheet. Another significant problem is being able to find all the plants with a specific use (e.g., shelter). It is not sufficient to just sort or filter column D, for example, to find all the values of shelter; this is because shelter may have been recorded in any of the columns D through F. It is possible to check all three columns using advanced filters and criteria tables, but this is well beyond the capabilities of the casual user. With this level of skill, the user would have been better off to use a database right from the start. Repeated columns, therefore can provide some checking of the use data, a good reporting format but poor querying in terms of plants for a given use.

Another common storage method is to have a separate category for each column and use check marks to specify whether they apply for a particular species. This is shown in Figure 12-20.

	A	B	C	D	E	F	G
1	genus	species	common_name	Shelter	Firewood	Hedging	Soil Stability
2	Dodonaea	viscosa	akeake	√		√	√
3	Cedrus	atlantica	atlas cedar	√			
4	Alnus	glutinosa	black alder	√	√		√

Figure 12-20. *Representing multiple values of use with categories as columns*

This is actually a very useful representation. As long as there are not too many categories, it is quite good for reporting purposes, as you can see all the uses on one line. There are no issues with spelling use names as these only appear once in the heading row. It is also possible to quite simply find all the plants with a specific use. If we want to find all Hedging plants, we can simply sort or filter column F. Simple filtering will also allow us to perform more complex queries such as *find plants that are suitable for Hedging AND Firewood*. The categories–as–columns arrangement therefore offers good reporting, good data entry consistency, and useful querying.

The last method is what we will call normalized ranges. This method actually mimics a relational database by introducing the equivalent of an intermediary class in Figure 12-18 and turning the Many–Many relationship into two 1–Many relationships. We now have a situation very similar to the orders spreadsheet described earlier. We would have a sheet with all the species information (with an ID column), a sheet with all the uses, and a third sheet for the pairings of species and uses with lookups or validations to the other sheets. This is shown in Figure 12-21. Columns B through D are looked up in the plants sheet, and column E can be validated from the use sheet.

	B2		▼	f_x	=VLOOKUP(A2,Plants,2, FALSE)	
	A	B	C	D	E	F
1	id	genus	species	common_name	use	
2	1	Dodonaea	viscosa	akeake	Shelter	
3	1	Dodonaea	viscosa	akeake	Hedging	
4	1	Dodonaea	viscosa	akeake	Soil Stability	
5	2	Cedrus	atlantica	atlas cedar	Shelter	
6	3	Alnus	glutinosa	black alder	Shelter	
7	3	Alnus	glutinosa	black alder	Firewood	
8	3	Alnus	glutinosa	black alder	Soil Stability	

Figure 12-21. Representing multiple values of usage with normalized ranges and lookups

With this method of keeping the data, we have good checking of the data, we can sort or filter column A to find all the usages for a particular plant, and we can sort or filter column E to find all the plants with a particular use. So far, so good. However, the reporting is awful. The format of the data is not in a form that anyone would want to print out and it is not particularly nice to use. If the data is going to be stored in this way, it might as well be in three tables in a database where we have access to better querying, data entry, and reporting features.

Implementing in XML

XML (Extensible Markup Language)[6] was designed as a way to exchange information. It is based on a hierarchy of tagged elements that contain both a description and a value for a piece of information. As an example, Listing 12-2 shows a tagged element to represent a piece of data representing a name. We have opening and closing tags which describe the content of the data (a first name) and between the tags is the value, "James."

Listing 12-2. An XML Tag to Represent a First Name

```
<first_name>James</first_name>
```

---

[6] http://www.w3.org/standards/xml/

181

Elements can also have attributes and elements can be nested inside each other. Listing 12-3 shows an XML definition of a student. Student is an element with an attribute, `studentID`, and the last name and first name are declared as elements.

Listing 12-3. *Using Elements and Attributes to Represent Student Data*

```
<student studentID="113452">
  <first_name>James</first_name>
  <last_name>Green</last_name>
</student>
```

If you are asking why `studentID` is an attribute and the names are elements, you are not alone! The student information could be reflected with many different combinations of attribute or element, although usually anything that is regarded as important to a human reader is represented by an element. The important thing to note about Listing 12-3 is that the XML contains both a definition of the structure of the data (a student has an ID, and first and last names) and also the value of the data (this student is James Green with ID 113452)

XML is very flexible, with elements able to be defined at any time. One of the few rules is that the overall structure is a tree with one root element, inside which all other elements need to be nested. Listing 12-3 is fine as it represents just one student; but to represent several students we need an encompassing root element such as `<university>` as in Listing 12-4.

Listing 12-4. *A Hierarchy to Represent Several Students*

```
<university>
  <student studentID="113452">
    <first_name>James</first_name>
    <last_name>Green</last_name>
  </student>
  <student studentID="113756">
    <first_name>Mary</first_name>
    <last_name>Smith</last_name>
    <degree>Science</degree>
  </student>
  <student studentID="116543">
    <first_name>Sally</first_name>
    <last_name>Hunter</last_name>
    <hostel>Helliers</hostel>
  </student>
</university>
```

XML allows us to keep different types of data about each of our students. In Listing 12-4 we see that Mary has information about a degree and Sally has information about a hostel. Representing the data in this way is extremely flexible since there is no predefined structure as is required for a relational database table. Extra information can easily be added because the description and the values are all kept together. The downside of this flexibility is that you will never quite know how a student is actually described, so querying the data will be difficult.

Representing Relationships

The hierarchical nature of XML allows us to nest elements inside each other so a 1–Many relationship is quite easy to represent. We could take an organization element with several department elements, each of which has employee elements nested within it. Let's have a look at how we could use XML to represent the Many–Many relationship in Figure 12-22.

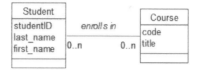

Figure 12-22. *Data model for students enrolling in courses*

We can think of the information in Figure 12-22 in two ways: as students each with a set of courses or as courses each with a set of students. Figure 12-23 shows these two versions of an XML tree that would represent some data about students and courses.

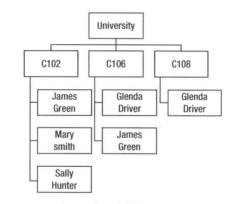

a) Students nested inside courses

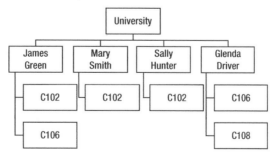

b) Courses nested inside students

Figure 12-23. *Two possible XML trees to represent students and courses*

183

In the trees in Figure 12-23, each box would be an element with its own nested elements and attributes. For example, each of the boxes for James Green would be represented with the code in Listing 12-3. Clearly, there is now an issue of repeated information. Each student will have their data repeated for every course in Figure 12-23a, while in Figure 12-23b the information for each course will be repeated. This is not necessarily a problem if XML is being used as a means of transferring the data between different applications, but it clearly would become a problem if anyone tried to update the data directly.

Another way to represent the model in Figure 12-22 is to introduce a third type of element (enroll) in very much the same way as we introduced an intermediate table for a relational database. Listing 12-5 shows the code to represent two courses, two students, and their enrollments in C102.

Listing 12-5. *A Hierarchy to Represent Students, Courses, and the Enrollments Relating Them*

```
<?xml version="1.0"?>
<university>
  <courses>
    <course>
      <code>C102</code>
      <title>Programming</title>
    </course>
    <course>
      <code>C106</code>
      <title>Databases</title>
    </course>
  </courses>
  <students>
    <student studentID = "113452">
      <first_name>James</first_name>
      <last_name>Green</last_name>
    </student>
    <student studentID = "113756">
      <first_name>Mary</first_name>
      <last_name>Smith</last_name>
    </student>
  </students>
  <enrollments>
    <enroll>
      <stud>113452</stud>
      <crse>C102</crse>
    </enroll>
    <enroll>
      <stud>113756</stud>
      <crse>C102</crse>
    </enroll>
  </enrollments>
</university>
```

Most database systems will have the facility to import and export data to and from XML files. For example, the file in Listing 12-5 can be imported directly into Access to create and populate three database tables (student, course, and enroll).

Defining XML types

The XML in the previous sections was very flexible. However, in practice we usually need more precision in the way data elements are described. It is possible to define a course as an element that has a code and a title with a DTD (Document Type Definition). The code in Listing 12-6 is a definition of a course. It says that a course is made up of a code and a title, and that codes and titles are character data. The lines of code at the bottom then provide some values for a course.

Listing 12-6. *A DTD for a Course*

```
<?xml version="1.0"?>
<!DOCTYPE course[
  <!ELEMENT course (code, title)>
  <!ELEMENT code (#CDATA)>
  <!ELEMENT title (#CDATA)>
  ]>
<course>
  <code>C102</code>
  <title>Programming</title>
</course>
```

Importing an XML document such as that in Listing 12-6 into Access would create a table with two text columns (code and title) and one row with values C102 and Programming. This is an excellent way of transferring information about the structure and the values of data between applications.

A more expressive method of defining XML data types is by using XML Schema Language. An XML schema document (XSD) is XML code to describe data. Listing 12-7 shows a very simple XSD to define a course. Because definitions of elements are likely to be reused in many different situations we may run into the situation in which two or more elements from different documents have the same name. For example, we may find in another definition that there is a different element named "title." XSD has the concept of a name space so that all elements can be uniquely identified. The second line of code in Listing 12-7 says that any definitions prefixed by "xs" come from this definition for our university. The rest of the code says that a course is a complex type made up of a sequence of code and title which are both strings (or character types).

Listing 12-7. *Very Basic XSD for a Course*

```
<?xml version="1.0"?>
<xs:schema xmlns:xs="http://university">
    <xs:element name="course">
      <xs:complexType>
        <xs:sequence>
          <xs:element name="code" type="xs:string"/>
          <xs:element name="title" type="xs:string"/>
        </xs:sequence>
      </xs:complexType>
    </xs:element>
</xs:schema>
```

XSD is a large language and will let you define constraints on values, specify cardinalities (e.g., the minimum and maximum number of courses a student could have), specify default values, declare that elements must have unique values, and so on. The full specification can be found at http://www.w3.org/XML/Schema. Essentially,

185

it allows you to specify the equivalent of database tables but with a platform independent text document. It is useful for transferring schema description between applications.

Querying XML

This section on querying XML data is only to give a brief idea of what is possible and to point you to further information. Consider the XML description of some student data in Listing 12-8.

Listing 12-8. *XML to Describe Some Student Data*

```
<?xml version="1.0"?>
<university>
  <student>
    <studentID>15673</studentID>
    <last_name>Smith</last_name>
    <first_name>Jim</first_name>
    <age>18</age>
  </student>
  <student>
    <studentID>23543</studentID>
    <last_name>Green</last_name>
    <first_name>Ruby</first_name>
    <age>22</age>
  </student>
</university>
```

The hierarchical structure means we can parse the text to find students which match particular criteria. XPath is a succinct language which allows the hierarchy to be traversed to retrieve elements satisfying different criteria. For example, the XPath code in Listing 12-9 would retrieve the last names of all students over age 20.

Listing 12-9. *XPath Expression to Retrieve the Last Names of Students Over 20*

```
/university/student[age>20]/last_name
```

The code will traverse the university tree and find all the elements defined as students and then find their last names—but just those which match the criteria that the value of the age element is greater than 20. XQuery is an extension to XPath that allows results to be transformed in various ways (e.g., sorted alphabetically) and even allows the equivalent of joins between sets of data. The specification for XPath and XQuery can be found at `http://www.w3.org/standards/xml/`.

NoSQL

This book has focused on small databases. We have been particularly interested in highly structured data where the emphasis is on being able to retrieve different types of information. This is only one small portion of the overall database world. The internet has given rise to huge data sets that often need to be stored on hundreds of computers across continents. Highly structured data models and their representation in relational or SQL databases are not an effective way to manage such data.

NoSQL databases offer a less structured way to manage large amounts of data. One example is a key–value database. Key data (say a string) is stored and is searchable, and the value is a reference to where the rest of the data can be found. There are no constraints on how that data is structured, so these databases are very flexible.

Other examples are document databases and big table databases (in which the rows can all have different structures.) While these types of databases have many advantages for storing large amounts of data, the downside is the ease of querying and finding connections between different pieces of data. Without a rigorous structure you cannot have the operations available in SQL such as joins. This kind of logic is generally handled in NoSQL databases with front-end programming. Graph databases can reflect associations between different pieces of data by maintaining links between them. Once again the actual data can be structured in any way and the prescribed links can provide fast access between items of data. Ad hoc queries are difficult.

SQL databases provide efficient storage and querying for well-structured data. NoSQL databases offer flexible ways of managing large amounts of data of many different types.

Summary

In this chapter, we have looked at alternatives to using a relational database to represent a data model.

Object–Oriented Databases

Object–oriented databases offer a number of advantages over relational databases in terms of complex data types (e.g., names and addresses), methods (e.g., outputting different formats of names), and accurately representing inheritance. The drawback is that complex queries may be more difficult to set up.

To represent a data model in an object–oriented language or database:

- Define a class for each class.

- Consider creating classes for complex data types such as addresses or names.

- Consider adding methods to classes (e.g., for formatting addresses or performing calculations).

- Give thought to how a user will identify objects (the equivalent of a primary key).

- For the Many part of a relationship, include a collection that has references to several objects (e.g., a `Customer` will have a collection of many `Order` objects).

- For the 1 part of a relationship, include a reference to the particular object (e.g., an `Order` will have a reference to one `Customer` object).

Spreadsheets

Spreadsheets are a marvelous tool for data analysis and calculations. They are not really designed for storing data but are commonly used for this purpose, as they are often considered to be simpler and more immediately useful than databases. For small data models with simple relationships between the classes, it is possible to design a spreadsheet that is both useful and accurate.

To represent very simple 1-Many relationships in a spreadsheet:

- Create a separate sheet for each class.

- Create a sheet where all the information will be brought together.

- Use exact match lookups to display information from other sheets.

- Use data validation features to provide the equivalent of referential integrity between sheets.

There are several ways to represent Many–Many relationships in a spreadsheet:

- Repeated columns (good for validation and reporting, but not querying)

- Categories as columns (good for validation, reporting, and querying)

- Normalized ranges (good for validation and querying, but poor for reporting and ease of use)

XML

XML provides a way of expressing both the structure of data and the values of data elements in a text format. It is useful for platform-independent specification of data and for transferring the description and values of data between applications.

- A simple XML document is a tree of elements specified by tags.

- We can represent relationships by using the hierarchical nature of the XML tree. For example, students can be nested within courses or vice versa.

- A Many–Many relationship can also be represented by defining three complex XML elements, such as students, courses, and enrollments (similar to the tables used to represent a Many–Many relationship in a relational database).

- Document Type Definitions (DTD) and XML Schema Definitions (XSD) can be used to define the structure of the data.

- XPath and XQuery are two languages which enable the retrieval of specific elements from an XML document.

APPENDIX

Testing Your Understanding

In this Appendix we will discuss the problems from the end of each chapter. I emphasize that these are discussions as opposed to answers. There may be other acceptable ways to approach the different scenarios.

EXERCISE 1-1

A school is planning some outdoor pursuits for its students. It wants to create a database of how parents can help. The secretary sets up the database table as in Figure A-1 to keep the information.

last_name	first_name	phone	contribution	contribution2
Smith	Jane	4623598	Food preparation	Driving
Green	Rob	8965431	Transport	
Henry	James	9576342	Camping Gear	Cooking
Wang	Li	9612345	Cooking	

Figure A-1. Initial database table for recording parent contributions

a) What problems can you foresee in making good use of the information in the table in Figure A-1?

The table was probably designed as in Figure A-1 because the school secretary prepared a list of people and asked them to fill in what they could do to help with the school camping trips. However the main use of the data will likely be the other way around—who can provide this help? If you want to find someone to help with driving then you will have to check both columns, so filtering or sorting the table to find the drivers will be difficult. There is also a category or keyword problem. Some people have called their willingness to get the children to a camp "driving," while others call it "transport." This makes any automated selection of appropriate people almost impossible. A human would need to check every row.

b) Suggest some better ways that this information could be stored.

One improvement would be to predetermine some categories: transport, provide equipment, and food preparation. A simple spreadsheet or table based on these categories, as shown in Figure A-2, would be much easier to manipulate. For example, some simple filtering of the transport column will find all the drivers very quickly.

189

last_name ▾	first_name ▾	phone ▾	transport ▾	food_preparation ▾	equipment ▾
Smith	Jane	4623598	Yes	Yes	
Green	Rob	8965431	Yes		
Henry	James	9576342	Yes		
Wang	Li	9612345		Yes	Yes

Figure A-2. A spreadsheet or database table using categories

The solution in Figure A-2 is fine if this is all the information the school wants to keep, and that may very well be the case. However, if the school later decides that it wants to elaborate on tasks such as food preparation, or keep dates about availability, then the design will be difficult to amend. We are actually storing information about two things, People and Contributions, and the relationship between them (i.e., who can provide what and possibly when). A solution similar to that proposed in Figure 2-1 for plants and uses would be a more general solution for this problem but it might not be worth the effort. There is always a tension between providing a good, cheap solution for the current problem and providing an extensible design which has the ability to evolve.

EXERCISE 1-2

a) What problems can you foresee in making good use of the information in the database table in Figure A-3?

week_start ▾	Mon ▾	Tue ▾	Wed ▾	Thur ▾	Fri ▾
17/10/2011	Jane	Sue	George	Sue	Jane
24/10/2011	Jane	Sue	Linda	Sue	Lee
31/10/2011	Sue	Sue	Lee	George	George

Figure A-3. An initial database table to record roster duties

This table is based on a report that the user has envisaged. It will be handy to print out for a given month and place by the phone or on the wall. That is pretty much all it will be useful for, though, and it could just as easily have been written on a piece of paper. One additional piece of information that could be available from this data is a report for each person showing the days on which they are rostered. The data is there but it is not at all easy to extract it with this design. Once again, it is useful to think about the data rather than the output. We are keeping information about two things: people and days, and the relationships between them.

b) Suggest some better ways that this information could be stored.

A table or spreadsheet similar to the one in Figure A-4 would enable many more views of the data. We can filter by name to get the roster for a person or select particular weeks to get the same information, as in Figure A-3.

week_start ▾	day ▾	name ▾
17/10/2011	Mon	Jane
17/10/2011	Tue	Sue
17/10/2011	Wed	George
17/10/2011	Thu	Sue
17/10/2011	Fri	Jane
24/10/2011	Mon	Jane
24/10/2011	Tue	Sue
24/10/2011	Wed	Linda
24/10/2011	Thu	Sue
24/10/2011	Fri	Lee
31/10/2011	Mon	Sue
31/10/2011	Tue	Sue
31/10/2011	Wed	Lee
31/10/2011	Thu	George
31/10/2011	Fri	George

Figure A-4. A more useful way to store data about roster duties

It is not particularly easy to get a report set out exactly as in Figure A-3 from the table in Figure A-4, although the information is all there. So here is the trade off. I really want the table format in Figure A-3, but I'm prepared to compromise on the formatting to get the additional views of the data that Figure A-4 allows.

EXERCISE 2-1

A small sports club keeps information about its members and the fees they pay. The secretary wants to be able to enter data as members pay and print a report similar to that in Figure A-5.

last_name ▾	first_name ▾	phone ▾	type ▾	gender ▾	fee ▾	date_paid ▾
Smith	Jane	563201	Full	F	220	21/09/2011
Wilson	Harry	375967	Full	M	220	19/09/2011
Green	Bert	439871	MidWeek	M	150	
Jones	Bert	295784	Social	F	80	
Smith	Sharon	387648	MidWeek	F	150	16/08/2011

Figure A-5. Membership data for a small club

a) Think about when the different pieces of data might be entered. Sketch an initial use case diagram for data entry.

191

At first sight we might think that entering the data is a one step task, but a closer inspection shows there are probably three different processes. The fees for the different membership types are probably decided early in the current year and can be entered then. Some membership data may already exist but we will need to add new members as they join the club. The fees may be paid at some later date (especially for existing members). So, an initial use case diagram should reflect these separate tasks.

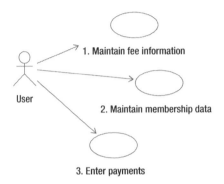

Figure A-6. *Possible use cases for entering the club data*

b) Consider what different things you are keeping information about and sketch a simple class diagram.

The different stages at which data is entered give us a bit of a clue that there are different classes involved. We have information about membership types and fees, information about members, and information about payments. An initial sketch of a class diagram is shown as follows.

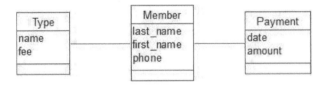

Figure A-7. *First attempt at a class diagram to represent the club data*

Let's consider the cardinalities. On face value we have that: one particular type (e.g., Full) will have a lot of members associated with it; a member will have just one type; a payment will be associated with just one member. How many payments might a member have? This will depend on whether we are keeping the information for just one year or over the long term. Sometimes someone like a club secretary will be concerned just with the job at hand of getting this year's information straight—and that may be all that is required. If you are going to the trouble of setting up a database, though, then having one that will cope long term is essential. (We then will have to worry about fees changing over time, but more of that later. Let's assume they stay constant for now.) The class diagram complete with cardinalities is shown in Figure A-8. Note that members might not have any payments (yet!) and there may be some membership types with no associated members at various times.

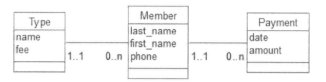

Figure A-8. *Class diagram to represent the club data, including cardinalities*

c) What options could you suggest to the club for different ways a report could be presented? Does your class diagram have the information readily available?

Being able to differentiate members by type might be useful for calculating summaries and subtotals of payments (having the type class will mean this information will be accurate). Finding members who have not paid is going to be essential. If we are only keeping payment records for a single year, this would be easy—just find members with no associated payment. If we are keeping the payment records long term, though, it becomes a bit trickier. We need to know for what year a payment is made, rather than when it was paid (and some members might be very tardy). Checking if a payment has been made in a particular year may not be satisfactory. We will look at options to deal with these sorts of issues in later chapters.

EXERCISE 3-1

Consider the following scenario and sketch some use cases and an initial data model. Assume that the main objectives for the system are to record student absences for the classroom teacher, for school reports, and for statistics for the Department of Education.

When parents call to say that children are sick, we have to let their classroom teachers know, and if it's sports day and the child is on a school team, the sports teacher might have to sort out substitutes. Then we need to count up all the days missed to put on the child's report. The Department of Education needs the totals each term, too.

Let's run through the steps in the summary section of Chapter 3.

1. Determine the main objective of the system.

    We agreed with the client that the main objectives are to record the absences for the classroom teacher, for school reports, and for statistics for the Department of Education.

2. Determine the jobs different users do in an average day.

    • Secretary takes phone calls and records name of each student.

193

- Secretary collates the absences for each classroom teacher and informs them of which students are away.

- Secretary gives list of absences to sports teacher if it is a sports day.

- Each student's absences are totaled for his or her report.

- All absences are totaled for Department of Education.

3. Brainstorm the data that could be associated with each job.

   a. Secretary takes phone calls and records name of each student.

   Because the absences need to be collated for each student, we need to ensure that the correct student is identified. This student data is going to be an essential part of the system. We will need to record names for all students and should consider introducing an ID number to distinguish students who might have the same name. We also need to record the current date.

   b. Secretary collates the absences for each classroom teacher and informs them of which students are away.

   We need to be able to associate each student with a classroom teacher. We will need the names of teachers and some contact information. How is the teacher informed? Do they get delivered a printed list or are they called on their phones? Maybe we could e-mail them. Recording contact information such as room numbers, phone numbers, and e-mail addresses for teachers would give us flexibility and is easy to do right from the start.

   c. Secretary gives list of sports team absences to sports teacher if it is a competition day.

   This isn't one of the main objectives, so recording members of sports teams looks like it is outside the scope of the problem for now. Being able to print a list of all today's absences is probably sufficient at this point, and we have all that information.

   d. Each student's absences are totaled for his or her report.

   We are collecting dates of absences and the IDs of the students so we can count absences for each student for any required time period (week, term, or year).

   e. All absences are totaled for Department of Education.

   Same as the preceding, but totaled over all students.

4. Agree on the scope of the project and decide on the relevant data.

   At a minimum we need:

   For each teacher: Name and contact details (maybe an ID)

   For each student: An ID, name, and classroom teacher

   For each absence: Student ID and date

5. Sketch data input use cases—consider exceptions—check existing forms.

   Figure A-9 shows some initial input use cases.

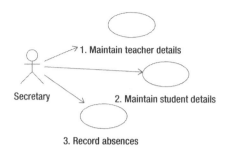

Figure A-9. *Use cases for data input*

Here are brief descriptions of the use cases depicted in Figure A-9.

1. Maintain teacher details: Record or update name and contact details.

2. Maintain student details: Assign IDs for new students. Record or update names and associate the student with an existing classroom teacher.

3. Record the date of each absence and the ID of the absent student.

6. Consider exceptions and complications.

One question that springs to mind is: how do we record that a student is away for several days at one time? We have a couple of choices; we could record each day as a separate absence or we could have one absence with a start date and end date. The former is the easiest option. However, if the school is likely to want some statistics about the types of absences (e.g., what is the average length of an absence? How many students are away for longer than a week at a time?), then we would have to rethink our approach. As the main objective is just to total the overall number of days, we will record each day as a separate absence for now. Another issue involves students that are absent without a call from their parents. Classroom teachers will be able to use existing use cases, but this raises the question as to whether there are different categories of absence. For now we will just add a comment to the data about absences.

7. Sketch a first data model.

A data model is shown in Figure A-10.

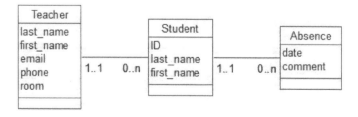

Figure A-10. *Class diagram to record student absences*

195

For the model in Figure A-10 the following statements are true:

- Each student has just one classroom teacher and could have many absences.

- Each teacher may be responsible as a classroom teacher for many students (but some teachers may not be classroom teachers).

- Each absence is for exactly one student.

8. Brainstorm the possible outputs given the data being collected.

We have all the information we need for reporting the number of absences for each student or for all students. What further information could we retrieve? We have decided not to keep durations of absences. What about the reason for an absence? It would be a simple addition to keep some categories of absences (illness, school trip, sports match, etc.). That may be worth discussing with the client.

Sketch information output use cases.

Figure A-11 shows some output use cases which satisfy the main objectives of the system.

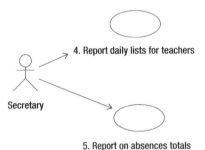

Figure A-11. *Use cases for reporting information*

Here are brief descriptions of the use cases depicted in Figure A-11.

4. Full list for sports teacher: Find all the absences with today's date. Print out names of associated students.

   Lists for classroom teachers: Find all the absences with today's date. Print out names of students and names of teachers, and group by teacher.

5. For Department of Education: Find all the absences with dates in the relevant time period and count them.

   For school reports: For each student, count all the absences with dates in the relevant time period.

EXERCISE 4-1

Figure A-12 shows a first draft of modeling the situation where a publishing company wants to keep information about authors and books. Consider the possible optionalities at each end of the relationships writes, and so determine some possible definitions for a book and an author.

Figure A-12. Consider possible optionalities for authors writing books

At first we might think that an author will always have at least one book he has written and a book will always have at least one author (even if we might not know who it is). This may be true for *actual* books and authors, but here we are concerned with *information* about books and authors. A publishing company might often see an opportunity for a book on a particular topic and record that information while they search for an author. Similarly, a publisher might retain a potential author and store information even though no books have yet been written for the publisher by that person.

Possible definitions might include: *a book is a work that has been written or is planned to be written; an author is a person who has or might in the future write a book.*

EXERCISE 4-2

Figure A-13 shows a possible data model for cocktail recipes. What is missing?

Figure A-13. Cocktails and their ingredients; what is missing?

Each cocktail may have a number of ingredients (Manhattan: Vermouth, Whisky; Margarita: Tequila, Triple Sec, Lime). What are missing are the quantities. As is often the case with a Many–Many relationship, an intermediate class is required. The quantities depend on a particular pairing of Cocktail and Ingredient. A better model is shown in Figure A-14, along with some possible data. The inclusion of the Recipe class allows us to keep information such as how much Rum is required for a Daiquiri as opposed to a Cable Car.

197

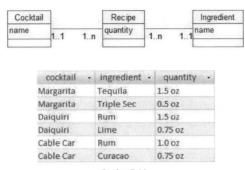

Recipe Table

Figure A-14. *An intermediate class, Recipe, can record quantities for each pairing of cocktail and ingredient.*

EXERCISE 4-3

Part of the data model about guests at a hostel is shown in Figure A-15. How could the model be amended to keep historical information about room occupancy?

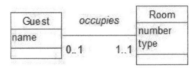

Figure A-15. *How could this be amended to keep historical information about room occupancy?*

The data model indicates that, for a hostel with single occupancy rooms, a room might be empty or have at most one occupant. Each current guest occupies one room. Over time, however, a room will have many different guests, and guests may return and occupy different rooms. This needs to be modeled as a Many–Many relationship as in Figure A-16. (As an aside, you can deduce from the optionality of 1 for a guest being associated with a room, that our definition of a guest is someone who has been assigned a room at some stage—not just any person who might or might not come to the hostel.)

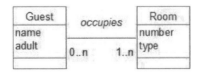

Figure A-16. *Guests and rooms modeled with a Many–Many relationship*

Now that we have a Many–Many relationship we need to ask the question: is anything missing? Clearly what is missing is information about when a particular guest occupied a particular room. This requires an intermediate class as in Figure A-17.

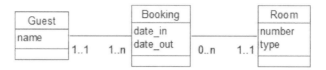

Figure A-17. Including a Booking class to keep information about the dates that guests occupy rooms

Each guest can have several bookings over time, as can a room. Each booking is for one guest in a particular room. A word of caution here though—our original data model (Figure A-16) indicated that a room could only have a single guest. Now that we have allowed many guests in a room over time, we have lost the information that at any one time a room can have only one guest. Our model in Figure A-17 would not prevent several people all having a simultaneous booking for one room. These sorts of problems are never simple! One way to record a business rule about simultaneous bookings would be to describe it in the use case for adding a booking for a room. It could say something such as: *no booking can be added to a room where an existing booking has overlapping dates.* A data model gives us a huge amount of insight, but on its own it is not a complete description of a problem.

EXERCISE 5-1

The class in Figure A-18 records information about a department. What other options are there for modeling information about the manager and location of a department?

Figure A-18. Initial attempt at modeling the information about a department

Let's first think about location. What might we want to do with this information? It may be useful to be able to find all the departments that are in the same location—to let them know the CEO is visiting, say. If we want to retrieve an object based on the value of an attribute, then we must ensure that the value is stored consistently in each object. Creating a new class can help with that. If we introduce a Location class, then we can store information about each location and set up a relationship between departments and location. Introducing a Location class also allows us to keep additional information about the location: address, phone, and so on.

It is unlikely that we will regularly want to retrieve department objects based on the manager's name, as for the most part managers will only be attached to a single department. However, there is a great deal of additional information we need to know about a manager. How to contact him would be a start. Do we already have this information? The company will surely have information stored about all its employees, so here we should model manager as a relationship to an existing Employee class.

A better model is shown in Figure A-19. If you are keen, try developing this new model to account for previous managers.

199

Figure A-19. *More flexible model for department information*

EXERCISE 5-2

A university wants to model information about the teaching of courses. A number of staff members may contribute to teaching a course and one staff member is denoted as the course supervisor. Suggest an initial data model.

We have two obvious classes for this situation: Course and StaffMember. There are two different relationships between the classes: teaches and supervises. A possible model is shown in Figure A-20. Reading from right to left, each course has one or more teachers and each course has a single supervisor. From left to right, staff members might teach and/or supervise any number of courses. In this model we haven't considered any historical information; nor have we considered other possible constraints, such as, does the supervisor need to be one of the teachers?

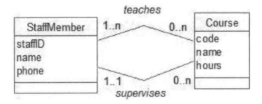

Figure A-20. *Modeling the teaching and supervision of courses with two relationships*

EXERCISE 5-3

How would you model the information about marriages? Think about all the different situations that could eventuate (for simplicity, do not worry at this stage about the gender of the participants).

We need to keep information about people—their names, at least. One person marries another person, so a self relationship is required as in Figure A-21.

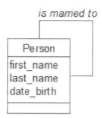

Figure A-21. *Modeling marriage with a self relationship*

Optionalities are easy—people are not required to be married to someone else. What about the cardinalities? Generally it is one marriage at a time (but not always). However, historically a person may have many marriages. This would require a Many–Many relationship. When we have a Many–Many relationship it is always prudent to ask, "What additional information could be useful about a particular pair of objects?" In this case the dates of the marriage would be useful. These can be kept in an intermediate class, Marriage. We could also keep details on the cause of the end of the marriage (divorce, separation, death of spouse, etc.). A class, EndType, to maintain these categories accurately would be useful, and something like the data model in Figure A-22 would capture much of this detail. Each marriage involves exactly two people (the two lines between Marriage and Person) and each person can be involved in any number of marriages. Some marriages have ended and so have an optional category associated with them.

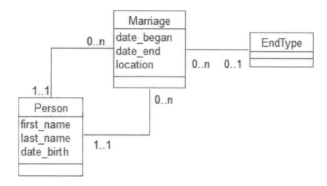

Figure A-22. *Including additional classes to capture marriage information*

EXERCISE 5-4

An orchestra keeps information about its musicians, repertoire, and concerts. A partial data model is shown in Figure A-23.

What false information could be deduced from this initial model?

Amend the model so that it can maintain the following information correctly:

- Which players are involved in particular works in a concert

- The works being presented at a concert
- The fee a player receives for appearing in a particular concert

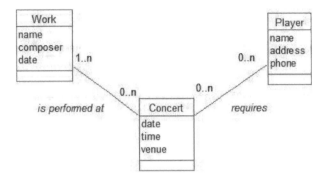

Figure A-23. *A partial model for an orchestra's concert information*

This model contains a fan trap: there are Many cardinalities at the outside ends of the two relationships. For example, if we have information that Joe Smith is required for Saturday's concert and that Beethoven's violin sonata is to be performed at Saturday's concert, we could incorrectly make the deduction that Joe performs in the violin sonata.

If we want to know which players are involved in particular works in a concert we need a ternary relationship that involves the three classes, Player, Concert, and Work, simultaneously. Figure A-24 shows the ternary relationship represented by a new class, Appearance.

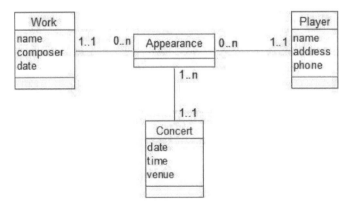

Figure A-24. *A ternary relationship represented by an additional class*

Each object of the Appearance class is related to one player, one work, and one concert.
It allows us to keep data as in the table in Figure A-25. We can see that Joe played in the Sonata
and the Symphony on Saturday, while Linda played only in the Sonata.

player	work	concert
Joe	Sonata	Saturday
Linda	Sonata	Saturday
Joe	Symphony	Saturday
Linda	Sonata	Monday
Mary	Duet	Monday

Figure A-25. *Example data represented by the class Appearance*

Do we need a relationship between Work and Concert so that we can know what is on the
program? From Figure A-25 we can see that Saturday's concert features the Sonata and the
Symphony. However, the program will probably be decided long before any players are involved,
so we need the information about works in a particular concert, independent of the players.
The binary relationship between Concert and Work in Figure A-26 can record that information;
a concert has one or more works on the program and a work might be performed at many
concerts.

What about the fee a player is paid for performing in a concert? If the fees go with each work,
then they could be included as attributes in Appearance. Joe is paid $30 for playing the Sonata
on Saturday and $50 for playing the Symphony, for example. If a fee is for the entire concert
(e.g., a travel allowance), then it is independent of the works and a new binary relationship
between Player and Concert will be required. The relationship will be Many–Many (a player
may be involved in many concerts and a concert will have many players). The new intermediate
class Player/Concert is required so that we have somewhere to include the fee for particular
pairings of player and concert.

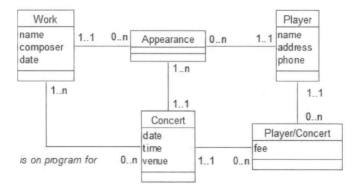

Figure A-26. *A more comprehensive model for concert information*

EXERCISE 6-1

Consider the model in Figure A-27 which describes purchases of a product by customers of a small mail order company The company changes the way it does business to allow customers to walk in off the street and pay cash. No customer needs to be associated with a cash purchase.

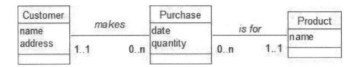

Figure A-27. *Customers purchase products.*

Discuss how effective the following changes to the data would be.

- Change the optionality at the customer end of the relationship to 0 so that not all purchases need a customer.

  This solution solves the immediate problem of a cash sale not requiring a customer. With care, it can be made to work. However, there is the problem of not having a record of the customer when a mail order purchase needs to be invoiced or delivered.

- Leave the optionality as 1 but include a dummy customer object with the name "Cash Customer."

  We now have to nominate a customer for the purchase. This is probably a bit safer than the preceding option. However, one of the objectives for the project was to provide statistics on customer habits. Mr. Cash Customer is likely to have a large number of purchases and this could skew the results for statistics such as average value or average number of purchases. It is possible, if you remember, to remove purchases made by "Cash Customer" before doing statistics, but it is a fiddle. It depends on how important these statistics are and how often they are required.

- Create subclasses of `Customer`: `Cash_Customer` and `Account_Customer`.

  This really doesn't achieve anything more than the preceding option and is much more difficult to implement. We are not collecting information about our cash customers, so having a class for them is pointless.

- Create subclasses of `Purchase`: `Cash_Purchase` and `Account_Purchase`.

  We will have many cash purchases (with no customer) and many account purchases (with a mandatory customer), so a class for each is a reasonable idea. It makes deriving statistics for the different customer types simple. It doesn't really have much advantage over the dummy cash customer for the present set of requirements, but if we want to start recording the method of payment (cash, EFTPOS, credit card, etc.) then they will be easy to add. Figure A-28 shows how this can be modeled.

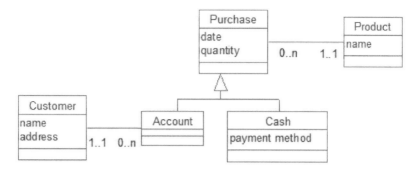

Figure A-28. A purchase can be for a customer with an account or can be an anonymous cash transaction.

EXERCISE 6-2

A farmer keeps information about the application of fertilizer to his crops (e.g., amount, date, etc.). His farm is made up of large sections which are divided into fields. Usually an application of fertilizer is applied to an entire section, but occasionally it is to an individual field. How would you model this?

We can start by having a class called Application which can record the date and the amount of fertilizer and which is associated with some sort of area—a section or a field. Sections and fields are both "areas" that have something in common (name, size, the fact that fertilizer can be applied, etc.), and so this is a candidate for generalization. Have a look at the model in Figure A-29.

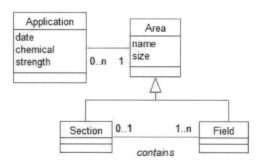

Figure A-29. Fertilizer applications are made to areas which are either sections or fields.

In addition to an area being either a section or a field we also have that fields may be one of many in a section. Now we can record that an application has been to a section and know which fields have received the treatment. We can also make an application to a single field if we wish.

205

Figure A-29 is a good solution; however using the composite pattern, as in Figure A-30, gives a more general solution. We can record an application for an entire farm, which is made up of sections which are made up of fields. We can also record the fertilizer application at any of these levels. This is analogous to the checks on buildings problem discussed in Chapter 6.

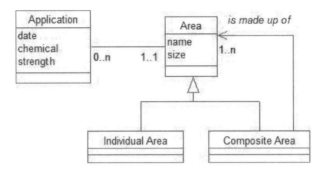

Figure A-30. *The composite pattern allows applications to all levels of area.*

EXERCISE 6-3

A volunteer library has staff, members, and books. It is necessary to know which books are on loan to whom and how to contact the borrower, and to record fees charged for overdue books. Reference books cannot be borrowed. Members are fined $5 per day for overdue books but staff do not receive fines. How might you model this situation? Some initial classes are shown in Figure A-31.

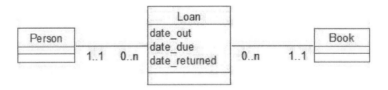

Figure A-31. *People can borrow books.*

We know that we have two types of books (ordinary and reference) and two types of people (staff and members). The important question now is: do we need inheritance? For people, the only difference in the problem stated is in the value of a fine for overdue books. There is no behavioral difference. We could create a Type class (with objects for staff and member) which is associated with each person. This class could record the value of the fine for that type ($5.00 for members, $0.00 for staff). Similarly we could categorize each book as being of a type and build into the use cases a rule that reference books cannot be associated with a loan. This different behavior, however, probably warrants considering an inheritance solution. Figure A-32 depicts a possible solution with an association to represent the different types of person and inheritance for the different types of book. Note that we have introduced an abstract Book class so that we can make changes to the ordinary and reference book classes independently.

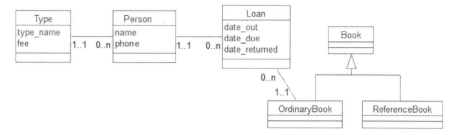

Figure A-32. *One of many possible ways to represent different types of books and people*

EXERCISE 7-1

a)   Figure A-33 shows an initial data model for a small library.Explain to the librarian what the initial data model means.

b)   Design tables for a relational database which would capture the information represented by the model. Include primary and foreign keys and other appropriate constraints.

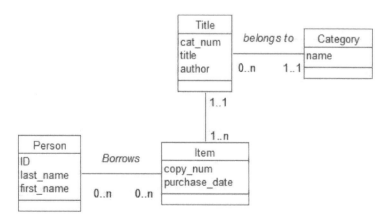

Figure A-33. *Draft data model for a small library*

a)   Here is a possible way to explain to the librarian what the data model means.

"The model shows that you are intending to keep information about people (who each have a number and names). You are also keeping information about the book titles you stock: author, title, and category. For each of these titles there is at least one copy and possibly more. These copies have a copy number and the date it was purchased. You will be keeping information about which people borrow a particular copy."

207

There are clearly important things missing from this model—we will get to some of them!

b) Now let's look at how to represent the model in a relational database.

For each class we need a table with fields to represent the attributes.

A direct translation gives us:

```
Person    (ID, last_name, first_name)

Title     (cat_num, title, author)

Item      (copy_num, purchase_date)

Category (name)
```

We need some types for the fields. ID should be an integer and you might consider some sort of auto-incrementing type. Depending on the cataloging system, cat_num will probably be a text field. $copy\_num$ will be an integer (1, 2, 3, etc.), $purchase\_date$ is obviously a date, and the other fields are all text. We should probably look more closely at the $author$ field. There are a few possibilities here; at the least it should be split into first and last names, but as people are likely to want to search by author it probably should be a class on its own. We won't worry about that for now.

What about constraints? All the fields seem very important to me and I see no reason not to make them all required (not null). The purchase date could perhaps be a date in the past, but then that might cause problems if planned future purchases need to be stored (and that increases the scope so we'll just leave that for now too.)

Primary keys are easy for the $Person$ (ID), $Title$ (cat_num), and $Category$ ($name$) tables, but the $Item$ table does not have an obvious candidate for a primary key. Every title will have a copy with $copy\_num = 1$ and they may have been purchased on the same date. So no field or combination of fields is suitable. We could add a unique identifier but we'll wait a bit to see what eventuates.

Now to represent the relationships. The 1–Many between $Title$ and $Category$ can be represented with a foreign key in the $Title$ table and similarly we need a foreign key in the $Item$ table referencing the $Title$ table. These must have the same datatypes as the tables they are referencing. To represent the Many–Many relationship $borrows$, we need to first add a new class ($Loan$) as in Figure A-34.

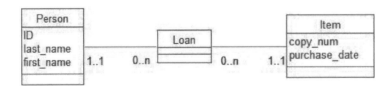

Figure A-34. *A new class to help represent the Many–Many relationship borrows*

At this stage we should realize (you probably did before now) that there is information about pairings of $Person$ and $Item$ that need to be stored ($date\_out$, due_date, etc). These will need to be discussed with the client. We'll just make a note of it for now. To represent the two 1–Many relationships in Figure A-34 we will need two foreign keys in the $Loan$ table referencing $Person$ and $Item$.

Below, I have recapped our progress so far. (I have used emboldened underlines to denote primary keys and italics to denote foreign keys.)

Person   (**ID**, last_name, first_name)

Title   (**cat_num**, title, author, *category*)

Item   (copy_num, purchase_date, *title_cat_num*)

Category   (**name**)

Loan   (<dates>, *item, person*)

We are nearly there; we just have the primary keys for the Item and Loan tables to decide. For the Item table it is now possible to use the combination of title_cat_num and copy_num as a primary key. Each title has a unique catalog number and each title will have only one copy1, one copy2, and so on. For the Loan table the combination item and person is not suitable; someone may check out the same item a second time. However, if we include the date it was taken out, then the three fields would be unique (assuming you don't check an item out twice in one day). It would also be possible to add a unique loan number to act as a primary key in the Loan table (we look at this choice in Chapter 8).

Listing A-1 shows the SQL to create these tables in SQL Server (we haven't covered all the required syntax for dealing with concatenated keys and foreign keys in this design book, but it is fairly self explanatory).

Listing A-1. SQL to Create Library Database

```
CREATE TABLE Category (name VARCHAR (20) PRIMARY KEY);

CREATE TABLE Person  (ID INT PRIMARY KEY,
                      last_name VARCHAR(20) NOT NULL,
                      first_name VARCHAR(20) NOT NULL);

CREATE TABLE Title   (cat_num VARCHAR(40) PRIMARY KEY,
                      title VARCHAR(80) NOT NULL,
                      author VARCHAR(80) NOT NULL,
                      category VARCHAR(20) NOT NULL FOREIGN KEY REFERENCES Category);

CREATE TABLE Item    (title_cat_num VARCHAR (40) FOREIGN KEY REFERENCES Title,
                      copy_num INT,
                      purchase_date DATE NOT NULL,
                      PRIMARY KEY (title_cat_num, copy_num));

CREATE TABLE Loan    (date_out DATE,
                      cat_num VARCHAR(40),
                      copy_num INT,
                      borrower INT FOREIGN KEY REFERENCES Person,
                      FOREIGN KEY (cat_num, copy_num) REFERENCES Item,
                      PRIMARY KEY (date_out, cat_num, copy_num, borrower) )
```

EXERCISE 8-3

Figure A-35 shows a version of the unnormalized insect data discussed in Example 1-3.

FarmID	FarmName	Field	Date	Visit	SampleID	Insect	Count
1	HighGate	F2	09-Feb-11	14	3	Beetle	2
1	HighGate	F2	09-Feb-11	14	2	Beetle	4
1	HighGate	F1	09-Feb-11	14	1	Beetle	4
1	HighGate	F1	18-Mar-11	15	1	Springtail	5
1	HighGate	F2	09-Feb-11	14	3	Springtail	3
1	HighGate	F2	09-Feb-11	14	2	Springtail	5
1	HighGate	F1	09-Feb-11	14	1	Springtail	6
1	High-Gate	F1	18-Mar-11	15	1	Beetle	7
2	Greyton	F2	09-Feb-11	16	1	Beetle	2
2	Greyton	F1	09-Feb-11	16	2	Beetle	4
2	Greyton	F1	09-Feb-11	16	2	Springtail	5
2	Greyton	F2	09-Feb-11	16	1	Springtail	3

Figure A-35. Unnormalized insect data

a) What are some of the updating problems that could occur?

The most obvious problems are likely to arise from inconsistent data caused by repeated information. The name of each farm is recorded several times and has inevitably resulted in a spelling error for HighGate. The fact that Visit 14 is on February 9th is recorded several times and a data input error is possible. Because the data was stored in a spreadsheet there is no primary key, so the insertion and deletion problems don't arise.

b) Which of the following functional dependencies hold?

- FarmID→FarmName? Yes. If I know the ID I can tell you the name (or I should be able to do so if the spelling errors are removed).

- FarmID→Visit? No. Farm 1 has two associated visits (14 and 15) in the data shown in Figure A-35. If this functional dependency was true that would mean only one visit per farm—clearly not the intention.

- Visit→Date? This is certainly true for the data shown, but will it always be true? It would mean that a visit was on a single day—something to be checked with the client. We'll say yes for now.

- Date→Visit? No. That would mean only one visit a day. February 9th has two associated visits: 14 and 16.

- Visit→FarmID? The data shown support this. In general we need to confirm that a visit is for just one farm (i.e., it doesn't include a tour around the country). We'll say yes.

- SampleID→Field? If we know the sample we should surely know which field it comes from, right? However, some rows with SampleID having a value 2 have F1 for the Field value while others have F2. So, no—we can't tell the value of Field from knowing the value of SampleID. This is because the SampleID field doesn't uniquely identify a sample. There are several SampleID 2 s from different visits. To identify a sample we need to also know on which visit it was collected.

- (SampleID, VisitID)→Field? Yes—see preceding! The data supports this. Sample 2 for Visit 14 is associated with only F2 and Sample 2 for Visit 16 is associated only with F1.

- (SampleID, Insect)→Count? In an actual sample, if we specify the insect then we should come up with a unique count. But remember, the SampleID field doesn't uniquely identify an actual sample. Take a look at the rows where SampleID = 2, and Insect = Beetle. (What a coincidence!)

- VisitID, SampleID, Insect→Count? See preceding. Now that we include the VisitID with SampleID, we can identify the actual test tube (or whatever) and know the number of Beetles.

c) Is (VisitID, SampleID, Insect) a suitable key?

From question 2, let's summarize the functional dependencies (FD) that hold for this data.

FD1: FarmID - > FarmName

FD2: VisitID - > Date, FarmID

FD3: SampleID, VisitID - > Field

FD4: VisitID, SampleID, Insect - > Count

What field values can I determine if I have values for (VisitID, SampleID and Insect)?

We know Count (FD4), Field (FD3), Date, and FarmID (FD2), and because I now know FarmID I can tell you FarmName (FD1). That's everything, so this set is a key. It is a primary key because if you remove any of the fields then you won't know everything (I'll leave that to the really keen readers to verify).

d) Decompose the data in Figure A-35 into a set of tables in 3rd Normal form.

Here are the fields (with the primary key underlined):

(FarmID, VisitID, SampleID, Date, FarmName, Field, Insect, Count)

Is this in 1st Normal Form?

Yes. We are not trying to put more than one piece of information in a cell.

Is this in 2nd Normal Form, or equivalently do the non-key fields depend on the whole key?

211

No. We can determine `FarmName` by just knowing `FarmID` (FD1), so it should be removed into another table with what it depends on. This leaves us with:

(FarmID, VisitID, SampleID, Date, FarmName, Field, Insect, Count)
(FarmID, FarmName) (new table)

`Date` and `FarmID` can be determined by knowing just `Visit` (FD2). Removing these two fields leaves us with:

(FarmID, VisitID, SampleID, Date, FarmName, Field, Insect, Count)
(VisitID, FarmID, Date) (new table)

`Field` can be determined by knowing just `SampleID` and `VisitID` (FD3). So this needs to be removed.

(FarmID, VisitID, SampleID, Date, FarmName, Field, Insect, Count)
(VisitID, SampleID, Field) (new table)

Finally we have the following four table (keys underlined, foreign keys italicized).

(FarmID, FarmName)

(VisitID, *FarmID*, Date)

(*VisitID*, SampleID, Field)

(*VisitID*, *SampleID*, Insect, Count) (remains of original table)

These tables would have been derived if we had started with the class diagram in Figure A-36.

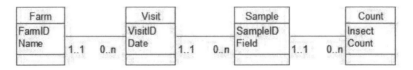

Figure A-36. *Class diagram for insect data*

The class diagram essentially says a farm gets many visits. Each visit has a number of associated samples and for each sample we can record the numbers of insects. I think you will see that starting with the class diagram would have been a great deal less trouble and would also have made us think about some other possible classes, such as `Field` and `Insect`. However, the two approaches are equivalent ways of arriving at similar outcomes.

EXERCISE 9-1

Here we have the ever–useful "customer orders product" example again. Design the table that will represent the Order class in Figure A-37. Consider constraints, primary and foreign keys, and updating rules.

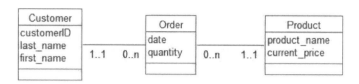

Figure A-37. Model for customers placing orders

Let's assume that customerID and product_name are primary keys for the Product and Customer tables. To represent the two relationships, these primary keys will be included as new foreign key fields in the Order table. We will have (foreign keys in italics):

Order (*customer, product,* date, quantity)

What is the primary key? A customer might order a product more than once, possibly on the same day and even for the same quantity. (You might order three dozen savories for your party, realize you've miscalculated the appetites of certain of your guests and immediately order another three dozen.) This is a (fairly rare) case where no combination of attributes can be guaranteed to be unique and a generated order number needs to be added. All attributes are necessary and so should have a NOT NULL constraint. If the date is when the order is placed then it should not be in the future—but if it is the date the order is to take effect, maybe a future date makes sense—let's not tie this down just now. As for updating rules, we must choose Disallow Delete (the default). If a customer or product is deleted we will still want to retain the order for accounting purposes (and as discussed in Chapter 9, we will probably want to retain the product and customer as well). A Nullify Delete would render the order information useless as we would be left with data such as, "On a particular date someone ordered six of something."

The SQL for creating the table would be something like that shown in Listing A-2.

Listing A-2. SQL to Create Order Table – Delete Disallowed is the Default Updating Rule

```
CREATE TABLE Order   (order_num INT PRIMARY KEY,
                      product INT NOT NULL FOREIGN KEY REFERENCES Product,
                      customer INT NOT NULL FOREIGN KEY REFERENCES Customer,
                      quantity INT NOT NULL,date DATE NOT NULL,);
```

EXERCISE 9-2

Think about the options available for setting up tables for makes and models of cars at a car sale yard.

We have makes, models, types, and actual cars. If we wind right back to Chapter 2, it is useful to think about attributes by which users might like to sort or search and have these as separate classes. (We did this for genus in the plant case so we could ensure all the Eucalyptus species were spelled correctly). Here we are likely to want to be able to find information about all Fords, or all Siestas, or even all sedans or all blue cars. An initial model may look like the one in Figure A-38.

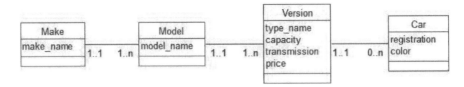

Figure A-38. *Possible model for keeping car information*

If we do a translation from class to tables we would start with the following tables (primary keys underlined and foreign keys in italics):

Make (make_name)

Model (model_name, *make_name*)

Version (type_name, capacity, transmission, price, *model_name*, *make_name*) (primary key?)

Car (registration, color,?)

Let's pause here. The primary key for the Model table being the combination of model_name and make_name seems reasonable. We can't guarantee model names will be unique across makes, and introducing a generated ID doesn't really seem to add much here.

The Version table is more problematic. We need all the fields except price for a primary key: a Ford Fiesta automatic 1.5 l sedan is a different version than a Ford Fiesta automatic 2.0 l sedan. There is no problem with having such a long primary key until we come to the Car table. That set of five attributes will be the foreign key and will need to be in every row of the Car table. This is going to become very cumbersome.

At this point it is probably worth considering a generated ID for the Version. We can then have the following tables.

Make (make_name)

Model (model_name, *make_name*)

Version (versionID, type_name, capacity, transmission, price, *model_name*, *make_name*)

Car (registration, color, *version*)

What about types (sedans, hatchbacks, etc.)? You have an option here of introducing a new table or of creating a constraint on the type_name field of the Version table. We could do similarly for colors. I'd probably favor a table for type: extra types will be constantly added as we start to consider three– or five–door hatchbacks and other variants. I don't even want to think about colors. If we could just assume red, green, and blue then it would be easy, but I'm sure you will find there are colors called cherry and fire and scarlet and…

EXERCISE 10-1

Figure A-39 shows the database tables and some possible data for the meal ordering problem discussed in Chapter 3. In the Order_Meal table, order and meal are foreign keys to the Orders and Meals tables respectively.

order_num	address	phone	driver	order_time	deliver_time
231	16 Lincoln Road	3475621	Billie	3/02/2012 2:34:00 p.m.	3/02/2012 3:03:00 p.m.
232	3a Breezes Road	3896834	Billie	3/02/2012 2:38:00 p.m.	
233	22 Waimea Tce	8563209	Jane	3/02/2012 2:56:00 p.m.	

Orders

name	type	price
Butter Chicken	Indian	8.95
Lamb Korma	Indian	8.95
MeatLovers	Pizza	15.99

Meals

order	meal	quantity
231	Butter Chicken	2
232	Lamb Korma	1
232	MeatLovers	1

Order_Meal

Figure A-39. Tables for meal delivery

Determine the queries that would provide the following information.

a) Determine the cost of a specific order (e.g., 232).

Which tables are required for this information? We don't actually need the Orders table. The Order_Meal table has the order number and the name of the meal and the Meals table has the prices. A join between Meals and Order_Meal with the condition that name = meal will give us the virtual table in Figure A-40.

name	type	price	order	meal	quantity
Butter Chicken	Indian	8.95	231	Butter Chicken	2
Lamb Korma	Indian	8.95	232	Lamb Korma	1
MeatLovers	Pizza	15.99	232	MeatLovers	1

Figure A-40. The result of a join between Meals and Order_Meal

The data in Figure A-40 has all the information we need. For each row we can multiply price by quantity. We can retrieve all the rows for order 232 and total those amounts.

Have a look at the SQL in Listing A-3 and see if you can understand it.

Listing A-3. SQL to Find the Cost of Order 232

```
SELECT SUM (quantity * price)
FROM Meals INNER JOIN Order_Meal on name = meal
WHERE order = 232
```

b) Prepare a list of undelivered orders.

We only need the Orders table to find this information. Any order without a delivery time is not yet delivered (or recorded as delivered). So a simple select operation to find rows with no value in the deliver_time field will achieve what we want. The code is shown in Listing A-4.

215

Listing A-4. SQL to Find Undelivered Orders

```
SELECT *
FROM Orders
WHERE deliver_time is NULL
```

The query in Listing A-4 will give us the order number, address, phone, driver and order time for each outstanding order. That is enough to call the driver and ask what is going on. If we also want to know which meals were ordered, then we would need to join the Orders table with the Meal_Order table to get the names and quantities of the dishes ordered.

c)   Determine the income from different types of meals in a given month.

This query has quite a few steps and you will need a bit of practice before being able to come up with the answer quickly. However, if taken slowly it is quite easy to follow. We need the Meals table (for the prices), the Order_Mealtable for the quantities, and the Order table to find the dates. Listing A-5 shows a join between these three tables.

Listing A-5. SQL to Join the Three Tables in the Meal Database

```
SELECT *
FROM (Meal INNER JOIN Order_Meal ON name = meal)
     INNER JOIN Orders ON order = order_num
```

Figure A-41 shows some of the most relevant columns resulting from the join in Listing A-5. The first three columns come from the Meals table, the next three are from the Order_Mealtable, and the remaining columns are from the Orders table.

name ▾	type ▾	price ▾	order ▾	meal ▾	quantity ▾	order_num ▾	order_time ▾
Butter Chicken	Indian	8.95	231	Butter Chicken	2	231	03-Feb-12
Lamb Korma	Indian	8.95	232	Lamb Korma	1	232	03-Feb-12
MeatLovers	Pizza	15.99	232	MeatLovers	1	232	03-Feb-12

Figure A-41. *Some of the columns from a join between Meals, Order_Meal, and Orders*

A WHERE clause will find the rows for the required time period. (e.g., WHERE Order_time >= 02/01/2012 AND Order_time < 03/01/2012will retrieve the rows for February 2012.) We can do a multiplication of quantity and price to find totals, similar to what we did in part a) of this question. A GROUP BY clause will allow us to find totals for each separate meal type.

Listing A-6 shows the final query. Try to identify the different parts.

Listing A-6. SQL to Find the Income from Different Types of Meals in February 2012

```
SELECT type, SUM (quantity * price)
FROM (Meal INNER JOIN Order_Meal ON name = meal)
     INNER JOIN Orders ON order = order_num
WHERE Order_time >= 02/01/2012 AND Order_time <= 03/01/2012
GROUP BY type
```

EXERCISE 11-1

In Exercise 3-1 we looked at the problem of a school recording student absences. The initial use cases are shown in Figure A-42 and a first data model in Figure A-43. Design some forms to satisfy the data entry requirements (use cases 1–3) and reports to satisfy the output use cases (4 and 5).

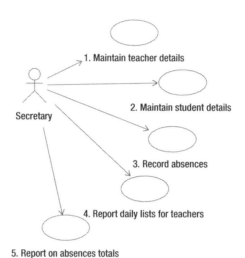

Figure A-42. Use cases for recording and reporting school absences

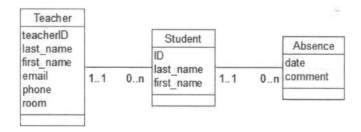

Figure A-43. Data model for recording school absences

Some representative data for the tables is shown in A-44: foreign keys, student and teacher, have been added to the Absence and Student tables respectively.

teacherID	▾	t_last_name	▾	t_first_name	▾
13		Smith		Judith	
14		Green		Trevor	
15		Howard		Jim	

Teacher

studentID	▾	s_last_name	▾	s_first_name	▾	teacher	▾
1003		Li		Bo			13
1006		Hanson		James			13
1008		Abell		Sue			13
1012		Grant		Linda			15
1014		Turner		Mark			15

Student

student	▾	date	▾
1003		09-Feb-12	
1003		10-Feb-12	
1008		10-Feb-12	
1014		10-Feb-12	

Absence

Figure A-44. *Some data for the school absences*

The forms to enter data about teachers and students are very straightforward as they each are based on a single table. The form to record absences requires an entry of a student ID and a date in the Absence table. However, the school secretary taking calls from parents will want to deal with names rather than IDs, so providing information about name is important for data entry purposes. Figure A-45 shows a form based on a join between the Absence and Student tables. A drop–down list shows the IDs and names of all students in alphabetical order for easy selection, read–only fields show the names of the students, and the date for new entries defaults to today's date.

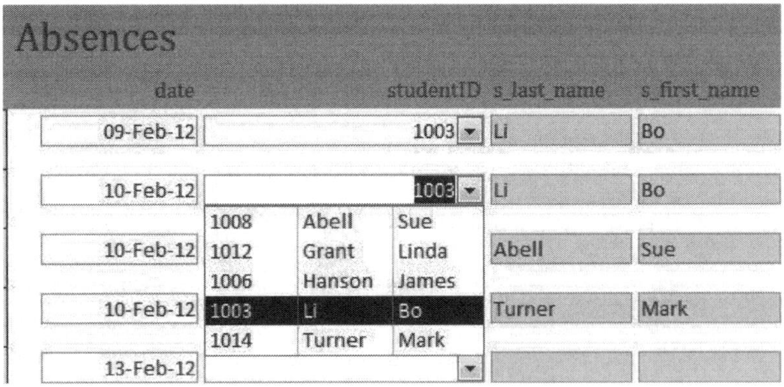

Figure A-45. *A form for entering absences*

For reporting to teachers, we need information from all three tables. Listing A-7 shows the SQL for a view which joins the tables. Note that we have an outer join on the Student table so that all students are included even if they have no absences.

Listing A-7. SQL to Retrieve Information from All Three Tables

```
CREATE VIEW AllInfo AS
SELECT * FROM Teacher INNER JOIN
(Student LEFT JOIN Absence ON studentID = student)
ON teacherID = teacher;
```

Figure A-46 shows some data resulting from the view in Listing A-7.

date	studentID	s_last_name	s_first_name	teacherID	t_last_name	t_first_name	room
09-Feb-12	1003	Li	Bo	13	Smith	Judith	14
10-Feb-12	1003	Li	Bo	13	Smith	Judith	14
	1006	Hanson	James	13	Smith	Judith	14
10-Feb-12	1008	Abell	Sue	13	Smith	Judith	14
	1012	Grant	Linda	15	Howard	Jim	13
10-Feb-12	1014	Turner	Mark	15	Howard	Jim	13

Figure A-46. *Data retrieved from view in A-8*

The data in Figure A-46 has everything we need for all our reports. We just need to select the relevant rows, then do some grouping and summarizing.

We can get the daily absences by selecting only those rows for the current day. Ordering that data by student name will be fine for the sports teacher, while grouping the data by teacher as in Figure A-47 will be a more useful way of getting the information to each classroom teacher.

Absences 10- Feb

Jim   Howard   Room: 13

    1014 Turner   Mark

Judith Smith   Room: 14

    1008 Abell   Sue

    1003 Li   Bo

Figure A-47. *Current absences grouped for each classroom teacher*

Adding some counts, selecting data from relevant time periods, and adding grouping can provide a number of different reports. Figure A-48 shows two reports: one showing total absences for each day, and the other showing total absences for each student in February.

Student Absences February

1003	Li	Bo	2
1006	Hanson	James	0
1008	Abell	Sue	1
1012	Grant	Linda	0
1014	Turner	Mark	1
		Total:	**4**

Absences grouped by student

Daily Absences

09-Feb-12		1
10-Feb-12		3
	Total	4

Absences grouped by date

Figure A-48. *Examples of reports possible with different groupings and summarizing*

Index

28531415R00141

Made in the USA
Middletown, DE
18 January 2016